International Guide to Accounting Journals

International Guide to Accounting Journals

By

J. DAVID SPICELAND
AND
SURENDRA P. AGRAWAL
Memphis State University

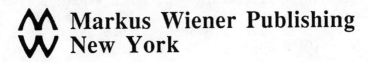 **Markus Wiener Publishing**
New York

CB

For information write to:
Markus Wiener Publishing, Inc.
2901 Broadway, New York, N.Y. 10025

Library of Congress Cataloging-in-Publication Data

Spiceland, J. David, 1949-
   An International Guide to Accounting Journals
   Includes index.
   1. Accounting--Periodicals--Bibliography.
2. Accounting literature--Publishing--Directories.
I. Agrawal, Suren, 1928-   . II. Title.
Z7164.C81S772 1987 [HF5657]   016.657'05   87-21035
ISBN 0-910129-63-0

Printed in the United States of America

4-6-90

Preface

The *International Guide to Accounting Journals* provides information relating to journals that publish unsolicited articles on accounting topics. The purpose is to assist accounting researchers in identifying appropriate publication outlets for their research.

The *Guide* includes information about journals published in 33 different countries. Journals were identified for inclusion based on an assessment of leading academic and professional journals, bibliographies, monographs, and reference sources of business libraries of the United States and Europe. Information is provided alphabetically by journal title with a separate listing by the country in which the journal is published. The primary source of information is editor response to a questionnaire mailed in the spring of 1987.

The information provided is intended to enable the author to determine the journal(s) most likely to be interested in publishing his/her manuscript. Among the data included are the journal's intended audience, the frequency with which articles are published on specific accounting topics, acceptance rate, and submission specifics.

We are grateful to the journal editors for their cooperation in providing the information for the *Guide*. We encourage readers to suggest journals to be included in future editions.

A special note of appreciation is due Lisa E. Shirley for her invaluable assistance in the compilation of these data.

August 1987
Memphis, Tennessee

TABLE OF CONTENTS

I. INFORMATION LISTED ALPHABETICALLY BY JOURNAL

Abacus

Primary readership: Academicians

Review process: 1 or 2 external blind reviewers

Invited articles: 0%

**Percentage of articles
on accounting topics:**   90

Approximate percentage of accounting-related articles devoted to:

Financial Accounting:	50	**Managerial:**	15
Computers/Systems:	5	**Tax:**	5
Auditing:	10	**Education:**	5
Professional:	5	Management:	5

Approximate percentage of accounting-related articles characterized as primarily:

Empirical:	20	**Experimental:**	20
Analytical:	20	**Descriptive:**	10
Historical and others:	30		

**Language(s) in which
articles are published:**   English

Accepts manuscripts in English for translation: N/A

Approximate acceptance rate: 10%

Review period: 3 months   **Lead time to publication after acceptance:** 4 months

Circulation: 1,400   **Frequency of publication:**   Semiannually

Sponsoring organization: Sydney University

Submission information:

Manuscript length: No limit

Number of copies: 3   **Submission fee:** $20

Style: Submit manuscripts on A4 papers, double-spaced. Use footnotes sparingly. Place them at the end of manuscript, double-spaced with an extra line between entries. Number footnotes consecutively throughout the text; use superior numbering without point. Cite books and articles in the text thus: (Jones, 1962, p. 21). List books and articles cited in alphabetical order at end of manuscript. Underline what is to be printed in italics.

**Manuscript
editor:**   Professor M. C. Wells

Abacus, Department of Accounting, University of Sydney

Lisco, 2006 Australia

Publisher: Sydney University Press

Press Building, University of Sydney

N.S.W., 2006, Australia

Academic Computing

Primary readership: Academicians

Review process: Not specified

Invited articles: Not specified

**Percentage of articles
on accounting topics:**
Approximate percentage of accounting-related articles devoted to: Not specified

Financial Accounting: **Managerial:**
Computers/Systems: **Tax:**
Auditing: **Education:**
Professional:

Approximate percentage of accounting-related articles characterized as primarily: Not specified

Empirical: **Experimental:**
Analytical: **Descriptive:**

**Language(s) in which
articles are published:**   English

Accepts manuscripts in English for translation: N/A

Approximate acceptance rate: Not specified

Review period: Not specified   **Lead time to publication after acceptance:** Not specified

Circulation: Not specified   **Frequency of publication:**   Monthly, except summer

Sponsoring organization:

Submission information:
Manuscript length: Not specified
Number of copies: Not specified **Submission fee:** None
Style: Not specified

**Manuscript
editor:**   Timothy J. Sloan
Academic Computing Publications, Inc., 200 West Virginia
McKinney, TX 75069, U. S. A.

Publisher: Same as above

Accountancy

Primary readership: Accounting (or tax) practitioners,businessmen

Review process: Editorial only

Invited articles: 81-99%

**Percentage of articles
on accounting topics:**   30

Approximate percentage of accounting-related articles devoted to:

Financial Accounting:	10	**Managerial:**	10
Computers/Systems:	25	**Tax:**	15
Auditing:	10	**Education:**	10
Professional:	5	**Other:**	15

Approximate percentage of accounting-related articles characterized as primarily: Not specified

Empirical: **Experimental:**

Analytical: **Descriptive:**

**Language(s) in which
articles are published:**   English

Accepts manuscripts in English for translation: N/A

Approximate acceptance rate: Low; prefer synopsis in advance from would-be contributors

Review period: 1-2 weeks   **Lead time to publication after acceptance:** Not specified

Circulation: 70,000 worldwide   **Frequency of publication:**   Monthly
                     (60,000 U.K.)

Sponsoring organization: Institute of Chartered Accountants In England and Wales

   Submission information:

Manuscript length: 1,000-3,500 words

Number of copies: 1   **Submission fee:**   None, honorarium is paid to the authors.

Style: Typed, single-side, double-spaced

**Manuscript
editor:**   Gillian Bird

Accountancy, The Journal of the Institute of Chartered Accountants in England and Wales, 40 Bernard St.
London WC1N 1LD, England

Publisher: Institute of Chartered Accountants in England and Wales
Chartered Accountants Hall, Moorgate Place
London EC2P 2BJ, England

Accountancy Age

Primary readership:	Academicians, accounting (or tax) practitioners (industry, public sector, and governmental), businessmen, computer specialists
Review process:	Editorial only

Invited articles: 41-60%

**Percentage of articles
on accounting topics:**   100

Approximate percentage of accounting-related articles devoted to:

Financial Accounting:	10	**Managerial:**	10
Computers/Systems:	10	**Tax:**	10
Auditing:	15	**Education:**	10
Professional:	30	**Other:**	5

Approximate percentage of accounting-related articles characterized as primarily:

Empirical:	20	**Experimental:**	
Analytical:		**Descriptive:**	80

**Language(s) in which
articles are published:**   English

Accepts manuscripts in English for translation: N/A

Approximate acceptance rate: Not specified

Review period: 1 week to 1 month   **Lead time to publication after acceptance:** Varies

Circulation: 85,000   **Frequency of publication:**   Weekly

Sponsoring organization: None

Submission information:

Manuscript length: 1,200 words

Number of copies: 2   **Submission fee:** None

Style: Highly readable and clear

**Manuscript
editor:**   Jill Papworth, Features Editor

Accountancy Age, VNU Publications, VNU House, 32-34 Broadwick St.

London W1A 2HG, England

Publisher: Same as above

Accountancy Ireland

Primary readership: Accounting (or tax) practitioners

Review process: Editorial only

Invited articles: 61-80%

**Percentage of articles
on accounting topics:** 75

Approximate percentage of accounting-related articles devoted to: Each issue is devoted to a particular topic

Financial Accounting: **Managerial:**

Computers/Systems: **Tax:**

Auditing: **Education:**

Professional:

Approximate percentage of accounting-related articles characterized as primarily: Not specified

Empirical: **Experimental:**

Analytical: **Descriptive:**

**Language(s) in which
articles are published:** English

Accepts manuscripts in English for translation: N/A

Approximate acceptance rate: N/A

Review period: 3 weeks   **Lead time to publication after acceptance:** 3 months

Circulation: 9,500   **Frequency of publication:** Bi-monthly

Sponsoring organization: Institute of Chartered Accountants in Ireland

Submission information:

Manuscript length: 2,500 words
Number of copies: 1   **Submission fee:** None
Style: No specific style listed

**Manuscript
editor:** B. J. Lynch
Accountancy Ireland, Chartered Accountants House, 87-89 Pembroke Road,
Dublin 4, Ireland

Publisher: Same as above

Accountant (England)

Primary readership: Accounting (or tax) practitioners, students

Review process: Editorial

Invited articles: None

**Percentage of articles
on accounting topics:** 90

Approximate percentage of accounting-related articles devoted to:

Financial Accounting:		**Managerial:**	
Computers/Systems:		**Tax:**	
Auditing:		**Education:**	
Professional:	80	Not specified, varies with each issue:	20

Approximate percentage of accounting-related articles characterized as primarily: Not specified

Empirical:	**Experimental:**	
Analytical:	**Descriptive:**	

**Language(s) in which
articles are published:** English

Accepts manuscripts in English for translation: N/A

Approximate acceptance rate: 90%

Review period: 2 months   **Lead time to publication after acceptance:** 1 month

Circulation: 10,500   **Frequency of publication:** Quarterly

Sponsoring organization: None

Submission information:

Manuscript length: 1,000 words per page of the journal

Number of copies: 1   **Submission fee:** None

Style: None

**Manuscript
editor:** Richard Waters, Editor
The Accountant, Lafferty Publications Ltd, 2 Pear Tree Court
London EC1R 0DS, England

Publisher: Lafferty Publications Ltd.
The Accountant, 3-4 Hardwick St.
London EC1 4RY, England

Accountant (Netherlands)

Primary readership: Not specified

Review process: Not specified

Invited articles: Not specified

**Percentage of articles
on accounting topics:**
Approximate percentage of accounting-related articles devoted to: Not specified

Financial Accounting:	**Managerial:**
Computers/Systems:	**Tax:**
Auditing:	**Education:**
Professional:	

Approximate percentage of accounting-related articles characterized as primarily: Not specified

Empirical:	**Experimental:**
Analytical:	**Descriptive:**

**Language(s) in which
articles are published:**   Dutch

Accepts manuscripts in English for translation:

Approximate acceptance rate: Not specified

Review period: Not specified   **Lead time to publication after acceptance:** Not specified

Circulation: 12,000   **Frequency of publication:**   Not specified

Sponsoring organization:

Submission information:
Manuscript length: Not specified
Number of copies: Not specified **Submission fee:** Not specified
Style: Not specified

**Manuscript
editor:**   H. Volten and H. H. Bos
Netherlands Instituut van Registeraccountants, Postbus 7984
1008 AD Amsterdam, Netherlands

Publisher: Same as above

Accountants' Journal (New Zealand)

Primary readership: Accounting (or tax) practitioners

Review process: Editorial only

Invited articles: 21-40%

**Percentage of articles
on accounting topics:**   80

Approximate percentage of accounting-related articles devoted to:

Financial Accounting:	10	Managerial:	10
Computers/Systems:	10	Tax:	10
Auditing:	15	Education:	5
Professional:	5	Investments; Law:	35

Approximate percentage of accounting-related articles characterized as primarily:

Empirical:	10	Experimental:	
Analytical:	30	Descriptive:	60

**Language(s) in which
articles are published:**   English

Accepts manuscripts in English for translation: N/A

Approximate acceptance rate: 30%

Review period: 3 months   **Lead time to publication after acceptance:** 3 months

Circulation: 13,673   **Frequency of publication:**   Monthly - except January

Sponsoring organization: New Zealand Society of Accountants

Submission information:

Manuscript length: 1,500 words

Number of copies: 2   **Submission fee:** None

Style: Informal but informative. Contact the editor for more information concerning manuscript publication.

**Manuscript
editor:**   Chris Wright
Accountants' Journal, Willbank House, 57 Willis St., P.O. Box 11342
Wellington, New Zealand

Publisher: Same as above

Accountants' Journal (Philippines)

Primary readership: Not specified

Review process: Not specified

Invited articles: Not specified

**Percentage of articles
on accounting topics:**
Approximate percentage of accounting-related articles devoted to: Not specified

Financial Accounting:	Managerial:
Computers/Systems:	Tax:
Auditing:	Education:
Professional:	

Approximate percentage of accounting-related articles characterized as primarily: Not specified

Empirical:	Experimental:
Analytical:	Descriptive:

**Language(s) in which
articles are published:**   Not specified

Accepts manuscripts in English for translation:

Approximate acceptance rate: Not specified

Review period: Not specified   **Lead time to publication after acceptance:** Not specified

Circulation: 15,000   **Frequency of publication:**   Not specified

Sponsoring organization: Philippine Institute of Certified Public Accountants

Submission information:
Manuscript length: Not specified
Number of copies: Not specified   **Submission fee:**   Not specified
Style: Not specified

**Manuscript
editor:**   Philippine Institute of Certified Public Accountants
    PICPA House, 700 Shaw Blvd.
    Mandaluyong, Metro-Manila, Philippines

Publisher: Same as above

Accountant's Magazine, The

Primary readership: Academicians, accounting (or tax) practitioners, businessmen

Review process: 1 external blind reviewer

Invited articles: 21-40%

**Percentage of articles
on accounting topics:**   50

Approximate percentage of accounting-related articles devoted to:

Financial Accounting:	15	Managerial:	10
Computers/Systems:	15	Tax:	15
Auditing:	15	Education:	5
Professional:	10	Other:	15

Approximate percentage of accounting-related articles characterized as primarily:

Empirical:	20	Experimental:	10
Analytical:	35	Descriptive:	15
Other	20		

**Language(s) in which
articles are published:**   English

Accepts manuscripts in English for translation: N/A

Approximate acceptance rate: 30%

Review period: 1-2 months   **Lead time to publication after acceptance:** 1-6 months

Circulation: 13,500   **Frequency of publication:**   Monthly

Sponsoring organization: The Institute of Chartered Accountants of Scotland

Submission information:

Manuscript length: 1,000 - 3,000 words

Number of copies: 1   **Submission fee:** None

Style: Articles should be typed, double-spaced, on A4 paper and submitted on an exclusive basis. Footnotes should be avoided. Sources should not be quoted unnecessarily; if unavoidable, it should be done briefly in the form of a numbered reference. Diagrams, tables, etc. should be provided on separate sheets and not folded. If they are intended to appear within the text, their locations should be clearly indicated.

**Manuscript
editor:**   Winifred Elliott

The Accountant's Magazine, 27 Queen St.

Edinburgh EH2 1LA, Scotland

Publisher: Same as above

Accounting and Business Research

Primary readership: Academicians, accounting (or tax) practitioners

Review process: 2 external blind reviewers

Invited articles: 1-20%

**Percentage of articles
on accounting topics:**   100

Approximate percentage of accounting-related articles devoted to:

Financial Accounting:	35	**Managerial:**	20
Computers/Systems:	5	**Tax:**	5
Auditing:	5	**Education:**	5
Professional:	5	Finance:	20

Approximate percentage of accounting-related articles characterized as primarily:

Empirical:	40	**Experimental:**	10
Analytical:	40	**Descriptive:**	10

**Language(s) in which
articles are published:**   English

Accepts manuscripts in English for translation: N/A

Approximate acceptance rate: 30%

Review period: 2-3 months   **Lead time to publication after acceptance:** 6 months

Circulation: 1,400   **Frequency of publication:**   Quarterly

Sponsoring organization: Institute of Chartered Accountants in England and Wales

Submission information:

Manuscript length: 3,000-7,000

Number of copies: 3   **Submission fee:** $34 for non-subscribers, none for subscribers.

Style: Manuscripts should be typed, double-spaced. Footnotes should be used only to avoid interrupting the continuity of the text and should not be used excessively. References should be listed at the end of the paper and referred to in the text. Entries should be arranged alphabetically by surname of the first author. Tables and figures should bear a number and title and should be referred to in the text. Sources should be clearly stated.

**Manuscript
editor:**   R. H. Parker

Accounting and Business Research, Amory Building, Rennes Drive

Exeter EX4 4RJ, England

Publisher: Institute of Chartered Accountants in England and Wales

P. O. Box 433, Moorgate Place

London EC 2P, England

Accounting and Finance

Primary readership:	Academicians
Review process:	2 external reviewers (authors known)
Invited articles:	0%

**Percentage of articles
on accounting topics:** 60

Approximate percentage of accounting-related articles devoted to:

Financial Accounting:	40	**Managerial:**	30
Computers/Systems:	10	**Tax:**	10
Auditing:		**Education:**	
Professional:	10		

Approximate percentage of accounting-related articles characterized as primarily:

Empirical:	60	**Experimental:**	
Analytical:	35	**Descriptive:**	5

**Language(s) in which
articles are published:** English

Accepts manuscripts in English for translation: N/A

Approximate acceptance rate: 20%

Review period: 2 months **Lead time to publication after acceptance:** 6-12 months

Circulation: 750 **Frequency of publication:** Semiannually

Sponsoring organization: Accounting Association of Australia & New Zealand (ARANZ)

Submission information:

Manuscript length: No longer than 30 pages

Number of copies: 3 **Submission fee:** $25, for those who are not members of ARANZ

Style: Double-spaced. Headings, figures, tables, and diagrams should be numbered consecutively and titled. Footnotes should be numbered consecutively with superscript arabic numerals. Footnotes must appear on the page they are referred to and not as a separate sheet at the end of the manuscript. References should be typed on separate sheets at the end of the manuscript.

**Manuscript
editor:**

Professor F. J. Finn, Editor

Accounting and Finance, Dept. of Commerce, University of Queensland

St. Lucia., Queensland, 4067 Australia

Publisher: Same as above

Accounting, Auditing and Accountability Journal

Primary readership: Academicians, accounting (or tax) practitioners,businessmen, decision makers

Review process: 2 external blind reviewers

Invited articles: 1-20%

**Percentage of articles
on accounting topics:**   100

Approximate percentage of accounting-related articles devoted to: Not specified

Financial Accounting: **Managerial:**

Computers/Systems: **Tax:**

Auditing: **Education:**

Professional:

Approximate percentage of accounting-related articles characterized as primarily:

Empirical:	25	**Experimental:**	
Analytical:	25	**Descriptive:**	25
Case study:	25		

**Language(s) in which
articles are published:**   English

Accepts manuscripts in English for translation: N/A

Approximate acceptance rate: 20%

Review period: 6 weeks   **Lead time to publication after acceptance:** 6-9 months

Circulation: 1,000 (estimated) **Frequency of publication:**   Semiannually

Sponsoring organization: None

Submission information:

Manuscript length: 5,000 words

Number of copies: 4   **Submission fee:** None

Style: Contact the editor for information concerning manuscript publication.

**Manuscript
editor:**   James Guthrie, Joint Editor

Accounting, Auditing and Accountability Journal, School of Accountancy, University of New South Wales

Sydney, 2033 Australia

U.S. Editor – Barbara Merino

Department of Accounting, North Texas State University

Denton, TX 76203-3677

Publisher: MCB University Press Ltd.

62 Toller Lane

Bradford BD8 9BY, England

Accounting, Business and Insurance

Primary readership:	Academicians
Review process:	2 external blind reviewers
Invited articles:	Not specified

**Percentage of articles
on accounting topics:** 40

Approximate percentage of accounting-related articles devoted to: Not specified

Financial Accounting:	**Managerial:**
Computers/Systems:	**Tax:**
Auditing:	**Education:**
Professional:	

Approximate percentage of accounting-related articles characterized as primarily: Not specified

Empirical:	**Experimental:**
Analytical:	**Descriptive:**

**Language(s) in which
articles are published:** Arabic, English

Accepts manuscripts in English for translation: N/A

Approximate acceptance rate: 50%

Review period: 2-3 weeks	**Lead time to publication after acceptance:** 2 months
Circulation: 1,000	**Frequency of publication:** Quarterly

Sponsoring organization: Faculty of Commerce, Cairo University

Submission information:

Manuscript length: 40 Pages	
Number of copies: 3	**Submission fee:** $15
Style: None specified	

**Manuscript
editor:** Dr. Mahmoud Bazaraa, Vice Dean
Accounting, Business and Insurance, Faculty of Commerce, Cairo University
Cairo, Egypt

Publisher: Not specified

Accounting Educators' Journal

Primary readership: People interested in the education of accountants

Review process: 1 or more blind reviewers

Invited articles: not specified

**Percentage of articles
on accounting topics:**   100

Approximate percentage of accounting-related articles devoted to:

Financial Accounting:		**Managerial:**	
Computers/Systems:		**Tax:**	
Auditing:		**Education:**	100
Professional:			

Approximate percentage of accounting-related articles characterized as primarily: Not specified

Empirical:	**Experimental:**
Analytical:	**Descriptive:**

**Language(s) in which
articles are published:**   English

Accepts manuscripts in English for translation: N/A

Approximate acceptance rate: New journal

Review period: Not specified   **Lead time to publication after acceptance:** Not specified

Circulation: Not specified   **Frequency of publication:**   Semiannually

Sponsoring organization: Department of Accounting, University of Nevada, Las Vegas

Submission information:

Manuscript length: Not specified

Number of copies: 3   **Submission fee:** $25 ($15 for subscribers)

Style: References in square brackets in text, 100-200 word abstract, footnotes at the end of text

**Manuscript
editor:**
   Prof. Ronald A. Milne
   Department of Accounting, College of Business Administration, University of Nevada - Las Vegas
   Las Vegas, NV 89154, U. S. A.,

Publisher: Same as above

Accounting Historians Journal, The

Primary readership: Academicians, business and academic historians, interested practicing professionals

Review process: External blind reviewers

Invited articles: 1-20%

Percentage of articles on accounting topics: 100

Approximate percentage of accounting-related articles devoted to: Not specified

Financial Accounting: **Managerial:**

Computers/Systems: **Tax:**

Auditing: **Education:**

Professional:

Approximate percentage of accounting-related articles characterized as primarily:

Empirical: 10   **Experimental:**

Analytical: 40   **Descriptive:** 30

Other: 20

Language(s) in which articles are published: English

Accepts manuscripts in English for translation: N/A

Approximate acceptance rate: 20%

Review period: 3 months   **Lead time to publication after acceptance:** 3-6 months

Circulation: 600   **Frequency of publication:** Semiannually

Sponsoring organization: The Academy of Accounting Historians

Submission information:

Manuscript length: 15 pages, double-spaced

Number of copies: 3   **Submission fee:** $25 for non-academy members; $15 for academy members

Style: The Accounting Review submission style is used; e .g., block citations of an article appear within the text, textual footnotes appear at the bottom of page, and references listed at the end of the article.

Manuscript editor: Gary J. Previts

The Accounting Historians Journal, Box 658, University Plaza, Georgia State University Atlanta, GA 30303, U. S. A.

Publisher: Same as above

Accounting Horizons

Primary readership: Academicians, practitioners

Review process: Blind reviews

Invited articles: Some

**Percentage of articles
on accounting topics:**   100

Approximate percentage of accounting-related articles devoted to: Not specified

Financial Accounting:	**Managerial:**
Computers/Systems:	**Tax:**
Auditing:	**Education:**
Professional:	

Approximate percentage of accounting-related articles characterized as primarily: Not specified

Empirical:	**Experimental:**
Analytical:	**Descriptive:**

**Language(s) in which
articles are published:**   English

Accepts manuscripts in English for translation: N/A

Approximate acceptance rate: Low

Review period: Not specified   **Lead time to publication after acceptance:** Not specified

Circulation: N/A   **Frequency of publication:**   Quarterly

Sponsoring organization: American Accounting Association

Submission information:

Manuscript length: not specified

Number of copies: 3   **Submission fee:** None

Style: That of The Accounting Review except references should be in footnotes; readable to non-researchers

**Manuscript
editor:**   R. K. Mautz
    Accounting Horizons, 684 East 4149 South
    Salt Lake City, UT 84107, U. S. A.

Publisher: American Accounting Association
    5717 Bessie Drive
    Sarasota, FL 33583, U. S. A.

Accounting News

Primary readership:	Accounting (or tax) practitioners, businessmen, CFOs, controllers, CPAs

Review process: Editorial only

Invited articles: Not specified

**Percentage of articles
on accounting topics:** 80

Approximate percentage of accounting-related articles devoted to: Not specified

Financial Accounting:	**Managerial:**
Computers/Systems:	**Tax:**
Auditing:	**Education:**
Professional:	

Approximate percentage of accounting-related articles characterized as primarily: Not specified

Empirical:	**Experimental:**
Analytical:	**Descriptive:**

**Language(s) in which
articles are published:** English

Accepts manuscripts in English for translation: N/A

Approximate acceptance rate: Varies

Review period: Varies   **Lead time to publication after acceptance:** 3 months

Circulation: 100,000   **Frequency of publication:** Quarterly

Sponsoring organization: None

Submission information:

Manuscript length: Varies

Number of copies: 2   **Submission fee:** None

Style: "How-to" articles, not theoretical

**Manuscript
editor:**
Jill Koenigsberg, Accounting Editor
Accounting News, Warren, Gorham & Lamont, Inc., One Penn Plaza, 40th Floor
New York, NY 10119, U. S. A.

Publisher: Warren, Gorham & Lamont, Inc.
210 South St.
Boston, MA 02111, U.S. A.

Accounting, Organizations and Society

Primary readership: Academicians

Review process: 2 or more external blind reviewers

Invited articles: 1-20%

**Percentage of articles
on accounting topics:** 100

Approximate percentage of accounting-related articles devoted to: Varies with each issue

Financial Accounting:	**Managerial:**
Computers/Systems:	**Tax:**
Auditing:	**Education:**
Professional:	

Approximate percentage of accounting-related articles characterized as primarily: Not specified

Empirical:	**Experimental:**
Analytical:	**Descriptive:**

**Language(s) in which
articles are published:** English

Accepts manuscripts in English for translation: N/A

Approximate acceptance rate: 15%

Review period: 3 months   **Lead time to publication after acceptance:** 3-6 months

Circulation: 1,500 +   **Frequency of publication:** 6 times a year

Sponsoring organization: None

Submission information:

Manuscript length: Open

Number of copies: 3   **Submission fee:** None

Style: Each table and figure should have number and brief title; placement in the text should be clearly indicated. No footnotes for literature citation. If footnotes are used, they should be used for elaboration and clarification and should be numbered consecutively throughout the text. The bibliography should include only those references cited in the text and should be arranged alphabetically by first author's last name.

Manuscript editor:

Professor A. G. Hopwood (for all articles except those relating to cognitive aspects of accounting)

Department of Accounting & Finance, London School of Economics and Political Science, Houghton St.

London WC2A 2AE, U.K.

Professor Barry Lewis (for articles relating to cognitive aspects of accounting)

Accounting, Organizations and Society, Graduate School of Business, University of Pittsburgh

Pittsburgh, PA 15260

Publisher: Pergamon Press - Journals Division

Maxwell House, Fairview Park

Elmsford, NY 10523, USA

Accounting Review, The

Primary readership: Academicians

Review process: 2 external blind reviewers

Invited articles: 1-20%

**Percentage of articles
on accounting topics:**   100

Approximate percentage of accounting-related articles devoted to: Varies by issue

Financial Accounting: **Managerial:**

Computers/Systems: **Tax:**

Auditing: **Education:**

Professional:

Approximate percentage of accounting-related articles characterized as primarily: Varies by issue

Empirical: **Experimental:**

Analytical: **Descriptive:**

**Language(s) in which
articles are published:**   English

Accepts manuscripts in English for translation: N/A

Approximate acceptance rate: 15%

Review period: 2 months   **Lead time to publication after acceptance:** 5 months

Circulation: 18,000   **Frequency of publication:**   Quarterly

Sponsoring organization: American Accounting Association

Submission information:

Manuscript length: 7,000 words maximum

Number of copies: 3   **Submission fee:** $25

Style: Double-spaced, except for indented quotations, footnotes, and references. Footnotes for extensions whose inclusion in the body of the manuscript might disrupt continuity. Footnotes numbered consecutively. Reference list must include only those works actually cited. Each table and figure should appear on a separate page and bear an arabic number and a title. A helpful guide is The Elements of Style by Strunk and White.

**Manuscript
editor:**   William R. Kinney, Jr.

The Accounting Review, GSBA, University of Michigan

Ann Arbor, Michigan 48109, U. S. A.

Publisher: Mr. Paul Gerhardt

American Accounting Association, 5717 Bessie Dr.

Sarasota, FL 33583, U. S. A.

Accounting Technician

Primary readership: Academicians, accounting (or tax) practitioners, students, and members

Review process: Not specified

Invited articles: 41-60%

**Percentage of articles
on accounting topics:** 100

Approximate percentage of accounting-related articles devoted to:

Financial Accounting:	20	**Managerial:**	20
Computers/Systems:	20	**Tax:**	20
Auditing:	10	**Education:**	10
Professional:			

Approximate percentage of accounting-related articles characterized as primarily:

Empirical:	5	**Experimental:**	5
Analytical:	65	**Descriptive:**	25

**Language(s) in which
articles are published:** English

Accepts manuscripts in English for translation: N/A

Approximate acceptance rate: 10-20%

Review period: 2 months   **Lead time to publication after acceptance:** 2 months

Circulation: 38,000   **Frequency of publication:** Monthly

Sponsoring organization: Association of Accounting Technicians

Submission information:

Manuscript length: 1,500 words
Number of copies: 1   **Submission fee:** 75 pounds (U.K.)
Style: None

**Manuscript
editor:** Graham Hambly
8A Hythe St.
Dartford, Kent DA1 1BX, England

Publisher: Association of Accounting Technicians
21 Jockey's Fields
London WC1R 4BN, England

Administrative Accountant

Primary readership: Accounting (or tax) practitioners

Review process: Editorial only

Invited articles: 1-20%

**Percentage of articles
on accounting topics:**   75

Approximate percentage of accounting-related articles devoted to: Not specified

Financial Accounting: **Managerial:**
Computers/Systems: **Tax:**
Auditing: **Education:**
Professional:

Approximate percentage of accounting-related articles characterized as primarily: Not specified

Empirical: **Experimental:**
Analytical: **Descriptive:**

**Language(s) in which
articles are published:**   English

Accepts manuscripts in English for translation: N/A

Approximate acceptance rate: 50%

Review period: 1 month   **Lead time to publication after acceptance:** 4 months

Circulation: 15,500   **Frequency of publication:**   Bi-monthly

Sponsoring organization: Institute of Administrative Accountants

Submission information:
Manuscript length: 1,000-1,500 words
Number of copies: 2   **Submission fee:** None
Style: None specified

**Manuscript
editor:**
      Derek Bradley
      Administrative Accountant, 8 Holmwood Ave, South Croydon
      Surrey, CR2 9HY, U. K.

Publisher: Institute of Administrative Accountants
      44 London Rd, Sevenoaks
      Kent, TN13 1AS, England

Advances in Accounting

Primary readership: Academicians, accounting (or tax) practitioners

Review process: 2 external blind reviewers and an associate editor

Invited articles: 1-20%

**Percentage of articles
on accounting topics:**   100

Approximate percentage of accounting-related articles devoted to:

Financial Accounting:	33	**Managerial:**	
Computers/Systems:		**Tax:**	
Auditing:	33	**Education:**	34
Professional:			

Approximate percentage of accounting-related articles characterized as primarily:

Empirical:	55	**Experimental:**	35
Analytical:	10	**Descriptive:**	

**Language(s) in which
articles are published:**   English

Accepts manuscripts in English for translation: N/A

Approximate acceptance rate: 20-25%

Review period: 60 days   **Lead time to publication after acceptance:** 6 months

Circulation: Not specified   **Frequency of publication:**   Annually

Sponsoring organization: JAI Press

Submission information:

Manuscript length: 20-25 pages with instrument if pertinent

Number of copies: 4   **Submission fee:** None

Style: All manuscripts should be typed, double-spaced on 8 1/2 by 11" white paper, single-sided. Tables, figures, and exhibits should appear on a separate page. Each should be numbered and have a title. Footnotes should be presented by citing the author's name and the year of publication in the body of the text. References should include those actually cited in the text. Contact the editor for more information regarding manuscript.

**Manuscript
editor:**   Bill N. Schwartz

Advances in Accounting, School of Business and Management, Temple University

Philadelphia, PA 19122, U. S. A.

Publisher: JAI Press

P.O. Box 1678, 36 Sherwood Place

Greenwich, CT 06836, U. S. A.

Advances in Accounting Information Systems

Primary readership: Academicians, accounting (or tax) practitioners

Review process: 2 blind reviewers

Invited articles: 0%

**Percentage of articles
on accounting topics:**   100

Approximate percentage of accounting-related articles devoted to:

Financial Accounting:	**Managerial:**	
Computers/Systems: 100	**Tax:**	
Auditing:	**Education:**	
Professional:		

Approximate percentage of accounting-related articles characterized as primarily:

Empirical:	**Experimental:**	50
Analytical: 50	**Descriptive:**	

**Language(s) in which
articles are published:**   English

Accepts manuscripts in English for translation: N/A

Approximate acceptance rate: 15-20

Review period: 2 months   **Lead time to publication after acceptance:** Not specified

Circulation: New journal   **Frequency of publication:**   Annually

Sponsoring organization:

Submission information:
Manuscript length: not specified
Number of copies: 3   **Submission fee:** None
Style: Available upon request.

**Manuscript
editor:**   Gary Grudnitski

Advances in Accounting Information Systems, Graduate School of Business, University of Texas
Austin, TX 78212-1172, U. S. A.

Publisher: JAI Press

P.O. Box 1678, 36 Sherwood Place
Greenwich, CT 06836, U. S. A.

Advances in International Accounting

Primary readership: Academicians, practitioners

Review process: 2 blind reviewers

Invited articles: none

**Percentage of articles
on accounting topics:**   100

Approximate percentage of accounting-related articles devoted to:

Financial Accounting:	**Managerial:**
Computers/Systems:	**Tax:**
Auditing:	**Education:**
Professional:	**Intn'l. standard setting:** 100

Approximate percentage of accounting-related articles characterized as primarily: Research- no "think pieces"

Empirical:	**Experimental:**
Analytical:	**Descriptive:**

**Language(s) in which
articles are published:**   English

Accepts manuscripts in English for translation: N/A

Approximate acceptance rate: 50%

Review period: 3-4 months   **Lead time to publication after acceptance:** 2 years

Circulation: 1,000   **Frequency of publication:**   Annually

Sponsoring organization: None

> **Submission information:**

Manuscript length: Not specified

Number of copies: 3   **Submission fee:** None

Style: Available upon request.

**Manuscript
editor:**   Kenneth S. Most

College of Business Administration, Florida International University

Miami, FL 33199, U. S. A.

Publisher: JAI Press

P.O. Box 1678, 36 Sherwood Place

Greenwich, CT 06836, U. S. A.

Advances in Public Interest Accounting

Primary readership: Academicians

Review process: 1-2 blind reviewers

Invited articles: 1-20%

**Percentage of articles
on accounting topics:** 100

Approximate percentage of accounting-related articles devoted to: Not specified

Financial Accounting: **Managerial:**

Computers/Systems: **Tax:**

Auditing: **Education:**

Professional:

Approximate percentage of accounting-related articles characterized as primarily: Not specified

Empirical: **Experimental:**

Analytical: **Descriptive:**

**Language(s) in which
articles are published:** English

Accepts manuscripts in English for translation: N/A

Approximate acceptance rate: 50%

Review period: 2 months   **Lead time to publication after acceptance:** 9 months

Circulation: Not specified   **Frequency of publication:** Annually

Sponsoring organization: None

Submission information:

Manuscript length: Not specified

Number of copies: 3   **Submission fee:** None

Style: All manuscripts should be typewritten and double-spaced on 8 1/2 x 11" paper, single-sided. Tables, figures, and exhibits should appear on a separate page. Each should be numbered and have a title. Footnotes should be presented by citing the author's name and the year of publication in the body of the text. Reference list should only include those actually cited in the text. Contact the editor for more information.

Manuscript editor:

Marilyn Neimark

Advances in Public Interest Accounting, Baruch College-CUNY, 17 Lexington Ave., Box 501 New York, NY 10010, U. S. A.

Publisher: JAI Press

P.O. Box 1678, 36 Sherwood Place

Greenwich, CT 06836, U. S. A.

AEDS Journal

Primary readership: Academicians, computer specialists

Review process: External reviewers (authors known)

Invited articles: 1-20%

**Percentage of articles
on accounting topics:**   5

Approximate percentage of accounting-related articles devoted to:

Financial Accounting:		**Managerial:**	
Computers/Systems:	40	**Tax:**	
Auditing:		**Education:**	40
Professional:	20		

Approximate percentage of accounting-related articles characterized as primarily:

Empirical:	25	**Experimental:**	25
Analytical:	25	**Descriptive:**	25

**Language(s) in which
articles are published:**   English

Accepts manuscripts in English for translation: N/A

Approximate acceptance rate: 50%

Review period: 6 weeks   **Lead time to publication after acceptance:** 9 months

Circulation: 2,500   **Frequency of publication:**   Quarterly

Sponsoring organization: Association for Educational Data Systems

Submission information:

Manuscript length: 10-25 typed, double-spaced

Number of copies: 4   **Submission fee:** None

Style: Manuscripts should be typed double-spaced on 8 1/2 x 11" paper with ample margins. Format of footnotes, references, etc. should be in the style described in the Publication Manual of the American Psychological Association.

**Manuscript
editor:**   Dennis W. Spuck

AEDS Journal, University of Houston-Clear Lake, 2700 Bay Area Blvd.

Houston, TX   77058, U. S. A.

Publisher: Association for Educational Data Systems

1201 Sixteenth St., N.W.

Washington, D.C.   20036, U. S. A.

Akron Business and Economic Review

Primary readership: Academicians

Review process: 3 external blind reviewers

Invited articles: 0%

**Percentage of articles
on accounting topics:**

Approximate percentage of accounting-related articles devoted to: Not specified

Financial Accounting:	**Managerial:**
Computers/Systems:	**Tax:**
Auditing:	**Education:**
Professional:	

Approximate percentage of accounting-related articles characterized as primarily: Not specified

Empirical:	**Experimental:**
Analytical:	**Descriptive:**

**Language(s) in which
articles are published:**   English

Accepts manuscripts in English for translation: N/A

Approximate acceptance rate: 15-20%

Review period: 6-8 weeks   **Lead time to publication after acceptance:** 9 months

Circulation: 2,500   **Frequency of publication:**   Quarterly

Sponsoring organization: University of Akron

Submission information:

Manuscript length: No limit

Number of copies: 3   **Submission fee:** None

Style: Bibliographic entries listed alphabetically at the end of the manuscript under the heading of "References." A reference in the text to a specific manuscript should be indicated by a bracketed number which reflects the author's "References." Each table and figure should bear a number and a title and a marginal notation made where in the text the table or figure should be placed. See publication for more information.

Manuscript editor: Dr. J. D. Williams, Editor

Akron Business and Economic Review, Kolbe Hall 107, University of Akron, CBA, 302 E. Buchtel Ave. Akron, OH 44325, U. S. A.

Publisher: Same as above

Akuntansi & Administrasi

Primary readership: Academicians, accounting (or tax) practitioners, businessmen, students

Review process: Editorial and 1 external blind reviewer

Invited articles: 21-40%

**Percentage of articles
on accounting topics:**   76

Approximate percentage of accounting-related articles devoted to:

Financial Accounting:	15	**Managerial:**	20
Computers/Systems:	11	**Tax:**	14
Auditing:	15	**Education:**	11
Professional:	11	**Other:**	3

Approximate percentage of accounting-related articles characterized as primarily:

Empirical:	5	**Experimental:**	5
Analytical:	20	**Descriptive:**	60
Other:	10		

**Language(s) in which
articles are published:**   Indonesian, English

Accepts manuscripts in English for translation: Yes

Approximate acceptance rate: Not specified

Review period: Not specified   **Lead time to publication after acceptance:** 2-3 months

Circulation: 10,000   **Frequency of publication:**   Monthly

Sponsoring organization: Indonesian Institute of Accountants

    Submission information:

Manuscript length: 3,000 to 5,000 words

Number of copies: 1   **Submission fee:** None

Style: None

**Manuscript
editor:**   Soemarso Sr

    Tata Usaha Akuntansi, Jalan Kapuas No. 5., Tromol pos No. 3579

    Jakarta, Indonesia

Publisher: Same as above

American Business Law Journal

Primary readership: Academicians, accounting (or tax) practitioners, businessmen

Review process: 3 external blind reviewers

Invited articles: 1-20%

Percentage of articles on accounting topics: 20

Approximate percentage of accounting-related articles devoted to:

Financial Accounting:	15	**Managerial:**	10
Computers/Systems:		**Tax:**	50
Auditing:	25	**Education:**	
Professional:			

Approximate percentage of accounting-related articles characterized as primarily:

Empirical:	100	**Experimental:**	
Analytical:		**Descriptive:**	

Language(s) in which articles are published: English

Accepts manuscripts in English for translation: N/A

Approximate acceptance rate: 18-20%

Review period: 2 months   **Lead time to publication after acceptance:** 6 months

Circulation: 2,500-3,000   **Frequency of publication:** Quarterly

Sponsoring organization: American Business Law Association

Submission information:

Manuscript length: 20-100 manuscript pages

Number of copies: 3   **Submission fee:** None

Style: All copy, including footnotes and indented portions, must be at least double-spaced with wide margins on one side only of white 8 1/2 x 11" paper. A removable cover page should be included. Tables should be typed on a separate page with explanatory heading and source. The text should indicate the appropriate place for insertion.

Manuscript editor: Virginia Marver

Amercian Business Law Journal, College of Business, University of Florida

Gainesville, FL 32611, U. S. A.

Publisher: Same as above

American Economist, The

Primary readership: Academicians

Review process: 100 external reviewers (authors known)

Invited articles: 1-20%

**Percentage of articles
on accounting topics:**   5

Approximate percentage of accounting-related articles devoted to:

Financial Accounting:	**Managerial:**	20
Computers/Systems:	**Tax:**	60
Auditing:	**Education:**	20
Professional:		

Approximate percentage of accounting-related articles characterized as primarily:

Empirical:	**Experimental:**	
Analytical: 50	**Descriptive:**	40
Other: 10		

**Language(s) in which
articles are published:**   English

Accepts manuscripts in English for translation: N/A

Approximate acceptance rate: 20%

Review period: 6 months   **Lead time to publication after acceptance:** 1 year

Circulation: 8,000   **Frequency of publication:**   Semiannually

Sponsoring organization: Omicron Delta Epsilon

Submission information:

Manuscript length: 10-15 pages

Number of copies: 3   **Submission fee:** None

Style: Copies should be on standard 8 1/2 x 11" paper. Double space all material throughout, including footnotes, references, and quoted matter. Leave 1 inch margin on all sides. Place all references (no more than 10), alphabetized by author, in a numbered list at the end of the paper. Footnotes should be substantive and typed on separate sheets following the last page of the article and numbered consecutively throughout the article.

**Manuscript
editor:**   Professor Michael Szenberg

The American Economist, Graduate School of Business, Pace University

New York, NY 10038, U. S. A.

Publisher: Dr. William D. Gunther

Department of Economics, P.O. Drawer AS, University of Alabama

University, AL 35486, U. S. A.

American Journal of Small Business

Primary readership: Academicians, consultants, government officials

Review process: 3 external blind reviewers

Invited articles: 1-20%

**Percentage of articles
on accounting topics:**   10

Approximate percentage of accounting-related articles devoted to: Not specified

Financial Accounting:	**Managerial:**
Computers/Systems:	**Tax:**
Auditing:	**Education:**
Professional:	

Approximate percentage of accounting-related articles characterized as primarily: Any research - based articles

Empirical:	**Experimental:**
Analytical:	**Descriptive:**

**Language(s) in which
articles are published:**   English

Accepts manuscripts in English for translation:

Approximate acceptance rate: 25%

Review period: 60 days   **Lead time to publication after acceptance:** 6 months

Circulation: about 800   **Frequency of publication:**   Quarterly

Sponsoring organization: University of Baltimore

Submission information:

Manuscript length: 15-25 pages, but length is not a major issue

Number of copies: 4   **Submission fee:** None

Style: Footnotes should be used only for clarification that is not appropriate for the body of the manuscript, consecutively numbered, and marked at the appropriate place in the text. Tables, charts, and graphs should be included only when they contribute materially to an understanding of the written presentation.   All publications cited in the text should be listed alphabetically by author's last name in the "References" section.

**Manuscript
editor:**

D. Ray Bagby, Executive Editor

American Journal of Small Business, University of Baltimore, 1420 N. Charles St. at Mt. Royal

Baltimore, MD 21201, U. S. A.

Publisher: American Journal of Small Business

P.O. Box 465

Hanover, PA 17331, U. S. A.

Annals of the School of Business Admin., Kobe University

Primary readership: Academicians, businessmen

Review process: Editorial only

Invited articles: 21-40%

**Percentage of articles
on accounting topics:**   30

Approximate percentage of accounting-related articles devoted to: Not specified

Financial Accounting: **Managerial:**

Computers/Systems: **Tax:**

Auditing: **Education:**

Professional:

Approximate percentage of accounting-related articles characterized as primarily: Not specified

Empirical: **Experimental:**

Analytical: **Descriptive:**

**Language(s) in which
articles are published:**   English, German, French, Russian

Accepts manuscripts in English for translation: N/A

Approximate acceptance rate: Articles accepted in the order of receipt; backlog published in the following year or as Working Papers.

Review period: **Lead time to publication after acceptance:** 5-6 months

Circulation: 600   **Frequency of publication:**   Annually

Sponsoring organization: School of Business Administration, Kobe University

Submission information:

Manuscript length: 5,000-12,000 words: 12-30 pages

Number of copies: 2   **Submission fee:** Not specified

Style: Double space all lines

**Manuscript
editor:**   Shigeki Sakakibara, Associate Professor

The Annals of the School of Business Administration, Kobe University, 2-1 Rokkodai, Nada-ku
Kobe 657, Japan

Publisher: Same as above

API Account

Primary readership: Accounting (or tax) practitioners, public service groups (non-profits)

Review process: Editorial only

Invited articles: 1-20%

**Percentage of articles
on accounting topics:**   90

Approximate percentage of accounting-related articles devoted to: Percentages change with each issue

Financial Accounting: **Managerial:**

Computers/Systems: **Tax:**

Auditing: **Education:**

Professional:

Approximate percentage of accounting-related articles characterized as primarily: Not specified

Empirical: **Experimental:**

Analytical: **Descriptive:**

**Language(s) in which
articles are published:**   English

Accepts manuscripts in English for translation: N/A

Approximate acceptance rate: 50%

Review period: 6 weeks   **Lead time to publication after acceptance:** 2 months

Circulation: 5,000   **Frequency of publication:**   Quarterly

Sponsoring organization: Accountants for the Public Interest

Submission information:

Manuscript length: 750-1,500 words

Number of copies: 1   **Submission fee:** None

Style: None

**Manuscript
editor:**   Marilyn Quinn, Editor
API Account, Accountants for the Public Interest, 888 17th St. N W., Suite 201
Washington, DC 20006, U. S. A.

Publisher: Same as above

Applied Business and Administration Quarterly

Primary readership: Academicians, accounting (or tax) practitioners, businessmen

Review process: Two external reviewers, blind reviewers

Invited articles: None

Percentage of articles on accounting topics: 40

Approximate percentage of accounting-related articles devoted to:

Financial Accounting:	50	**Managerial:**	50
Computers/Systems:		**Tax:**	
Auditing:		**Education:**	
Professional:			

Approximate percentage of accounting-related articles characterized as primarily:

Empirical:	50	**Experimental:**	50
Analytical:		**Descriptive:**	

Language(s) in which articles are published: English

Accepts manuscripts in English for translation: N/A

Approximate acceptance rate: 30%

Review period: 2-3 months   **Lead time to publication after acceptance:** 3 months

Circulation: 3,000   **Frequency of publication:**   Quarterly

Sponsoring organization: Wright State University

Submission information:

Manuscript length: 15 pages

Number of copies: 3   **Submission fee:** None

Style: None

Manuscript editor: Nabil Hassan
Department of Accountancy, College of Business and Administration
Wright State University, Dayton, OH 45435, U. S. A.

Publisher: Same as above

Arkansas Business and Economic Review

Primary readership: Academicians, businessmen

Review process: 2 external blind reviewers

Invited articles: 0%

**Percentage of articles
on accounting topics:**   10

Approximate percentage of accounting-related articles devoted to:

Financial Accounting:		**Managerial:**	
Computers/Systems:		**Tax:**	
Auditing:		**Education:**	100
Professional:			

Approximate percentage of accounting-related articles characterized as primarily:

Empirical:		**Experimental:**	
Analytical:	50	**Descriptive:**	50

**Language(s) in which
articles are published:**   English

Accepts manuscripts in English for translation: N/A

Approximate acceptance rate: 25%

Review period: 6 weeks   **Lead time to publication after acceptance:** 4-6 months

Circulation: 3,900   **Frequency of publication:**   Quarterly

Sponsoring organization: None

Submission information:

Manuscript length: 12 double-spaced pages not including tables

Number of copies: 3   **Submission fee:** None

Style: Typed double-spaced pages; standard research-based reports and articles with endnotes.

**Manuscript
editor:**   Dr. Phillip Taylor, Director BBER

Arkansas Business and Economic Review, College of Business Administration, University of Arkansas
Fayetteville, AR 72701, U. S. A.

Publisher: Same as above

Armed Forces Comptroller

Primary readership: Academicians, accounting (or tax) practitioners, businessmen, computer specialists, government comptrollers

Review process: Editorial only

Invited articles: 41-60%

Percentage of articles on accounting topics: 30

Approximate percentage of accounting-related articles devoted to:

Financial Accounting:	10	**Managerial:**	10
Computers/Systems:	10	**Tax:**	
Auditing:	10	**Education:**	10
Professional:	10	**Other:**	40

Approximate percentage of accounting-related articles characterized as primarily:

Empirical:		**Experimental:**	
Analytical:		**Descriptive:**	70
Other:	30		

Language(s) in which articles are published: English

Accepts manuscripts in English for translation: N/A

Approximate acceptance rate: 80%

Review period: 3 weeks   **Lead time to publication after acceptance:** 3-4 months

Circulation: 19,000   **Frequency of publication:** Quarterly

Sponsoring organization: ASMC (American Society of Military Comptrollers)

Submission information:

Manuscript length: 3,000-4,000 words, (210-500 lines, double-spaced)

Number of copies: 2   **Submission fee:** None

Style: Manuscripts should be typed double-spaced on one side of paper, 65 characters per line. All references should be given within the articles and will not be carried as a separate footnote. Contact the editor for more information concerning manuscript publication.

Manuscript editor: Edmund W. Edmonds, Jr. COL USAF (Ret.)

Armed Forces Comptroller, Executive Director, American Society of Military Comptrollers, P.O. Box 91

Mount Vernon, VA 22121-0091, U. S. A.

Publisher: Same as above

Asia Pacific Journal of Management

Primary readership: Not specified

Review process: Not specified

Invited articles: Not specified

**Percentage of articles
on accounting topics:**
Approximate percentage of accounting-related articles devoted to: Not specified

Financial Accounting:	**Managerial:**	
Computers/Systems:	**Tax:**	
Auditing:	**Education:**	
Professional:		

Approximate percentage of accounting-related articles characterized as primarily: Not specified

Empirical:	**Experimental:**
Analytical:	**Descriptive:**

**Language(s) in which
articles are published:**   English

Accepts manuscripts in English for translation: Not specified

Approximate acceptance rate: Not specified

Review period: Not specified   **Lead time to publication after acceptance:** Not specified

Circulation: Not specified   **Frequency of publication:**   Not specified

Sponsoring organization: National University of Singapore

Submission information:

Manuscript length: 4,000 to 6,000 words

Number of copies: 3   **Submission fee:** Not specified

Style: Manuscripts should be typed, triple-spaced on only one side of the paper. Tables and exhibits must be typed on separate sheets, be appropriately numbered , and authors should clearly indicate where they are to be inserted in the text. References cited in the text should be presented at the end of the article in alphabetical order of the first author's surname.

**Manuscript
editor:**   Editor In Chief

Asia Pacific Journal of Management, School of Management, National University of Singapore
Singapore 0511, Singapore

Publisher: Same as above

Asian Finance

Primary readership: Not specified

Review process: Not specified

Invited articles: Not specified

**Percentage of articles
on accounting topics:**
Approximate percentage of accounting-related articles devoted to: Not specified

Financial Accounting: **Managerial:**

Computers/Systems: **Tax:**

Auditing: **Education:**

Professional:

Approximate percentage of accounting-related articles characterized as primarily: Not specified

Empirical: **Experimental:**

Analytical: **Descriptive:**

**Language(s) in which
articles are published:**   English

Accepts manuscripts in English for translation: Not specified

Approximate acceptance rate: Not specified

Review period: Not specified   **Lead time to publication after acceptance:** Not specified

Circulation: Not specified   **Frequency of publication:**   Monthly

Sponsoring organization: None

Submission information:

Manuscript length: Not specified

Number of copies: Not specified   **Submission fee:**   Not specified

Style: Not specified

**Manuscript
editor:**   The Editor
Suite 9D, Hyde Centre, 223 Gloucester Road
Hong Kong

Publisher: Same as above

Attorney-CPA, The

Primary readership: Academicians, accounting (or tax) practitioners, attorney-CPAs

Review process: Editorial only

Invited articles: 41-60%

**Percentage of articles
on accounting topics:** 90

Approximate percentage of accounting-related articles devoted to:

Financial Accounting:	10	**Managerial:**	
Computers/Systems:		**Tax:**	80
Auditing:		**Education:**	
Professional:	10		

Approximate percentage of accounting-related articles characterized as primarily: Not specified

Empirical:	**Experimental:**
Analytical:	**Descriptive:**

**Language(s) in which
articles are published:** English

Accepts manuscripts in English for translation: N/A

Approximate acceptance rate: 80%

Review period: 30 days   **Lead time to publication after acceptance:** 2-4 months

Circulation: 1,600   **Frequency of publication:** Bi-monthly

Sponsoring organization: American Association of Attorney-Certified Public Accountants, Inc.

Submission information:

Manuscript length: 3-5 pages
Number of copies: 3   **Submission fee:** None
Style: None

**Manuscript
editor:** Ronald M. Devore
24196 Alicia Parkway, Suite K
Mission Viejo, CA 92691, U. S. A.

Publisher: Same as above

Audit Report

Primary readership: Accounting (or tax) practitioners

Review process: Editorial only

Invited articles: 1-20%

**Percentage of articles
on accounting topics:**   100

Approximate percentage of accounting-related articles devoted to:

Financial Accounting:		**Managerial:**
Computers/Systems:		**Tax:**
Auditing:	100	**Education:**
Professional:		

Approximate percentage of accounting-related articles characterized as primarily: Not specified

Empirical:	**Experimental:**
Analytical:	**Descriptive:**

**Language(s) in which
articles are published:**   English

Accepts manuscripts in English for translation: N/A

Approximate acceptance rate: Not specified

Review period: 1 day   **Lead time to publication after acceptance:** 1 month

Circulation: Not disclosed   **Frequency of publication:**   Monthly

Sponsoring organization: None

Submission information:

Manuscript length: Not specified

Number of copies: 1   **Submission fee:** None

Style: Not specified

**Manuscript
editor:**   David Shellan
Audit Report, Chapter Three Publications Ltd., 8A Hythe St.
Dartford, Kent, DA1 1BY, England

Publisher: Same as above

Auditing: A Journal of Practice and Theory

Primary readership: Academicians, accounting (tax) practitioners

Review process: 2 external reviewers (authors known)

Invited articles: 0%

**Percentage of articles
on accounting topics:**   100

Approximate percentage of accounting-related articles devoted to:

Financial Accounting:		**Managerial:**	
Computers/Systems:		**Tax:**	
Auditing:	100	**Education:**	
Professional:			

Approximate percentage of accounting-related articles characterized as primarily:

Empirical:	50	**Experimental:**	5
Analytical:	30	**Descriptive:**	10
Other	5		

**Language(s) in which
articles are published:**   English

Accepts manuscripts in English for translation: N/A

Approximate acceptance rate: 20%

Review period: 30-45 days   **Lead time to publication after acceptance:** 3 months

Circulation: 1,750   **Frequency of publication:**   Semiannually

Sponsoring organization: American Accounting Association, Auditing Section

Submission information:

Manuscript length: 7,000 words maximum

Number of copies: 4   **Submission fee:** None

Style: Each table and figure should appear on a separate page and bear an arabic number, a title, and the reference should appear next to the figure or reference. Authors should indicate by marginal notation where the table or figure should be inserted. Footnotes should be numbered consecutively with superscript arabic numerals. Reference list should follow the text and should include only those works actually cited.

**Manuscript
editor:**   Andrew D. Bailey, Jr.

Faculty of Accounting and MIS, College of Business, Ohio State University

Columbus, OH 43210-1399, U. S. A.

Kurt Pany, Editor

Department of Accounting, College of Business, Arizona State University

Tempe, AZ 85287, U. S. A.

Publisher: American Accounting Association

5717 Bessie Drive

Sarasota, FL 33583

Australian Accountant

Primary readership: Academicians, accounting (tax) practitioners, businessmen, computer specialists, government accountants, auditors, taxation specialists, students

Review process: 2 external reviewers (authors known)

Invited articles: 41-60%

Percentage of articles on accounting topics: 80

Approximate percentage of accounting-related articles devoted to: Not specified

Financial Accounting: **Managerial:**

Computers/Systems: **Tax:**

Auditing: **Education:**

Professional:

Approximate percentage of accounting-related articles characterized as primarily:

Empirical:	20	**Experimental:**	
Analytical:	30	**Descriptive:**	30
Other:	20		

Language(s) in which articles are published: English

Accepts manuscripts in English for translation: N/A

Approximate acceptance rate: 5-10%

Review period: 5 months   **Lead time to publication after acceptance:** 2-3 months

Circulation: 69,000   **Frequency of publication:** 11 issues per year

Sponsoring organization: Australian Society of Accountants

Submission information:

Manuscript length: 1,000-1,500 words

Number of copies: 1   **Submission fee:** None

Style: Non-academic. Contact the editor for more information concerning manuscript publication.

Manuscript editor: Tim Atkinson

Australian Accountant, 5th Floor, Accountancy House, 170 Queen St.

Melbourne, 3000 Australia

Publisher: Same as above

Australian Journal of Management

Primary readership: Academicians

Review process: Editorial only, 2 external reviewers (authors known)

Invited articles: 1-20%

Percentage of articles on accounting topics: 35

Approximate percentage of accounting-related articles devoted to:

Financial Accounting:	80	**Managerial:**	10
Computers/Systems:		**Tax:**	
Auditing:	10	**Education:**	
Professional:			

Approximate percentage of accounting-related articles characterized as primarily:

Empirical:	70	**Experimental:**	15
Analytical:	15	**Descriptive:**	

Language(s) in which articles are published: English

Accepts manuscripts in English for translation: N/A

Approximate acceptance rate: Not specified

Review period: 4-6 weeks   **Lead time to publication after acceptance:** 6 months

Circulation: Not specified   **Frequency of publication:** Semiannually

Sponsoring organization: Australian Graduate School of Management

Submission information:

Manuscript length: No length requirements, content is the only important element.
Number of copies: Not specified **Submission fee:** Not specified
Style: Not specified

Manuscript editor: Professor Peter Dodd
Australian Graduate School of Management, University of NSW, P. O. Box 1
Kensington, 2033 Australia

Publisher: Same as above

Australian Tax Forum

Primary readership: Academicians, accounting (or tax) practitioners

Review process: Editorial, 1-2 external blind reviewers

Invited articles: 41-60%

Percentage of articles on accounting topics: 90

Approximate percentage of accounting-related articles devoted to:

Financial Accounting:	**Managerial:**	
Computers/Systems:	**Tax:**	100
Auditing:	**Education:**	
Professional:		

Approximate percentage of accounting-related articles characterized as primarily:

Empirical:	**Experimental:**	
Analytical: 30	**Descriptive:**	40
Policy-oriented analysis: 30		

Language(s) in which articles are published: English

Accepts manuscripts in English for translation: N/A

Approximate acceptance rate: 20%

Review period: 2-4 months   **Lead time to publication after acceptance:** 3 months

Circulation: 1,000   **Frequency of publication:** Quarterly

Sponsoring organization: Faculty of Law and Center of Policy Studies, Monash University

Submission information:

Manuscript length: No limit

Number of copies: 3   **Submission fee:** None

Style: Style guide available from the editor; this journal requires a "disk" version on 5 1/2" computer disk formatted in ASCII characters.

Manuscript editor:
Richard Krever
Faculty of Law, Monash University
Clayton, Victoria, 3168 Australia

Publisher: Same as above

Bankers Magazine

Primary readership: Bank officers

Review process: Not specified

Invited articles: Not specified

**Percentage of articles
on accounting topics:**
Approximate percentage of accounting-related articles devoted to: Not specified

Financial Accounting: **Managerial:**
Computers/Systems: **Tax:**
Auditing: **Education:**
Professional:

Approximate percentage of accounting-related articles characterized as primarily: Not specified

Empirical: **Experimental:**
Analytical: **Descriptive:**

**Language(s) in which
articles are published:**   English

Accepts manuscripts in English for translation: N/A

Approximate acceptance rate: 10%

Review period: 2 to 3 weeks   **Lead time to publication after acceptance:** 3 to 5 months

Circulation: 5,000   **Frequency of publication:**   Bi-monthly

Sponsoring organization:

Submission information:
Manuscript length: 10 to 20 pages
Number of copies: Not specified **Submission fee:** None
Style: Not specified

**Manuscript
editor:**   Philip Ruppel
Bankers Magazine, 1633 Broadway
New York, NY 10019, U. S. A.

Publisher: Warren, Gorham & Lamont, Inc.
210 South St.
Boston, MA 02111, U. S. A.

Behavioral Research in Accounting

Primary readership: Academicians

Review process: Double blind review

Invited articles: Not specified

**Percentage of articles
on accounting topics:**   100

Approximate percentage of accounting-related articles devoted to: Not specified

Financial Accounting:	**Managerial:**
Computers/Systems:	**Tax:**
Auditing:	**Education:**
Professional:	

Approximate percentage of accounting-related articles characterized as primarily: Not specified

Empirical:	**Experimental:**
Analytical:	**Descriptive:**

**Language(s) in which
articles are published:**   English

Accepts manuscripts in English for translation: N/A

Approximate acceptance rate: Not specified

Review period: Not specified   **Lead time to publication after acceptance:** Not specified

Circulation: Not specified   **Frequency of publication:**   Not specified

Sponsoring organization: Accounting, Behavior, and Organizations Section of American Accounting Association

Submission information:

Manuscript length: Not specified

Number of copies: Four   **Submission fee:** $25

Style: Same as for The Accounting Revirew

**Manuscript
editor:**   K. J. Euske, Code 54 Ee

Behavioral Research in Accounting, Naval Postgraduate School

Monterey, CA 93943, U. S. A.

Publisher: American Accounting Association

5717 Bessie Drive

Sarasota, FL 33583, U. S. A.

Betrieb, Der

Primary readership: Accounting (or tax) practitioners, businessmen, academicians, computer specialists

Review process: Editorial only

Invited articles: 41-60%

**Percentage of articles
on accounting topics:**   45

Approximate percentage of accounting-related articles devoted to:

Financial Accounting:	5	**Managerial:**	15
Computers/Systems:	3	**Tax:**	75
Auditing:	2	**Education:**	
Professional:			

Approximate percentage of accounting-related articles characterized as primarily:

Empirical:		**Experimental:**	
Analytical:	70	**Descriptive:**	30

**Language(s) in which
articles are published:**   German

Accepts manuscripts in English for translation: No

Approximate acceptance rate: 40%

Review period: 1 to 4 weeks   **Lead time to publication after acceptance:** 2-8 weeks

Circulation: 25,000   **Frequency of publication:**   Weekly

Sponsoring organization: None

Submission information:

Manuscript length: 20-24 manuscript pages

Number of copies: 1   **Submission fee:** None

Style: None

**Manuscript
editor:**   Dr. Gunther Ackermann
Kasernenstrasse 67
D-4000 Dusseldorf 1, West Germany

Publisher: Handelsblatt, GmbH
P. O. Box 1102
4 Dusseldorf 1, West Germany

Bilans

Primary readership: Accounting (or tax) practitioners

Review process: 3 external blind reviewers

Invited articles: 1-20%

**Percentage of articles
on accounting topics:**   95

Approximate percentage of accounting-related articles devoted to:

Financial Accounting:		**Managerial:**	
Computers/Systems:		**Tax:**	
Auditing:	45	**Education:**	5
Professional:	50		

Approximate percentage of accounting-related articles characterized as primarily:

Empirical:		**Experimental:**	
Analytical:		**Descriptive:**	100

**Language(s) in which
articles are published:**   French, English

Accepts manuscripts in English for translation: N/A

Approximate acceptance rate: Not specified

Review period: Not specified   **Lead time to publication after acceptance:** Not specified

Circulation: 14,500   **Frequency of publication:**   Bi-monthly

Sponsoring organization: Ordre des C. A. du Quebec

Submission information:

Manuscript length: Not specified
Number of copies: Not specified   **Submission fee:** Not specified
Style: None specified

**Manuscript
editor:**   Pierre Bouchard

Bilans, Ordre des Comptables Agrees du Quebec, 680 rue Sherbrooke, W.
Montreal, Quebec H3A 2S3, Canada

Publisher: Same as above

Bilanz & Buchhaltung

Primary readership: Academicians, accounting (or tax) practitioners, businessmen

Review process: Editorial only

Invited articles: 61-80%

**Percentage of articles
on accounting topics:**

Approximate percentage of accounting-related articles devoted to: Not specified

Financial Accounting:	**Managerial:**
Computers/Systems:	**Tax:**
Auditing:	**Education:**
Professional:	

Approximate percentage of accounting-related articles characterized as primarily: Not specified

Empirical:	**Experimental:**
Analytical:	**Descriptive:**

**Language(s) in which
articles are published:**   German

Accepts manuscripts in English for translation: Yes

Approximate acceptance rate: Not specified

Review period: 3 weeks   **Lead time to publication after acceptance:** 6 weeks

Circulation: 4,000   **Frequency of publication:**   Monthly

Sponsoring organization: None

Submission information:

Manuscript length: 10-15 pages (23 lines per page)

Number of copies: 1   **Submission fee:**   None

Style: Avoid shortcuts; reference list at end of paper

**Manuscript
editor:**   Karin Rothenspieler

Gabler Vertag

Taunus strasse 54, 6200 Wiesbaden, West Germany

Publisher: Same as above

Bombay Chartered Accountant Journal

Primary readership: Not specified

Review process: Not specified

Invited articles: Not specified

**Percentage of articles
on accounting topics:**
Approximate percentage of accounting-related articles devoted to: Not specified

Financial Accounting: **Managerial:**

Computers/Systems: **Tax:**

Auditing: **Education:**

Professional:

Approximate percentage of accounting-related articles characterized as primarily: Not specified

Empirical: **Experimental:**

Analytical: **Descriptive:**

**Language(s) in which
articles are published:**   English

Accepts manuscripts in English for translation: N/A

Approximate acceptance rate: Not specified

Review period: Not specified   **Lead time to publication after acceptance:** Not specified

Circulation: 4,500   **Frequency of publication:**   Not specified

Sponsoring organization: Not specified

Submission information:
Manuscript length: Not specified
Number of copies: Not specified   **Submission fee:** Not specified
Style: Not specified

**Manuscript
editor:**   B. V. Dalal and A. A. Thakkar
Bombay Chartered Accountants' Society, 69-71 Don-bin-Shir, Ghoga St.
Bombay 400001 India

Publisher: Same as above

Bookkeeping Science

Primary readership: Academicians, accounting (or tax) practitioners, computer specialists

Review process: External reviewers

Invited articles: 1-20%

**Percentage of articles
on accounting topics:**   90

Approximate percentage of accounting-related articles devoted to:

Financial Accounting:	50	**Managerial:**	10
Computers/Systems:	15	**Tax:**	
Auditing:	3	**Education:**	5
Professional:		**Other :**	17

Approximate percentage of accounting-related articles characterized as primarily:

Empirical:	10	**Experimental:**	50
Analytical:	30	**Descriptive:**	10

**Language(s) in which
articles are published:**   Russian

Accepts manuscripts in English for translation: Yes

Approximate acceptance rate: 50%

Review period: 2-3 months   **Lead time to publication after acceptance:** 2-3 months

Circulation: 185,000   **Frequency of publication:**   Monthly

Sponsoring organization: Ministry of Finance (U. S. S. R.)

Submission information:

Manuscript length: Not more than 10 manuscript pages

Number of copies: 2   **Submission fee:** Honorarium of 150 rubles

Style: None

**Manuscript
editor:**   Peter S. Bezrukikh

Bookkeeping Science, Moscow, Shdovaya Triumfalnaya 4/10

U. S. S. R.

Publisher: Same as above

British Accounting Review

Primary readership: Academicians

Review process: 1 external blind reviewer

Invited articles: 1-20%

**Percentage of articles
on accounting topics:**   90

Approximate percentage of accounting-related articles devoted to:

Financial Accounting:	10	**Managerial:**	10
Computers/Systems:	10	**Tax:**	5
Auditing:	5	**Education:**	40
Professional:	10	Other:	10

Approximate percentage of accounting-related articles characterized as primarily:

Empirical:	20	**Experimental:**	10
Analytical:	30	**Descriptive:**	30
Other:	10		

**Language(s) in which
articles are published:**   English

Accepts manuscripts in English for translation: N/A

Approximate acceptance rate: 50%

Review period: 10 weeks   **Lead time to publication after acceptance:** 3-6 months

Circulation: 800+   **Frequency of publication:**   Three issues per year

Sponsoring organization: British Accounting Association

Submission information:

Manuscript length: 10,000 words maximum

Number of copies: 3   **Submission fee:**   None for 1987

Style: Manuscripts should be original works, typed on A4 paper, double-spaced, and the Harvard Reference system should be used. Footnotes should be used sparingly. Short abstract should accompany the manuscript.

**Manuscript
editor:**   R. H. Gray, Joint Editor

British Accounting Review, Department of Economics, U.C.N.W.

Bangor, Gwynedd, LL57 2DG, N. Wales, U. K.

Publisher: Same as above

British Tax Review

Primary readership: Academicians, accounting (or tax) practitioners

Review process: Editorial only

Invited articles: 81-99%

**Percentage of articles
on accounting topics:**
Approximate percentage of accounting-related articles devoted to:

Financial Accounting:	**Managerial:**	
Computers/Systems:	**Tax:**	100
Auditing:	**Education:**	
Professional:		

Approximate percentage of accounting-related articles characterized as primarily:

Empirical:	**Experimental:**	
Analytical:	**Descriptive:**	100

**Language(s) in which
articles are published:** English

Accepts manuscripts in English for translation: N/A

Approximate acceptance rate: Varies

Review period: Varies   **Lead time to publication after acceptance:** Varies

Circulation: 3,000   **Frequency of publication:** Monthly

Sponsoring organization: None

Submission information:
Manuscript length: Varies
Number of copies: 2   **Submission fee:** None
Style: None

**Manuscript
editor:** John Avery Jones, Esq.
British Tax Review, 11 New Fetter Lane
London, EC4P 4EE, England

Publisher: Same as above

Broadcast Financial Journal

Primary readership: Membership - financial professionals in broadcasting

Review process: Editorial only

Invited articles: 41-60%

**Percentage of articles
on accounting topics:**   50

Approximate percentage of accounting-related articles devoted to:

Financial Accounting:	20	**Managerial:**	20
Computers/Systems:	20	**Tax:**	10
Auditing:		**Education:**	
Professional:	20	Professional news :	10

Approximate percentage of accounting-related articles characterized as primarily:

Empirical:	25	**Experimental:**	
Analytical:		**Descriptive:**	75

**Language(s) in which
articles are published:**   English

Accepts manuscripts in English for translation: N/A

Approximate acceptance rate: 75%

Review period: 30 days   **Lead time to publication after acceptance:** 60 days

Circulation: 1,600   **Frequency of publication:**   Bi-monthly

Sponsoring organization: Broadcast Financial Management Association

Submission information:

Manuscript length: Up to 2,500 words and graphics

Number of copies: 2   **Submission fee:** None

Style: Typed double-spaced, wide margins, AP style

**Manuscript
editor:**
          Peter M. Deuel, Editor
          Broadcast Financial Journal, BFM, 701 Lee St., Suite 1010
          Des Plaines, IL 60016, U. S. A.

Publisher: Same as above

Bulletin Comptable & Financier

Primary readership: Accounting (or tax) practitioners, businessmen, internal and external auditors

Review process: Editorial only

Invited articles: Not specified

**Percentage of articles
on accounting topics:**   45

Approximate percentage of accounting-related articles devoted to:

Financial Accounting:	45	**Managerial:**	10
Computers/Systems:	10	**Tax:**	10
Auditing:	10	**Education:**	
Professional:	5	Finance:	10

Approximate percentage of accounting-related articles characterized as primarily:

Empirical:		**Experimental:**	
Analytical:	25	**Descriptive:**	75

**Language(s) in which
articles are published:**   French

Accepts manuscripts in English for translation: No

Approximate acceptance rate: Not specified

Review period: Not specified   **Lead time to publication after acceptance:** Not specified

Circulation: Not specified   **Frequency of publication:**   Quarterly

Sponsoring organization: None

Submission information:

Manuscript length: Not specified

Number of copies: Not specified   **Submission fee:** Not specified

Style: Not specified

**Manuscript
editor:**   Jl Icart

Editions Francis Lefebvre, 5 rue Jacques Bingen

75017 Paris, France

Publisher: Same as above

Business

Primary readership:	Academicians, accounting (tax) practitioners, businessmen
Review process:	2 external blind reviewers
Invited articles:	21-40%
Percentage of articles on accounting topics:	15

Approximate percentage of accounting-related articles devoted to: Not specified

Financial Accounting:	**Managerial:**
Computers/Systems:	**Tax:**
Auditing:	**Education:**
Professional:	

Approximate percentage of accounting-related articles characterized as primarily:

Empirical:	60	**Experimental:**	
Analytical:		**Descriptive:**	40

Language(s) in which articles are published: English

Accepts manuscripts in English for translation: N/A

Approximate acceptance rate: 25%

Review period: 6-8 weeks   **Lead time to publication after acceptance:** 3-6 months

Circulation: 5,000   **Frequency of publication:** Quarterly

Sponsoring organization: College of Business Administration, Georgia State University

Submission information:

Manuscript length: 6,000-9,000 words

Number of copies: 2   **Submission fee:** None

Style: Manuscripts should be typed double-spaced. Footnotes should be typed on separate pages at the end of the manuscript. Avoid use of reference citations--i.e., bracketed notes in the text. Bibliographical material is acceptable, but should be kept to a minimum. Charts and tables should be kept to a minimum, but illustrations such as photographs and artwork is desired. See current issues for style.

Manuscript editor: Margaret Stanley

Business, Business Publishing Division, College of Business Administration, Georgia State University
Atlanta, GA   30303-3093, U. S. A.

Publisher: Same as above

Business and Economic Review

Primary readership: Businessmen

Review process: Not specified

Invited articles: Not specified

**Percentage of articles
on accounting topics:**
Approximate percentage of accounting-related articles devoted to: Not specified

Financial Accounting:	**Managerial:**
Computers/Systems:	**Tax:**
Auditing:	**Education:**
Professional:	

Approximate percentage of accounting-related articles characterized as primarily: Not specified

Empirical:	**Experimental:**
Analytical:	**Descriptive:**

**Language(s) in which
articles are published:**   English

Accepts manuscripts in English for translation: N/A

Approximate acceptance rate: 7%

Review period: 1 month   **Lead time to publication after acceptance:** 3-6 months

Circulation: 5,500   **Frequency of publication:**   Quarterly

Sponsoring organization: University of South Carolina

Submission information:

Manuscript length: 10-20 pages
Number of copies: Not specified   **Submission fee:** None
Style: Available upon request.

**Manuscript
editor:**   Jan C. Stucker
University of South Carolina, College of Business Administration, Division of Research
Columbia, SC 29208, U. S. A.

Publisher: Same as above

Business and Professional Ethics Journal

Primary readership: Academicians

Review process: 2 external blind reviewers

Invited articles: 1-20%

**Percentage of articles
on accounting topics:**   5

Approximate percentage of accounting-related articles devoted to:

Financial Accounting:	**Managerial:**
Computers/Systems:	**Tax:**
Auditing:	**Education:**
Professional:	**Ethics:** 100

Approximate percentage of accounting-related articles characterized as primarily:

Empirical:	20	**Experimental:**	
Analytical:	80	**Descriptive:**	

**Language(s) in which
articles are published:**   English

Accepts manuscripts in English for translation: N/A

Approximate acceptance rate: 15%

Review period: 3-6 months   **Lead time to publication after acceptance:** 1-2 years

Circulation: Not specified   **Frequency of publication:**   Quarterly

Sponsoring organization: Rensselaer Polytechnic Institute, University of Delaware, University of Florida

Submission information:

Manuscript length: 15-30 pages, typed double-spaced
Number of copies: 5   **Submission fee:** None
Style: None

**Manuscript
editor:**   Robert J. Baum

Business and Professional Ethics Journal, Dept. of Philosophy, University of Florida

Gainesville, FL   32611, U. S. A.

Publisher: Science & Technology Studies Division, Rensselaer Polytechnic Institute

Business and Professional Ethics Journal

Troy, NY   12181, U. S. A.

Business and Society

Primary readership: Academicians, businessmen, students

Review process: Not specified

Invited articles: Not specified

**Percentage of articles
on accounting topics:**

Approximate percentage of accounting-related articles devoted to: Not specified

Financial Accounting: **Managerial:**
Computers/Systems: **Tax:**
Auditing: **Education:**
Professional:

Approximate percentage of accounting-related articles characterized as primarily: Not specified

Empirical: **Experimental:**
Analytical: **Descriptive:**

**Language(s) in which
articles are published:** English

Accepts manuscripts in English for translation: N/A

Approximate acceptance rate: 20%

Review period: 1 to 4 months   **Lead time to publication after acceptance:** 1 month

Circulation: 23,000   **Frequency of publication:** Semiannually

Sponsoring organization: Roosevelt University

Submission information:
Manuscript length: 4,000 words
Number of copies: Not specified **Submission fee:** None
Style: Available upon request.

**Manuscript
editor:** Gilbert Ghez

Roosevelt University,Walter E. Heller College of Business Administration, 430 S. Michigan Ave. Chicago, IL 60605, U. S. A.

Publisher: Same as above

Business Horizons

Primary readership: Academicians, businessmen

Review process: Not specified

Invited articles: Not specified

**Percentage of articles
on accounting topics:**
Approximate percentage of accounting-related articles devoted to: Not specified

Financial Accounting: **Managerial:**
Computers/Systems: **Tax:**
Auditing: **Education:**
Professional:

Approximate percentage of accounting-related articles characterized as primarily: Not specified

Empirical: **Experimental:**
Analytical: **Descriptive:**

**Language(s) in which
articles are published:**   English

Accepts manuscripts in English for translation: N/A

Approximate acceptance rate: 10%

Review period: 1 1/2 months   **Lead time to publication after acceptance:** 6-10 months

Circulation: 6,000   **Frequency of publication:**   Bi-monthly

Sponsoring organization: Indiana University

    Submission information:
Manuscript length: 5 -25 pages
Number of copies: 2   **Submission fee:** None
Style: Not specified

**Manuscript
editor:**   Joseph R. Hartley
    Business Horizons, Graduate School of Business, Indiana University
    Bloomington, IL 47405, U. S. A.

Publisher: Same as above

Business Insights

Primary readership: Academicians, accounting (or tax) practitioners, businessmen, computer specialists

Review process: 2 external blind reviewers

Invited articles: 0%

**Percentage of articles
on accounting topics:** 13

Approximate percentage of accounting-related articles devoted to:

Financial Accounting:	15	**Managerial:**	20
Computers/Systems:	20	**Tax:**	20
Auditing:	20	**Education:**	
Professional:		**Other:**	5

Approximate percentage of accounting-related articles characterized as primarily:

Empirical:	30	**Experimental:**	
Analytical:	25	**Descriptive:**	20
Other:	25		

**Language(s) in which
articles are published:** English

Accepts manuscripts in English for translation:

Approximate acceptance rate: 25-40%

Review period: 3 months   **Lead time to publication after acceptance:** One issue

Circulation: 2,200   **Frequency of publication:** Semiannually

Sponsoring organization: University of Southern Mississippi, College of Business Administration

Submission information:

Manuscript length: 10-15 pages

Number of copies: 3   **Submission fee:** None

Style: See pages 85-86 in Cabell's Directory of Publishing Opportunities in Business and Economics,3rd edition, 1985. Consult the editor for more information concerning manuscript publication.

Manuscript editor: Colleen Cameron

Business Insights, Box 5094, University of Southern Mississippi

Hattiesburg, MS 39406-5094, U. S. A.

Publisher: Same as above

Business Quarterly

Primary readership: Businessmen

Review process: Not specified

Invited articles: Not specified

Percentage of articles on accounting topics:
Approximate percentage of accounting-related articles devoted to: Not specified

Financial Accounting: **Managerial:**
Computers/Systems: **Tax:**
Auditing: **Education:**
Professional:

Approximate percentage of accounting-related articles characterized as primarily: Not specified

Empirical: **Experimental:**
Analytical: **Descriptive:**

Language(s) in which articles are published: English

Accepts manuscripts in English for translation: N/A

Approximate acceptance rate: 30%

Review period: 6 months   **Lead time to publication after acceptance:** 2-4 months

Circulation: 12,000   **Frequency of publication:** Quarterly

Sponsoring organization: The University of Western Ontario

Submission information:
Manuscript length: 4-6 pages
Number of copies: Not specified   **Submission fee:** None
Style: Available upon request.

Manuscript editor: Doreen Sanders
The University of Western Ontario, 1393 Western Rd.
London, Ontario N6A 5B9, Canada

Publisher: Same as above

Buyouts & Acquisitions

Primary readership: Not specified

Review process: Not specified

Invited articles: Not specified

**Percentage of articles
on accounting topics:**
Approximate percentage of accounting-related articles devoted to: Not specified

Financial Accounting: **Managerial:**
Computers/Systems: **Tax:**
Auditing: **Education:**
Professional:

Approximate percentage of accounting-related articles characterized as primarily: Not specified

Empirical: **Experimental:**
Analytical: **Descriptive:**

**Language(s) in which
articles are published:**   English

Accepts manuscripts in English for translation: N/A

Approximate acceptance rate: Not specified

Review period: Not specified   **Lead time to publication after acceptance:** Not specified

Circulation: Not specified   **Frequency of publication:**   Bi-monthly

Sponsoring organization: None

   Submission information:
Manuscript length: Not specified
Number of copies: 2   **Submission fee:** None
Style: Not specified

**Manuscript
editor:**   Steve Barth
          Quality Services Co., 5290 Overpass Rd.
          Santa Barbara, CA 93111, U. S. A.

Publisher: Same as above

CA Magazine

Primary readership:	Accounting (or tax) practitioners, businessmen
Review process:	2-3 external blind reviewers
Invited articles:	Not specified

**Percentage of articles
on accounting topics:**

Approximate percentage of accounting-related articles devoted to: Not specified

Financial Accounting:	**Managerial:**
Computers/Systems:	**Tax:**
Auditing:	**Education:**
Professional:	

Approximate percentage of accounting-related articles characterized as primarily: Not specified

Empirical:	**Experimental:**
Analytical:	**Descriptive:**

**Language(s) in which
articles are published:**   English, French

Accepts manuscripts in English for translation: N/A

Approximate acceptance rate:

Review period: 6 weeks   **Lead time to publication after acceptance:** 4-6 months

Circulation: 57,000   **Frequency of publication:**   Monthly

Sponsoring organization: The Canadian Institute of Chartered Accountants

Submission information:

Manuscript length: 3,000-4,000 words

Number of copies: 3   **Submission fee:** $75-100, Honorarium

Style: Manuscripts should be typed--double-spaced with one-inch margins--on one side of 8 1/2 x 11" paper. Footnotes should be kept to minimum. If included, they should be submitted on a separate sheet of paper at the end of the article. Each major table or figure should be on a separate sheet, numbered, titled, and referred to in the text. Contact the editor for more information concerning manuscript publication.

**Manuscript
editor:**   Judy Margolis, Managing Editor

CA Magazine, 150 Bloor Street W.

Toronto, Ontario M5S 2Y2 , Canada

Publisher: Same as above

California Management Review

Primary readership: Academicians, accounting (or tax) practitioners, businessmen

Review process: Dozens of external blind reviewers

Invited articles: 1-20%

**Percentage of articles
on accounting topics:**   5

Approximate percentage of accounting-related articles devoted to:

Financial Accounting:		**Managerial:**	25
Computers/Systems:	25	**Tax:**	25
Auditing:	25	**Education:**	
Professional:			

Approximate percentage of accounting-related articles characterized as primarily:

Empirical:	25	**Experimental:**	25
Analytical:	25	**Descriptive:**	25

**Language(s) in which
articles are published:**   English

Accepts manuscripts in English for translation: N/A

Approximate acceptance rate: 10%

Review period: 6-12 weeks   **Lead time to publication after acceptance:** 3-6 months

Circulation: 5,500   **Frequency of publication:**   Quarterly

Sponsoring organization: Graduate Schools of Business and Management of the University of California

Submission information:

Manuscript length: 15-25 typed double-spaced pages

Number of copies: 3   **Submission fee:** None

Style: All manuscripts should be typed double-spaced. Footnotes, tables, charts, and diagrams should be placed on separate pages. Footnotes should be numbered consecutively in the text and compiled at the end of the article. See current issue of publication for more information.

**Manuscript
editor:**   David Vogel

California Management Review, University of California, 350 Barrows Hall
Berkeley, CA 94720, U. S. A.

Publisher: Same as above

Certificate

Primary readership: Accounting (or tax) practitioners

Review process: Editorial only

Invited articles: Not specified

**Percentage of articles
on accounting topics:**

Approximate percentage of accounting-related articles devoted to: Not specified

Financial Accounting:	**Managerial:**
Computers/Systems:	**Tax:**
Auditing:	**Education:**
Professional:	

Approximate percentage of accounting-related articles characterized as primarily: Not specified

Empirical:	**Experimental:**
Analytical:	**Descriptive:**

**Language(s) in which
articles are published:**   English

Accepts manuscripts in English for translation: N/A

Approximate acceptance rate: 90%

Review period: 1 month   **Lead time to publication after acceptance:** 2 months

Circulation: 3,000   **Frequency of publication:**   6 times per year

Sponsoring organization: District of Columbia Institute of CPAs

    Submission information:

Manuscript length: 600+ words

Number of copies: 1   **Submission fee:** None

Style: Not specified

**Manuscript
editor:**   Ed Carl

    Certificate, AICPA, 1620 Eye St., N. W.

    Washington, DC 20006-4063, U. S. A.

Publisher: Same as above

Certified Accountant

Primary readership: Accounting (or tax) practitioners

Review process: Editorial

Invited articles: 61-80%

**Percentage of articles
on accounting topics:**   100

Approximate percentage of accounting-related articles devoted to: Not specified

Financial Accounting:	**Managerial:**
Computers/Systems:	**Tax:**
Auditing:	**Education:**
Professional:	

Approximate percentage of accounting-related articles characterized as primarily: Not specified

Empirical:	**Experimental:**
Analytical:	**Descriptive:**

**Language(s) in which
articles are published:**   English

Accepts manuscripts in English for translation: N/A

Approximate acceptance rate: Not specified

Review period: Immediate   **Lead time to publication after acceptance:** 3 months

Circulation: 37,000   **Frequency of publication:**   Monthly

Sponsoring organization: Chartered Association of Certified Accountants

Submission information:

Manuscript length: 1,000-1,500 words

Number of copies: 1   **Submission fee:**   Not specified

Style: Direct, practical, with specific examples.

**Manuscript
editor:**   Richard Garlick
Certified Accountant, 8A Hythe St.
Dartford, Kent DA1 1BX, England

Publisher: The Chartered Association of Certified Accountants
29 Lincoln's Inn Fields
London WC2A 3EE, England

CGA Magazine

Primary readership: academicians, accounting (or tax) practitioners, businessmen

Review process: 3 external blind reviewers

Invited articles: 21-40%

**Percentage of articles
on accounting topics:**   80

Approximate percentage of accounting-related articles devoted to:

Financial Accounting:	10	**Managerial:**	5
Computers/Systems:	15	**Tax:**	25
Auditing:	15	**Education:**	10
Professional:	10	International:	10

Approximate percentage of accounting-related articles characterized as primarily:

Empirical:	30	**Experimental:**	
Analytical:		**Descriptive:**	70

**Language(s) in which
articles are published:**   English, French

Accepts manuscripts in English for translation: yes

Approximate acceptance rate: 50%

Review period: 6 weeks   **Lead time to publication after acceptance:** Varies, up to 8 months

Circulation: 35,000   **Frequency of publication:**   Monthly

Sponsoring organization: Certified General Accountants' Association of Canada

Submission information:

Manuscript length: 21,000 words

Number of copies: 2   **Submission fee:** Not specified

Style: None

**Manuscript
editor:**   Toni Dabbs

CGA Magazine, CGA Association of Canada, 740-1176 W. Georgia St.
Vancouver, B. C. V63 4A2, Canada

Publisher: Same as above

Chartered Accountant in Australia, The

Primary readership: Academicians, accounting (or tax) practitioners, businessmen, students

Review process: Not specified

Invited articles: Not specified

Percentage of articles on accounting topics:
Approximate percentage of accounting-related articles devoted to: Not specified

Financial Accounting:	**Managerial:**
Computers/Systems:	**Tax:**
Auditing:	**Education:**
Professional:	

Approximate percentage of accounting-related articles characterized as primarily: Not specified

Empirical:	**Experimental:**
Analytical:	**Descriptive:**

Language(s) in which articles are published: English

Accepts manuscripts in English for translation: N/A

Approximate acceptance rate: 40%

Review period: 1 to 2 months **Lead time to publication after acceptance:** 1-2 months

Circulation: 17,500 **Frequency of publication:** Monthly

Sponsoring organization: Institute of Chartered Accountants in Australia

Submission information:
Manuscript length: 1,500-2,000 words
Number of copies: 3 **Submission fee:** None
Style: Available upon request.

Manuscript editor:
Ms. Jo Avigdor
Institute of Chartered Accountants in Australia, Box 3921
Sydney, 2001 Australia

Publisher: Same as above

Chartered Accountant, The

Primary readership: Academicians, accounting (or tax) practitioners, businessmen, computer specialists

Review process: Editorial only

Invited articles: 1-20%

Percentage of articles on accounting topics: 15

Approximate percentage of accounting-related articles devoted to:

Financial Accounting:	15	**Managerial:**	15
Computers/Systems:	10	**Tax:**	20
Auditing:	10	**Education:**	10
Professional:	10	**Other :**	10

Approximate percentage of accounting-related articles characterized as primarily:

Empirical:	20	**Experimental:**	20
Analytical:	20	**Descriptive:**	30
Other :	10		

Language(s) in which articles are published: English

Accepts manuscripts in English for translation: N/A

Approximate acceptance rate: 20%

Review period: 1 month   **Lead time to publication after acceptance:** 2-3 months

Circulation: 60,000   **Frequency of publication:** Monthly

Sponsoring organization: The Institute of Chartered Accountants of India

Submission information:

Manuscript length: 3,000 words

Number of copies: 2   **Submission fee:** None

Style: None

Manuscript editor:
S. K. Dasgupta
P. B. No. 7100, Indraprastha Marg
New Delhi-110002, India

Publisher: Same as above

CMA - The Management Accounting Magazine

Primary readership: Academicans, accounting (or tax) practitioners, businessmen

Review process: 2-3 external blind reviewers

Invited articles: 41-60%

**Percentage of articles
on accounting topics:**   60

Approximate percentage of accounting-related articles devoted to:

Financial Accounting:	7	**Managerial:**	14
Computers/Systems:	20	**Tax:**	2
Auditing:	7	**Education:**	2
Professional:	27	**Economics, management:**	21

Approximate percentage of accounting-related articles characterized as primarily:

Empirical:		**Experimental:**	
Analytical:	20	**Descriptive:**	40
	40		

**Language(s) in which
articles are published:**   English, French

Accepts manuscripts in English for translation: N/A

Approximate acceptance rate: 33%

Review period: 1 month   **Lead time to publication after acceptance:** 1 year

Circulation: 40,973   **Frequency of publication:**   Bi-monthly

Sponsoring organization: The Society of Management Accountants of Canada

Submission information:

Manuscript length: 1,500-2,500 words

Number of copies: 2   **Submission fee:** None

Style: We welcome articles on Accounting, Management, and Economics which are of practical interest to readers such as case studies, descriptions of practices and applications, surveys, etc. The style should be informal and anecdotal, preferably featuring interviews with authorities and practitioners.

**Manuscript
editor:**   Mrs. J. M. Hewer

CMA Magazine, Society of Management Accountants, P.O. Box 176 MPO

Hamilton, Ontario L8N 3C3, Canada

Publisher: Same as above

Columbia Journal of World Business

Primary readership: Academicians, accounting (or tax) practitioners, businessmen

Review process: External blind reviewers

Invited articles: 41-60%

**Percentage of articles
on accounting topics:**   5

Approximate percentage of accounting-related articles devoted to: Not specified

Financial Accounting:	**Managerial:**
Computers/Systems:	**Tax:**
Auditing:	**Education:**
Professional:	

Approximate percentage of accounting-related articles characterized as primarily: Articles should apply to middle management.

Empirical:		**Experimental:**	
Analytical:	50	**Descriptive:**	50

**Language(s) in which
articles are published:**   English

Accepts manuscripts in English for translation: N/A

Approximate acceptance rate: Not specified

Review period: 5-7 months   **Lead time to publication after acceptance:** Usually 4-12 months

Circulation: 2,500   **Frequency of publication:**   Quarterly

Sponsoring organization: Columbia University

Submission information:

Manuscript length: 15-30 pages, typed, double spaced, 3,000-5,000 words

Number of copies: 3   **Submission fee:** None

Style: Not specified.

**Manuscript
editor:**

    Mary Anne Devanna, Editor-in-Chief

    Columbia Journal of World Business, 315 Uris Hall, Columbia University

    New York, NY 10027, U. S. A.

Publisher: Same as above

COM-AND, Computer Audit News & Developments

Primary readership: Academicians, accounting (or tax) practitioners, businessmen, computer specialists, EDP auditors, CPAs, security professionals

Review process: Editorial only

Invited articles: 41-60%

Percentage of articles on accounting topics: 60

Approximate percentage of accounting-related articles devoted to:

Financial Accounting:		Managerial:	
Computers/Systems:	50	Tax:	
Auditing:	50	Education:	
Professional:			

Approximate percentage of accounting-related articles characterized as primarily:

Empirical:	20	Experimental:	
Analytical:	30	Descriptive:	50

Language(s) in which articles are published: English

Accepts manuscripts in English for translation: N/A

Approximate acceptance rate: 50%

Review period: 1 month   **Lead time to publication after acceptance:** 2-4 months

Circulation: N/A   **Frequency of publication:** Every other month

Sponsoring organization: None

Submission information:

Manuscript length: 2-15 pages , double spaced

Number of copies: 1   **Submission fee:** None

Style: Practical business writing style; seeking how to apply concepts

Manuscript editor: Javier F. Kuong

COM-AND, Management Advisory Publications, P.O. Box 151
Wellesley Hills, MA 0218, U. S. A..

Publisher: Same as above

COM-SAC, Computer Security, Auditing & Controls

Primary readership: Academicians, accounting (or tax) practitioners, businessmen, computer specialists, auditors, CPAs, security professionals

Review process: Editorial only

Invited articles: 41-60%

Percentage of articles on accounting topics: 60

Approximate percentage of accounting-related articles devoted to:

Financial Accounting:		Managerial:	
Computers/Systems:	50	Tax:	
Auditing:	50	Education:	
Professional:			

Approximate percentage of accounting-related articles characterized as primarily:

Empirical:		Experimental:	10
Analytical:	30	Descriptive:	30
Other:	30		

Language(s) in which articles are published: English

Accepts manuscripts in English for translation: N/A

Approximate acceptance rate: 50%

Review period: 1 month   **Lead time to publication after acceptance:** 2-6 months

Circulation: N/A   **Frequency of publication:** Semiannually

Sponsoring organization: None

Submission information:

Manuscript length: 2-20 pages of draft work

Number of copies: 2   **Submission fee:** None

Style: Prefer double-spaced, typed or word processed with proper headings, business writing. Practical oriented papers are preferred.

Manuscript editor: J. F. Kuong

COM-SAC, Management Advisory Publications, P.O. Box 151

Wellesley Hills, MA 02181, U. S. A.

Publisher: Same as above

Commercial Investment Real Estate Journal

Primary readership: Academicians, businessmen, commercial real estate brokers, bankers, attorneys

Review process: 3 external blind reviewers

Invited articles: 61-80%

**Percentage of articles
on accounting topics:**   3

Approximate percentage of accounting-related articles devoted to: Not specified

Financial Accounting:	**Managerial:**
Computers/Systems:	**Tax:**
Auditing:	**Education:**
Professional:	

Approximate percentage of accounting-related articles characterized as primarily: Not specified

Empirical:	**Experimental:**
Analytical:	**Descriptive:**

**Language(s) in which
articles are published:**   English

Accepts manuscripts in English for translation: N/A

Approximate acceptance rate: 40%

Review period: 1 month   **Lead time to publication after acceptance:** 6-8 months

Circulation: 10,000   **Frequency of publication:**   Quarterly

Sponsoring organization: Commercial Investment Real Estate Council

Submission information:

Manuscript length: 10-25 double-spaced manuscript pages

Number of copies: 1   **Submission fee:** None

Style: All articles should be submitted in typewritten form on plain 8 1/2 x 11" paper, typed double-spaced. Furnish footnotes where needed. Include charts, graphs, photographs, and illustrations whenever possible to emphasize and clarify points in the article. Contact editor for more information.

**Manuscript
editor:**   Maureen Glass

Commercial Investment Real Estate Journal, 430 N. Michigan Ave., Suite 500

Chicago, IL 60611, U. S. A.

Publisher: Realtors National Marketing Institute

Same as above

Compensation Planning Journal

Primary readership: Accounting (or tax) practitioners, tax lawyers, pension plan advisers

Review process: Not specified

Invited articles: Not specified

**Percentage of articles
on accounting topics:**
Approximate percentage of accounting-related articles devoted to: Not specified

Financial Accounting: **Managerial:**
Computers/Systems: **Tax:**
Auditing: **Education:**
Professional:

Approximate percentage of accounting-related articles characterized as primarily: Not specified

Empirical: **Experimental:**
Analytical: **Descriptive:**

**Language(s) in which
articles are published:**   English

Accepts manuscripts in English for translation: N/A

Approximate acceptance rate: 50%

Review period: 4 to 6 weeks   **Lead time to publication after acceptance:** 1-2 months

Circulation: 2,000   **Frequency of publication:**   Monthly

Sponsoring organization: None

   Submission information:
Manuscript length: 15-21 pages
Number of copies: Not specified   **Submission fee:** None
Style: Not specified

**Manuscript
editor:**   Patrick Rockelli
   Tax Management, Inc., 1231 25th St., N. W. , Suite 401
   Washington, DC 20037, U. S. A.

Publisher: Same as above

Comptabilite Et Mecanographie

Primary readership: Not specified

Review process: Not specified

Invited articles: Not specified

**Percentage of articles
on accounting topics:**
Approximate percentage of accounting-related articles devoted to: Not specified

Financial Accounting:	**Managerial:**
Computers/Systems:	**Tax:**
Auditing:	**Education:**
Professional:	

Approximate percentage of accounting-related articles characterized as primarily: Not specified

Empirical:	**Experimental:**
Analytical:	**Descriptive:**

**Language(s) in which
articles are published:**   French

Accepts manuscripts in English for translation: Not specified

Approximate acceptance rate: Not specified

Review period: Not specified   **Lead time to publication after acceptance:** Not specified

Circulation: Not specified   **Frequency of publication:**   Not specified

Sponsoring organization: Not specified

        Submission information:
Manuscript length: Not specified
Number of copies: Not specified   **Submission fee:** Not specified
Style: Not specified

**Manuscript
editor:**   Jean Deit
        14 rue de la Somme
        94000 Cachan, France

Publisher: Same as above

Computers in Accounting

Primary readership: Academicians, accounting (or tax) practitioners, students

Review process: Not specified

Invited articles: Not specified

**Percentage of articles
on accounting topics:**   100

Approximate percentage of accounting-related articles devoted to: Not specified

Financial Accounting:		**Managerial:**	
Computers/Systems:	100	**Tax:**	
Auditing:		**Education:**	
Professional:			

Approximate percentage of accounting-related articles characterized as primarily: Not specified

Empirical:	**Experimental:**
Analytical:	**Descriptive:**

**Language(s) in which
articles are published:**   English

Accepts manuscripts in English for translation: N/A

Approximate acceptance rate: Not specified

Review period: Not specified   **Lead time to publication after acceptance:** Not specified

Circulation: Not specified   **Frequency of publication:**   Bi-monthly

Sponsoring organization:

Submission information:

Manuscript length: Not specified
Number of copies: Not specified   **Submission fee:** None
Style: Available upon request.

**Manuscript
editor:**   Robert A. Behren, CPA; Alex Cohen, CPA
Computers in Accounting, 964 Third Ave.
New York, NY 10155, U. S. A.

Publisher: Same as above

Connecticut CPA Quarterly, The

Primary readership: Membership of the CSCPA

Review process: Editorial only

Invited articles: 0%; academic articles are not solicited. If received they will be considered on merit, timeliness and relevance to theme of issue of that quarter. Wholesale submissions are not welcome.

**Percentage of articles
on accounting topics:**   50

Approximate percentage of accounting-related articles devoted to: Not specified

Financial Accounting: **Managerial:**

Computers/Systems: **Tax:**

Auditing: **Education:**

Professional:

Approximate percentage of accounting-related articles characterized as primarily:

Empirical: **Experimental:**

Analytical: **Descriptive:**   10

Practice: 90

**Language(s) in which
articles are published:**   English

Accepts manuscripts in English for translation: N/A

Approximate acceptance rate: 1%

Review period: Depends on time of year   **Lead time to publication after acceptance:** 6 weeks

Circulation: 5,600   **Frequency of publication:**   Quarterly

Sponsoring organization: The Connecticut Society of CPAs (CSCPA)

Submission information:

Manuscript length: 6-9 manuscript pages

Number of copies: 1   **Submission fee:** none

Style: Not specified

Manuscript editor: Andrea Massa

Connecticut CPA Quarterly, 179 Allyn St., Suite 501

Hartford, CT 06103, U. S. A.

Publisher: Same as above

Contaduria Administracion

Primary readership: Not specified

Review process: Not specified

Invited articles: Not specified

**Percentage of articles
on accounting topics:**

Approximate percentage of accounting-related articles devoted to: Not specified

Financial Accounting: **Managerial:**

Computers/Systems: **Tax:**

Auditing: **Education:**

Professional:

Approximate percentage of accounting-related articles characterized as primarily: Not specified

Empirical: **Experimental:**

Analytical: **Descriptive:**

**Language(s) in which
articles are published:**   Spanish

Accepts manuscripts in English for translation: Not specified

Approximate acceptance rate: Not specified

Review period: Not specified   **Lead time to publication after acceptance:** Not specified

Circulation: Not specified   **Frequency of publication:**   Not specified

Sponsoring organization: Not specified

Submission information:

Manuscript length: Not specified

Number of copies: Not specified   **Submission fee:** Not specified

Style: Not specified

**Manuscript
editor:**   C. P. Jaime Bladinieres

Universidad Nacional Autonoma de Mexico, Facultad de Contaduria y Administracion

VIlla Obregon, Ciudad Universitaria, Mexico 20 D. F. , Mexico

Publisher: Same as above

Contemporary Accounting Research

Primary readership: Academicians

Review process: 2 external reviewers (authors known)

Invited articles: 0%

**Percentage of articles
on accounting topics:**   100

Approximate percentage of accounting-related articles devoted to: Not specified

Financial Accounting:	**Managerial:**
Computers/Systems:	**Tax:**
Auditing:	**Education:**
Professional:	

Approximate percentage of accounting-related articles characterized as primarily: Not specified

Empirical:	**Experimental:**
Analytical:	**Descriptive:**

**Language(s) in which
articles are published:**   English, French

Accepts manuscripts in English for translation:

Approximate acceptance rate:

Review period: 9 weeks   **Lead time to publication after acceptance:** 4-5 months

Circulation: 1,100   **Frequency of publication:** Semiannually

Sponsoring organization: Canadian Academic Accounting Association

Submission information:

Manuscript length: No limit

Number of copies: 3   **Submission fee:** None

Style: Footnotes for extensions where inclusion in the body of text might disrupt continuity. All footnotes numbered consecutively, presented on separate pages immediately following the text, and referred to throughout the text with superscript arabic numerals. Each table, figure, etc. should be presented on a separate page and have an arabic numeral and title. Author should indicate in text where table, etc. should be inserted.

**Manuscript
editor:**   Haim Falk

Contemporary Accounting Research, McMaster University, Faculty of Business, 1280 Main Street West
Hamilton, Ontario L8S 4M4, Canada.

Publisher: CAAA Secretariat

Room 34E, Crossroads Bldg, Erindale Campus, Univ. of Toronto, 3359 Mississauga Rd.
Mississauga, Ontario L5L 1C6, Canada

Controller Magazin

Primary readership: Accounting (or tax) practitioners, businessmen

Review process: Editorial only

Invited articles: 61-80%

**Percentage of articles
on accounting topics:**   60

Approximate percentage of accounting-related articles devoted to:

Financial Accounting:	10	**Managerial:**	50
Computers/Systems:	30	**Tax:**	
Auditing:		**Education:**	5
Professional:	5		

Approximate percentage of accounting-related articles characterized as primarily:

Empirical:	50	**Experimental:**	
Analytical:	20	**Descriptive:**	30

**Language(s) in which
articles are published:**   German, sometimes English

Accepts manuscripts in English for translation: Yes

Approximate acceptance rate: 70%

Review period: **Lead time to publication after acceptance:** 3 months

Circulation: 3,800   **Frequency of publication:**   Monthly

Sponsoring organization: Controllers' Academy

Submission information:

Manuscript length: 10-15 pages

Number of copies: **Submission fee:**   Not specified

Style: none

**Manuscript
editor:**   Dr. Al Deyhle

Controller Magazin, Controller Akademie und Management Service Verlag, Untertaxetweg 5
D-8035 Gauting, W. Germany

Publisher: Same as above

Controllers' Quarterly

Primary readership: Accounting (or tax) practitioners

Review process: External reviews

Invited articles: Not specified

**Percentage of articles
on accounting topics:**
Approximate percentage of accounting-related articles devoted to: Not specified

Financial Accounting:	**Managerial:**
Computers/Systems:	**Tax:**
Auditing:	**Education:**
Professional:	

Approximate percentage of accounting-related articles characterized as primarily: Not specified

Empirical:	**Experimental:**
Analytical:	**Descriptive:**

**Language(s) in which
articles are published:**   English

Accepts manuscripts in English for translation: N/A

Approximate acceptance rate: Not specified

Review period: Not specified   **Lead time to publication after acceptance:** Not specified

Circulation: Not specified   **Frequency of publication:**   Quarterly

Sponsoring organization: National Association of Accountants

Submission information:
Manuscript length: Not specified
Number of copies: Not specified **Submission fee:** None
Style: Not specified

**Manuscript
editor:**   Erwin S. Koval
National Association of Accountants, 10 Paragon Drive
Montvale, NJ 07645-1760, U. S. A.

Publisher: Same as above

Cooperative Accountant

Primary readership: Agricultural cooperative accountants

Review process: Not specified

Invited articles: Not specified

**Percentage of articles
on accounting topics:**
Approximate percentage of accounting-related articles devoted to: Not specified

Financial Accounting:	**Managerial:**
Computers/Systems:	**Tax:**
Auditing:	**Education:**
Professional:	

Approximate percentage of accounting-related articles characterized as primarily: Not specified

Empirical:	**Experimental:**
Analytical:	**Descriptive:**

**Language(s) in which
articles are published:**   English

Accepts manuscripts in English for translation: Not specified

Approximate acceptance rate: Not specified

Review period: Not specified   **Lead time to publication after acceptance:** Not specified

Circulation: 2,000   **Frequency of publication:**   Not specified

Sponsoring organization: Not specified

Submission information:
Manuscript length: Not specified
Number of copies: Not specified **Submission fee:** Not specified
Style: Not specified

**Manuscript
editor:**   Dr. John B. Sperry
National Society of Accountants for Cooperatives
Moseley, VA   23210, U. S. A.

Publisher: Same as above

Coordinator

Primary readership: Women accountants

Review process: Not specified

Invited articles: Not specified

**Percentage of articles
on accounting topics:**
Approximate percentage of accounting-related articles devoted to: Not specified

Financial Accounting: **Managerial:**
Computers/Systems: **Tax:**
Auditing: **Education:**
Professional:

Approximate percentage of accounting-related articles characterized as primarily: Not specified

Empirical: **Experimental:**
Analytical: **Descriptive:**

**Language(s) in which
articles are published:**   English

Accepts manuscripts in English for translation: Not specified

Approximate acceptance rate: Not specified

Review period: Not specified   **Lead time to publication after acceptance:**   Not specified

Circulation: 7,500   **Frequency of publication:**   Not specified

Sponsoring organization: American Society of Women Accountants

     Submission information:
Manuscript length: Not specified
Number of copies: Not specified   **Submission fee:**   Not specified
Style: Not specified

**Manuscript
editor:**   Miriam Green
   American Society of Women Accountants, 35 E. Wacker Dr., Rm. 1036
   Chicago, IL 60601, U. S. A.

Publisher: Same as above

Corporate Accounting

Primary readership: Accounting (or tax) practitioners, vice presidents of finance, treasurers, and controllers

Review process: Editorial only

Invited articles: 81-99%

**Percentage of articles
on accounting topics:** 100

Approximate percentage of accounting-related articles devoted to:

Financial Accounting:	13	**Managerial:**	13
Computers/Systems:	13	**Tax:**	13
Auditing:	13	**Education:**	13
Professional:	13	Other:	9

Approximate percentage of accounting-related articles characterized as primarily:

Empirical:	75	**Experimental:**	
Analytical:		**Descriptive:**	25

**Language(s) in which
articles are published:** English

Accepts manuscripts in English for translation: N/A

Approximate acceptance rate:

Review period: 2-3 weeks   **Lead time to publication after acceptance:** 3 months

Circulation: 8,000   **Frequency of publication:** Quarterly

Sponsoring organization: None

Submission information:

Manuscript length: 10-15 pages

Number of copies: 2   **Submission fee:** None

Style: Type manuscripts on one side of the paper only, on 8 1/2 x 11" good-quality white bond paper, using double or triple spacing and liberal margins on all sides. Place references, footnotes, etc., at the end of the article, separate from the text. Footnotes and reference citations should generally follow the Chicago Manual of Style and should be double- or triple-spaced. See recent publication for more information.

Manuscript editor:

Barry J. Brinker, CPA, Managing Editor

Corporate Accounting, WG&L, One Penn Plaza - 40th Fl.

New York, NY 10119, U. S. A.

Publisher: Warren, Gorham & Lamont, Inc.

210 South St.

Boston, MA 02111, U. S. A.

Cost and Management

Primary readership: Academicians, accounting (or tax) practitioners, businessmen, computer specialists, other professionals

Review process: Editorial only

Invited articles: 61-80%

Percentage of articles on accounting topics: 80

Approximate percentage of accounting-related articles devoted to:

Financial Accounting:	30	Managerial:	30
Computers/Systems:	5	Tax:	5
Auditing:	10	Education:	10
Professional:	10		

Approximate percentage of accounting-related articles characterized as primarily:

Empirical:	20	Experimental:	30
Analytical:	40	Descriptive:	10

Language(s) in which articles are published: English

Accepts manuscripts in English for translation: N/A

Approximate acceptance rate: 80%

Review period: 3-4 months   **Lead time to publication after acceptance:** 3-4 months

Circulation: 5,000   **Frequency of publication:** Bi-monthly

Sponsoring organization: None

Submission information:

Manuscript length: 2,000 - 5,000 words

Number of copies: 2   **Submission fee:** $6.60

Style: None

Manuscript editor:
Mr. D. P. Bhattacharyya FCMA, C/O Md. Abdur Rashid FCMA, Additional Director
Cost and Management, Institute of Cost and Management Accountants of Bangladesh
ICMA Bhaban, Nilkhet, Dhaka-5, Bangladesh

Publisher: Same as above

CPA   Marketing Report

Primary readership: Accounting (or tax) practitioners

Review process: Editorial only

Invited articles: 1-20%

**Percentage of articles
on accounting topics:**   100

Approximate percentage of accounting-related articles devoted to: Not specified

Financial Accounting:	**Managerial:**
Computers/Systems:	**Tax:**
Auditing:	**Education:**
Professional:	

Approximate percentage of accounting-related articles characterized as primarily: Not specified

Empirical:	**Experimental:**
Analytical:	**Descriptive:**

**Language(s) in which
articles are published:**   English

Accepts manuscripts in English for translation: N/A

Approximate acceptance rate: Not specified

Review period: 1 month   **Lead time to publication after acceptance:** Depends on editorial calendar

Circulation: N/A   **Frequency of publication:**   Monthly

Sponsoring organization: None

Submission information:

Manuscript length: Any length (could be condensed)

Number of copies: 2   **Submission fee:** None

Style: Not specified

**Manuscript
editor:**   Suzanne Verity

CPA Marketing Report, Professional Publications, P.O. Box 81067
Atlanta, GA   30366, U. S. A.

Publisher: Same as above

CPA Journal, The

Primary readership: Academicians, accounting (or tax) practitioners

Review process: Editorial only; External reviewers (authors known) - number depends on particular article

Invited articles: 1-20%

**Percentage of articles
on accounting topics:**   100

Approximate percentage of accounting-related articles devoted to:

Financial Accounting:	7.5	**Managerial:**	7.5
Computers/Systems:	7.5	**Tax:**	7.5
Auditing:	7.5	**Education:**	7.5
Professional:	7.5	**Other:**	47.5

Approximate percentage of accounting-related articles characterized as primarily:

Empirical:	30	**Experimental:**	10
Analytical:	30	**Descriptive:**	30

**Language(s) in which
articles are published:**   English

Accepts manuscripts in English for translation: N/A

Approximate acceptance rate: 25-30%

Review period: 15-30 days   **Lead time to publication after acceptance:** 2 months

Circulation: 50,000   **Frequency of publication:**   Monthly

Sponsoring organization: New York State Society of CPAs

Submission information:

Manuscript length: 2,500-3,500 words

Number of copies: 2   **Submission fee:** None

Style: Avoid numerous footnotes and citations. Tables and figures should be numbered, titled so references made within the text can refer to the key. Tables and figures should be on separate sheets. See recent publication for more information.

**Manuscript
editor:**   Kirk Batzer, Feature Article Editor

The CPA Journal, 600 Third Ave.

New York, NY 10016, U. S. A.

Publisher: Same as above

CPA Personnel Report

Primary readership: Accounting (or tax) practitioners

Review process: Editorial only

Invited articles: 1-20%

**Percentage of articles
on accounting topics:**   100

Approximate percentage of accounting-related articles devoted to: Not specified

Financial Accounting: **Managerial:**

Computers/Systems: **Tax:**

Auditing: **Education:**

Professional:

Approximate percentage of accounting-related articles characterized as primarily: Not specified

Empirical: **Experimental:**

Analytical: **Descriptive:**

**Language(s) in which
articles are published:**   English

Accepts manuscripts in English for translation: N/A

Approximate acceptance rate: not specified

Review period: 1 month   **Lead time to publication after acceptance:** Depends on editorial calendar

Circulation: N/A   **Frequency of publication:**   Monthly

Sponsoring organization: None

Submission information:
Manuscript length: Any length (could be condensed)

Number of copies: 2   **Submission fee:**   None

Style: Not specified

**Manuscript
editor:**   Suzanne Verity
CPA Personnel Report, Professional Publications, P.O. Box 81067
Atlanta, GA   30366, U. S. A.

Publisher: Same as above

Current Accounts

Primary readership: Academicians, accounting (or tax) practitioners, businessmen

Review process: Editorial only

Invited articles: Not specified

**Percentage of articles
on accounting topics:**   70

Approximate percentage of accounting-related articles devoted to: Not specified

Financial Accounting: **Managerial:**

Computers/Systems: **Tax:**

Auditing: **Education:**

Professional:

Approximate percentage of accounting-related articles characterized as primarily: Not specified

Empirical: **Experimental:**

Analytical: **Descriptive:**

**Language(s) in which
articles are published:**   English

Accepts manuscripts in English for translation: N/A

Approximate acceptance rate: Not specified

Review period: 3 weeks   **Lead time to publication after acceptance:** 1 month

Circulation: 7,000   **Frequency of publication:**   Monthly

Sponsoring organization: Georgia Society of CPAs

Submission information:

Manuscript length: 1,500 words

Number of copies: 1   **Submission fee:** None

Style: News style, feature material.

**Manuscript
editor:**
Betsy Casey, Editor, Communications Manager
Current Accounts, GSCPAs, 3340 Peachtree Rd., N.E., Suite 1980, Tower Place
Atlanta, GA 30026, U. S. A.

Publisher: Same as above

Data Management

Primary readership: Data processing management professionals

Review process: Not specified

Invited articles: Not specified

**Percentage of articles
on accounting topics:**
Approximate percentage of accounting-related articles devoted to: Not specified

Financial Accounting: **Managerial:**

Computers/Systems: **Tax:**

Auditing: **Education:**

Professional:

Approximate percentage of accounting-related articles characterized as primarily: Not specified

Empirical: **Experimental:**

Analytical: **Descriptive:**

**Language(s) in which
articles are published:**   English

Accepts manuscripts in English for translation: N/A

Approximate acceptance rate: Not specified

Review period: 1 1/2 months   **Lead time to publication after acceptance:** 3-4 months

Circulation: 50,000   **Frequency of publication:**   Monthly

Sponsoring organization: None

   Submission information:
Manuscript length: 2,000 words or 6-10 pages
Number of copies: Not specified **Submission fee:** None
Style: Available upon request.

**Manuscript
editor:**   Bill Zaleed
          Data Management, 505 Busse Highway
          Park Ridge, IL   60068, U. S. A.

Publisher: Same as above

Decision Sciences

Primary readership: Academicians, accounting (or tax) practitioners, businessmen, computer specialists

Review process: External blind reviewers

Invited articles: 1-20%

Percentage of articles on accounting topics: 10

Approximate percentage of accounting-related articles devoted to:

Financial Accounting:	10	Managerial:	10
Computers/Systems:	10	Tax:	10
Auditing:	10	Education:	20
Professional:	10	Other:	20

Approximate percentage of accounting-related articles characterized as primarily:

Empirical:	40	Experimental:	10
Analytical:	40	Descriptive:	10

Language(s) in which articles are published: English

Accepts manuscripts in English for translation: N/A

Approximate acceptance rate: 60%

Review period: 3 months   **Lead time to publication after acceptance:** 6 months

Circulation: 4,000   **Frequency of publication:** Quarterly

Sponsoring organization: Decision Sciences Institute

Submission information:

Manuscript length: 25 pages

Number of copies: 3   **Submission fee:** $15 for members, $30 for non-members

Style: All manuscripts should be typewritten double-spaced on 8 1/2 x 11" paper. Figures, charts, and tables should be numbered consecutively. Footnotes should be typed double-spaced and appear at the end of the paper. References should be listed alphabetically by author at the end of the paper and referred to in the body of the text by bracketed numbers. See publication for more information.

Manuscript editor:
Dr. Robert E. Markland

Decision Sciences, College of Business Administration, University of South Carolina

Columbia, SC 29208-0361, U. S. A.

Publisher: Decision Sciences Institute

140 Decatur St., S.E.

Atlanta, GA 30303-3083, U. S. A.

Defense Management Journal

Primary readership: Academicians, businessmen

Review process: 1-2 external blind reviewers

Invited articles: 61-80%

**Percentage of articles
on accounting topics:**   5

Approximate percentage of accounting-related articles devoted to:

Financial Accounting:	50	**Managerial:**	50
Computers/Systems:		**Tax:**	
Auditing:		**Education:**	
Professional:			

Approximate percentage of accounting-related articles characterized as primarily:

Empirical:	50	**Experimental:**	
Analytical:	25	**Descriptive:**	25

**Language(s) in which
articles are published:**   English

Accepts manuscripts in English for translation: N/A

Approximate acceptance rate: 25%

Review period: 3 months   **Lead time to publication after acceptance:** 6-9 months

Circulation: 100,000   **Frequency of publication:**   Semiannually

Sponsoring organization: Department of Defense

Submission information:

Manuscript length: 3,000 words (12 double-spaced, typewritten pages)

Number of copies: 3   **Submission fee:** None

Style: Manuscripts should be typed double-spaced on one side of 8 1/2 x 11" paper, leaving at least a 1-inch circumferential margin. References and footnotes should be typed on a separate sheet and should be numbered consecutively in the order of their appearance in the text. Complete source data must be provided.

**Manuscript
editor:**
David R. Lampe

Defense Management Journal, 716-R Church St.

Alexandria, VA 22314, U. S. A.

Publisher: Same as above

Detroit Business Review

Primary readership:	Academicians, practitioners, businessmen
Review process:	2 external reviewers, blind reviewers
Invited articles:	21-40%

**Percentage of articles
on accounting topics:** 20

Approximate percentage of accounting-related articles devoted to: Not specified

Financial Accounting:	**Managerial:**
Computers/Systems:	**Tax:**
Auditing:	**Education:**
Professional:	

Approximate percentage of accounting-related articles characterized as primarily:

Empirical:	**Experimental:**	
Analytical:	**Descriptive:**	100

**Language(s) in which
articles are published:** English

Accepts manuscripts in English for translation: N/A

Approximate acceptance rate: 50%

Review period: 2 months	**Lead time to publication after acceptance:** 6 months
Circulation: 1,000	**Frequency of publication:** Semiannually

Sponsoring organization: University of Detroit

Submission information:

Manuscript length: 15 pages	
Number of copies: 3	**Submission fee:** None
Style: None	

**Manuscript
editor:** Suk H. Kim
College of Business and Administration
University of Detroit , Detroit, MI 48221, U. S. A.

Publisher: Same as above

Directors & Boards

Primary readership: Academicians, businessmen, students

Review process: Not specified

Invited articles: Not specified

**Percentage of articles
on accounting topics:**
Approximate percentage of accounting-related articles devoted to: Not specified

Financial Accounting:	**Managerial:**
Computers/Systems:	**Tax:**
Auditing:	**Education:**
Professional:	

Approximate percentage of accounting-related articles characterized as primarily: Not specified

Empirical:	**Experimental:**
Analytical:	**Descriptive:**

**Language(s) in which
articles are published:**   English

Accepts manuscripts in English for translation: N/A

Approximate acceptance rate: 75% for invited articles, 10% for unsolicited manuscripts.

Review period: 1 month   **Lead time to publication after acceptance:** 3 to 6 months

Circulation: 5,000   **Frequency of publication:**   Quarterly

Sponsoring organization: None

Submission information:

Manuscript length: 1,000 to 2,500 words

Number of copies: 2   **Submission fee:** None

Style: Available upon request.

**Manuscript
editor:**   James Kristie
M L R Enterprises Inc., 229 S. 18th St.
Philadelphia, PA 19103, U. S. A.

Publisher: Same as above

Economie Et Comptabilite

Primary readership: Not specified

Review process: Not specified

Invited articles: Not specified

**Percentage of articles
on accounting topics:**
Approximate percentage of accounting-related articles devoted to: Not specified

Financial Accounting: **Managerial:**
Computers/Systems: **Tax:**
Auditing: **Education:**
Professional:

Approximate percentage of accounting-related articles characterized as primarily: Not specified

Empirical: **Experimental:**
Analytical: **Descriptive:**

**Language(s) in which
articles are published:**   French

Accepts manuscripts in English for translation: Not specified

Approximate acceptance rate: Not specified

Review period: Not specified   **Lead time to publication after acceptance:** Not specified

Circulation: 6,000   **Frequency of publication:**   Not specified

Sponsoring organization: Institut Francais des Experts Comptables

Submission information:
Manuscript length: Not specified
Number of copies: Not specified   **Submission fee:**   Not specified
Style: Not specified

**Manuscript
editor:**   Institut Francais des Experts Comptables
        139 rue du Faubourg Saint-Honore
        75008 Paris, France

Publisher: Same as above

Esso Italiana Informazioni Economiche

Primary readership: Not specified

Review process: Not specified

Invited articles: Not specified

**Percentage of articles
on accounting topics:**
Approximate percentage of accounting-related articles devoted to: Not specified

Financial Accounting:	**Managerial:**
Computers/Systems:	**Tax:**
Auditing:	**Education:**
Professional:	

Approximate percentage of accounting-related articles characterized as primarily: Not specified

Empirical:	**Experimental:**
Analytical:	**Descriptive:**

**Language(s) in which
articles are published:**   Italian

Accepts manuscripts in English for translation: Not specified

Approximate acceptance rate: Not specified

Review period: Not specified   **Lead time to publication after acceptance:** Not specified

Circulation: 10,000   **Frequency of publication:**   Not specified

Sponsoring organization: Esso Italiana

Submission information:
Manuscript length: Not specified
Number of copies: Not specified   **Submission fee:** Not specified
Style: Not specified

**Manuscript
editor:**   Raffaele Massimo
Esso Italiana, Stampa Informazione, Viale Castello della Magliana 25
00148 Rome, Italy

Publisher: Same as above

Estate Planning

Primary readership: Academicians, accounting (or tax) practitioners, lawyers, trust officers, insurance advisers, financial planners, others interested in estate planning

Review process: 1 external reviewer (authors known)

Invited articles: 61-80%

Percentage of articles on accounting topics:

Approximate percentage of accounting-related articles devoted to:

Financial Accounting:		Managerial:	
Computers/Systems:		Tax:	85
Auditing:		Education:	
Professional:		Other:	15

Approximate percentage of accounting-related articles characterized as primarily: Not specified

Empirical:	Experimental:
Analytical:	Descriptive:

Language(s) in which articles are published: English

Accepts manuscripts in English for translation: N/A

Approximate acceptance rate: 60%

Review period: 4-5 weeks **Lead time to publication after acceptance:** 4 weeks

Circulation: 13,000 **Frequency of publication:** 6 times a year

Sponsoring organization: None

Submission information:

Manuscript length: 4,000-5,000 words

Number of copies: 2 **Submission fee:** None

Style: Double-spaced; footnotes limited to citations; practical rather than theoretical analysis

Manuscript editor:
Joseph Graft
Estate Planning, One Penn Plaza, 40th Fl.
New York, NY 10119, U. S. A.

Publisher: Warren, Gorham & Lamont, Inc.
210 South Sreet
Boston, MA 02111, U. S. A.

Estates

Primary readership: Accounting (or tax) practitioners, tax lawyers, tax planners

Review process: Not specified

Invited articles: Not specified

Percentage of articles on accounting topics:
Approximate percentage of accounting-related articles devoted to: Not specified

Financial Accounting:	**Managerial:**
Computers/Systems:	**Tax:**
Auditing:	**Education:**
Professional:	

Approximate percentage of accounting-related articles characterized as primarily: Not specified

Empirical:	**Experimental:**
Analytical:	**Descriptive:**

Language(s) in which articles are published: English

Accepts manuscripts in English for translation: N/A

Approximate acceptance rate: 50%

Review period: 4-6 weeks   **Lead time to publication after acceptance:** 1-2 months

Circulation: 4,000   **Frequency of publication:** Monthly

Sponsoring organization: None

Submission information:
Manuscript length: 15-20 pages
Number of copies: Not specified   **Submission fee:** None
Style: Not specified

Manuscript editor: Patrick Rockelli
Estates, Tax Management, Inc., 1231 25th St., N. W., Suite 401
Washington, DC 20037, U. S. A.

Publisher: Same as above

European Taxation

Primary readership: Academicians, accounting (or tax) practitioners, businessmen

Review process: Not specified

Invited articles: 21-40%

**Percentage of articles
on accounting topics:**

Approximate percentage of accounting-related articles devoted to:

Financial Accounting:	**Managerial:**
Computers/Systems:	**Tax:** 100
Auditing:	**Education:**
Professional:	

Approximate percentage of accounting-related articles characterized as primarily: Not specified

Empirical:	**Experimental:**
Analytical:	**Descriptive:**

**Language(s) in which
articles are published:** English

Accepts manuscripts in English for translation: N/A

Approximate acceptance rate: 100%, for solicited manuscripts only

Review period: 2-3 months **Lead time to publication after acceptance:** 2-3 months

Circulation: World-wide **Frequency of publication:** Monthly

Sponsoring organization: None

Submission information:

Manuscript length: 15-25 typewritten pages (double-spaced)

Number of copies: 2 **Submission fee:** None

Style: Editorial changes are made in-house, if necessary

**Manuscript
editor:**
W. G. Kuiper, Editor in Chief
International Bureau of Fiscal Documentation, P.O. Box 20237
1000 HE Amsterdam, The Netherlands

Publisher: Same as above

Examiner, The

Primary readership: Acccounting (or tax) practitioners, insurance, and financial institutional examiners

Review process: 1 external reviewer (authors known)

Invited articles: 81-99%

**Percentage of articles
on accounting topics:** 100

Approximate percentage of accounting-related articles devoted to:

Financial Accounting:	20	**Managerial:**	
Computers/Systems:		**Tax:**	20
Auditing:	20	**Education:**	20
Professional:	20		

Approximate percentage of accounting-related articles characterized as primarily:

Empirical:		**Experimental:**	
Analytical:		**Descriptive:**	100

**Language(s) in which
articles are published:** English

Accepts manuscripts in English for translation: N/A

Approximate acceptance rate: 80%

Review period: 2 months   **Lead time to publication after acceptance:** 1-6 months

Circulation: Not specified   **Frequency of publication:** Quarterly

Sponsoring organization: Society of Financial Examiners

Submission information:

Manuscript length: 6-13 pages, 8 1/2 by 11", double-spaced
Number of copies: 2   **Submission fee:** None
Style: Not specified

**Manuscript
editor:** Phyllis H. Johnson
The Examiner, SOFE, 5 W. Hargett St., Suite 1100
Raleigh, NC 27601, U. S. A.

Publisher: Olson Management Group, Inc.
Same as above

Executive Accountant

Primary readership: Academicians, accounting (or tax) practitioners, businessmen

Review process: Editorial only

Invited articles: 41-60%

**Percentage of articles
on accounting topics:** 40

Approximate percentage of accounting-related articles devoted to:

Financial Accounting:	20	**Managerial:**	20
Computers/Systems:	10	**Tax:**	10
Auditing:	10	**Education:**	10
Professional:	10	**Other:**	10

Approximate percentage of accounting-related articles characterized as primarily:

Empirical:	10	**Experimental:**	20
Analytical:	20	**Descriptive:**	20
Other :	30		

**Language(s) in which
articles are published:** English

Accepts manuscripts in English for translation: N/A

Approximate acceptance rate: Not specified

Review period: 1 month   **Lead time to publication after acceptance:** Within the next two issues

Circulation: 5,000   **Frequency of publication:** Quarterly

Sponsoring organization: Association of Cost & Executive Accountants

Submission information:
Manuscript length: 3,000-5,000 words
Number of copies: 2   **Submission fee:** None
Style: Typed double-spaced.

**Manuscript
editor:** Sushil K. Das Gupta
Executive Accountant, Association of Cost & Executive Accountants
London N4 3HF, England

Publisher: Same as above

Financial Accountability & Management

Primary readership: Academicians

Review process: 1 or 2 external blind reviewers

Invited articles: 1-20%

**Percentage of articles
on accounting topics:**   80

Approximate percentage of accounting-related articles devoted to: In the not-for-profit sector

Financial Accounting:	20	**Managerial:**	50
Computers/Systems:	10	**Tax:**	
Auditing:	10	**Education:**	5
Professional:	5		

Approximate percentage of accounting-related articles characterized as primarily: Not specified

Empirical: **Experimental:**

Analytical: **Descriptive:**

**Language(s) in which
articles are published:**   English only, but national variations on spelling and grammar are acceptable.

Accepts manuscripts in English for translation: N/A

Approximate acceptance rate: 50%, because FAM is a new journal, building contributor interest.

Review period: 4 months   **Lead time to publication after acceptance:** currently 9 months

Circulation: 1,200   **Frequency of publication:**   Quarterly

Sponsoring organization: no

Submission information:

Manuscript length: 2,000-8,000 words

Number of copies: 3   **Submission fee:** None

Style: The main text should be followed by any appendices, by any footnotes (which should be kept to an essential minimum, identified in the text by superscript numerals and listed together at the end), and by the list of source references. Tables and figures should be numbered in order of their appearance with arabic numerals, and each should have a concise, descriptive title (and source where relevant).

**Manuscript
editor:**

Professor John Perrin

Financial Accountability & Management, Department of Economics, University of Exeter

Exeter EX4 4RJ, England

Publisher: Journals Dept., Basil Blackwell Ltd.

108 Cowley Road

Oxford OX4 1JF, England

Financial Analysts Journal

Primary readership: Financial analysts, businessmen

Review process: Not specified

Invited articles: Not specified

**Percentage of articles
on accounting topics:**
Approximate percentage of accounting-related articles devoted to: Not specified

Financial Accounting:	**Managerial:**
Computers/Systems:	**Tax:**
Auditing:	**Education:**
Professional:	

Approximate percentage of accounting-related articles characterized as primarily: Not specified

Empirical:	**Experimental:**
Analytical:	**Descriptive:**

**Language(s) in which
articles are published:** English

Accepts manuscripts in English for translation: N/A

Approximate acceptance rate: 10%

Review period: 3 months   **Lead time to publication after acceptance:** 4 months

Circulation: 20,000   **Frequency of publication:** Bi-monthly

Sponsoring organization: Financial Analysts Federation

Submission information:

Manuscript length: 4,000 words

Number of copies: Not specified **Submission fee:** None

Style: Available upon request.

**Manuscript
editor:** Mr. Charles D'Ambrosio
Financial Analysts Journal, 1633 Broadway, 14th Floor
New York, NY 10019, U. S. A.

Publisher: Same as above

Financial Management

Primary readership: Academicians, businessmen

Review process: 2-3 external blind reviewers

Invited articles: 1-20%

**Percentage of articles
on accounting topics:** 20

Approximate percentage of accounting-related articles devoted to:

Financial Accounting:		**Managerial:**	
Computers/Systems:		**Tax:**	
Auditing:		**Education:**	
Professional:		**Finance:**	100

Approximate percentage of accounting-related articles characterized as primarily:

Empirical:	60	**Experimental:**	
Analytical:		**Descriptive:**	40

**Language(s) in which
articles are published:** English

Accepts manuscripts in English for translation: N/A

Approximate acceptance rate: 20%

Review period: 8 weeks   **Lead time to publication after acceptance:** 3 months

Circulation: 8,200   **Frequency of publication:** Quarterly

Sponsoring organization: Financial Management Association

Submission information:

Manuscript length: No limit

Number of copies: 3   **Submission fee:** $40 for non-FMA menbers, $20 for FMA members

Style: Place references in a numbered, alphabetical list at the end of the article . Cite references in the text by placing the appropriate reference number in brackets. Tables, charts, and graphs should appear on separate pages labeled in numerical order and grouped at the end of the paper. Refer to all as exhibits, not tables or figures, and include marginal notation in the text for the approximate placement of the exhibits.

Manuscript editor: Robert A. Taggart

Financial Management Association, Boston University, School of Business, 704 Commonwealth Ave. Boston, MA 02215, U. S. A.

Publisher: Financial Management Association

University of South Florida, College of Business
Tampa, FL 33620, U. S. A.

Financial Planning Today

Primary readership: Accounting (or tax) practitioners, lawyers, businessmen, insurance underwriters

Review process: Not specified

Invited articles: Not specified

**Percentage of articles
on accounting topics:**
Approximate percentage of accounting-related articles devoted to: Not specified

Financial Accounting: **Managerial:**
Computers/Systems: **Tax:**
Auditing: **Education:**
Professional:

Approximate percentage of accounting-related articles characterized as primarily: Not specified

Empirical: **Experimental:**
Analytical: **Descriptive:**

**Language(s) in which
articles are published:**   English

Accepts manuscripts in English for translation: N/A

Approximate acceptance rate: Not specified

Review period: 1 month   **Lead time to publication after acceptance:** 1-2 months

Circulation: Not specified   **Frequency of publication:**   Quarterly

Sponsoring organization: None

Submission information:
Manuscript length: 1,500-10,000 words
Number of copies: Not specified   **Submission fee:**   Not specified
Style: Footnotes should be at the end of the manuscript. More information available upon request.

**Manuscript
editor:**   B. E. Newmark
Financial Planning Today, Box 5359
Lakeworth, FL 33461, U. S. A.

Publisher: Same as above

Financial Review, The

Primary readership: Academicians, bankers, security industry professionals

Review process: Not specified

Invited articles: Not specified

**Percentage of articles
on accounting topics:**

Approximate percentage of accounting-related articles devoted to: Not specified

Financial Accounting:	**Managerial:**
Computers/Systems:	**Tax:**
Auditing:	**Education:**
Professional:	

Approximate percentage of accounting-related articles characterized as primarily: Not specified

Empirical:	**Experimental:**
Analytical:	**Descriptive:**

**Language(s) in which
articles are published:**   English

Accepts manuscripts in English for translation: N/A

Approximate acceptance rate: 20%

Review period: 2 months   **Lead time to publication after acceptance:** 4-9 months

Circulation: 1,200   **Frequency of publication:**   Quarterly

Sponsoring organization: Eastern Finance Association

Submission information:

Manuscript length: Not specified

Number of copies: Not specified   **Submission fee:** $10 for members; $15 for non-members

Style: Not specified

**Manuscript
editor:**   James Boness

State University of New York, Buffalo, School of Management

Buffalo, NY 14214, U. S. A.

Publisher: Same as above

Georgia Journal of Accounting

Primary readership: Academicians, accounting (or tax) practitioners, businessmen

Review process: 2-3 external blind reviewers

Invited articles: 61-80%

**Percentage of articles
on accounting topics:**   100

Approximate percentage of accounting-related articles devoted to: Varies

Financial Accounting: **Managerial:**
Computers/Systems: **Tax:**
Auditing: **Education:**
Professional:

Approximate percentage of accounting-related articles characterized as primarily: Not specified

Empirical: **Experimental:**
Analytical: **Descriptive:**

**Language(s) in which
articles are published:**   English

Accepts manuscripts in English for translation: N/A

Approximate acceptance rate: Unknown

Review period: 2 months   **Lead time to publication after acceptance:** N/A

Circulation: 2,500   **Frequency of publication:**   Annually

Sponsoring organization: Changes yearly with issue

Submission information:

Manuscript length:

Number of copies: 2   **Submission fee:** None

Style: Double-spaced

**Manuscript
editor:**   Paul Streer (NOTE: Editors are changed annually)

Georgia Journal of Accounting, J. M. Tull School of Accounting, College of Business, University of Georgia
Athens, GA 30602, U. S. A.

Publisher: Same as above

Government Accountants Journal, The

Primary readership: Government financial management professionals

Review process: 2 external blind reviewers

Invited articles: 1-20%

**Percentage of articles
on accounting topics:** 80

Approximate percentage of accounting-related articles devoted to: Not specified

Financial Accounting: **Managerial:**

Computers/Systems: **Tax:**

Auditing: **Education:**

Professional:

Approximate percentage of accounting-related articles characterized as primarily: Not specified

Empirical: **Experimental:**

Analytical: **Descriptive:**

**Language(s) in which
articles are published:** English

Accepts manuscripts in English for translation: N/A

Approximate acceptance rate: 50%

Review period: 2 months   **Lead time to publication after acceptance:** Up to one year

Circulation: 13,000   **Frequency of publication:** Quarterly

Sponsoring organization: Association of Government Accountants

Submission information:

Manuscript length: 10-12 pages, double-spaced

Number of copies: 3   **Submission fee:** None

Style: Not specified

**Manuscript
editor:** Charles E. Hamilton
The Government Accountants Journal, 727 S. 23rd St.
Arlington, VA 22202, U. S. A.

Publisher: Same as above

Government Finance Review

Primary readership: Government finance officers

Review process: Not specified

Invited articles: Not specified

**Percentage of articles
on accounting topics:**   10

Approximate percentage of accounting-related articles devoted to:

Financial Accounting:	**Managerial:**
Computers/Systems:	**Tax:**
Auditing:	**Education:**
Professional:	**Governmental:** 100

Approximate percentage of accounting-related articles characterized as primarily: Not specified

Empirical:	**Experimental:**
Analytical:	**Descriptive:**

**Language(s) in which
articles are published:**   English

Accepts manuscripts in English for translation: N/A

Approximate acceptance rate: Not specified

Review period: Not specified   **Lead time to publication after acceptance:**   Not specified

Circulation: 12,000   **Frequency of publication:**   Bi-monthly

Sponsoring organization: Government Finance Officers Association

Submission information:

Manuscript length: 10 pages, typed double-spaced.

Number of copies: **Submission fee:**   None

Style: Not specified

**Manuscript
editor:**   Barbara Weiss

Government Finance Review, 1750 K St. N.W., Suite 200

Washington, DC   20006, U. S. A.

Publisher: Government Finance Officers Association

180 N. Michigan Ave., Suite 800

Chicago, IL   60601, U. S. A.

Governmental Finance

Primary readership: Accounting (or tax) practitioners, public finance officials

Review process: Not specified

Invited articles: Not specified

**Percentage of articles
on accounting topics:**
Approximate percentage of accounting-related articles devoted to: Not specified

Financial Accounting: **Managerial:**
Computers/Systems: **Tax:**
Auditing: **Education:**
Professional:

Approximate percentage of accounting-related articles characterized as primarily: Not specified

Empirical: **Experimental:**
Analytical: **Descriptive:**

**Language(s) in which
articles are published:** English

Accepts manuscripts in English for translation: N/A

Approximate acceptance rate: Not specified

Review period: 6 months   **Lead time to publication after acceptance:** 4-6 months

Circulation: 10,000   **Frequency of publication:** Quarterly

Sponsoring organization: Municipal Finance Officers Association of the U. S. and Canada

Submission information:
Manuscript length: 15 -20 manuscript pages
Number of copies: 2   **Submission fee:** None
Style: Available upon request.

**Manuscript
editor:** Editor
Governmental Finance, 180 North Michigan Avenue, # 800
Chicago, IL 60601, U. S. A.

Publisher: Same as above

Harvard Business Review

Primary readership:	Academicians, businessmen
Review process:	In-house reviewers
Invited articles:	Not specified

**Percentage of articles
on accounting topics:**
Approximate percentage of accounting-related articles devoted to: Not specified

Financial Accounting:	**Managerial:**
Computers/Systems:	**Tax:**
Auditing:	**Education:**
Professional:	

Approximate percentage of accounting-related articles characterized as primarily: Not specified

Empirical:	**Experimental:**
Analytical:	**Descriptive:**

**Language(s) in which
articles are published:**   English

Accepts manuscripts in English for translation: N/A

Approximate acceptance rate: 5%

Review period: 2 months   **Lead time to publication after acceptance:** 4-6 months

Circulation: 240,000   **Frequency of publication:**   Bi-monthly

Sponsoring organization: Harvard University

Submission information:
Manuscript length: 2,000-6,000 words
Number of copies: Original   **Submission fee:** None
Style: Not specified

**Manuscript
editor:**   Kenneth R. Andrews
Harvard University, Graduate School of Business, Soldiers Field
Boston, MA   02163, U. S. A.

Publisher: Same as above

Healthcare Financial Management

Primary readership: Health care financial managers

Review process: 3 external blind reviewers

Invited articles: Not specified

Percentage of articles on accounting topics: 50

Approximate percentage of accounting-related articles devoted to:

Financial Accounting:	25	**Managerial:**	35
Computers/Systems:	20	**Tax:**	10
Auditing:	5	**Education:**	
Professional:	5		

Approximate percentage of accounting-related articles characterized as primarily:

Empirical:		**Experimental:**	10
Analytical:		**Descriptive:**	10
"How-to" articles:	80		

Language(s) in which articles are published: English

Accepts manuscripts in English for translation: N/A

Approximate acceptance rate: 50%

Review period: 2 months   **Lead time to publication after acceptance:** 3-6 months

Circulation: 25,000   **Frequency of publication:** Monthly

Sponsoring organization: Healthcare Financial Management Association

Submission information:

Manuscript length: 10-15 double-spaced typed pages

Number of copies: 4   **Submission fee:** None

Style: Double-spaced with 1" inch margins. Footnotes alphabetically in the text and put in the same consecutive order on the footnote page at the end of the manuscript. If a bibliography is included as well as footnotes, it should be placed at the end of the manuscript. If charts, tables, or graphs are used, they should be referred to as exhibits in the text and numbered consecutively throughout the text. Contact the editor for more information.

Manuscript editor: Leslie Silkworth, Editor

Healthcare Financial Management, HFMA, 1900 Spring Rd, Suite 500

Oak Brook, IL 60521, U. S. A.

Publisher: Same as above

Hong Kong Manager, The

Primary readership: Academicians, accounting (or tax) practitioners, businessmen, computer specialists

Review process: 2 external blind reviewers

Invited articles: 81-99%

**Percentage of articles
on accounting topics:**   20

Approximate percentage of accounting-related articles devoted to:

Financial Accounting:	10	**Managerial:**	40
Computers/Systems:	20	**Tax:**	
Auditing:		**Education:**	10
Professional:	20		

Approximate percentage of accounting-related articles characterized as primarily:

Empirical:		**Experimental:**	
Analytical:	50	**Descriptive:**	50

**Language(s) in which
articles are published:**   English, Chinese

Accepts manuscripts in English for translation: Yes

Approximate acceptance rate: 70%

Review period: 1 month   **Lead time to publication after acceptance:** 2 months

Circulation: 5,600   **Frequency of publication:**   Bi-monthly

Sponsoring organization: The Hong Kong Management Association

Submission information:

Manuscript length: 5,000-7,000 words

Number of copies: 3   **Submission fee:** None

Style: All articles should be typed double-spaced on size A4 paper. Contact the editor for more information concerning article publication.

**Manuscript
editor:**   Mr. John Hung
The Hong Kong Manager, 14/F, Fairmont House, 8 Cotton Tree Drive
Central , Hong Kong

Publisher: Same as above

Hospital & Health Services Administration

Primary readership: Health care executives

Review process: 5 external blind reviewers

Invited articles: 1-20%

**Percentage of articles
on accounting topics:**   5

Approximate percentage of accounting-related articles devoted to:

Financial Accounting:	15	**Managerial:**	15
Computers/Systems:		**Tax:**	
Auditing:		**Education:**	
Professional:	70		

Approximate percentage of accounting-related articles characterized as primarily:

Empirical:	10	**Experimental:**	
Analytical:		**Descriptive:**	90

**Language(s) in which
articles are published:**   English

Accepts manuscripts in English for translation: N/A

Approximate acceptance rate: 50%

Review period: 2 months   **Lead time to publication after acceptance:** 10 months

Circulation: 21,500   **Frequency of publication:**   Quarterly

Sponsoring organization: Foundation at the American College and Healthcare Executives

    Submission information:

Manuscript length: 15-25 double-spaced pages

Number of copies: 4   **Submission fee:** None

Style: Copies should be typed and double-spaced on 8 1/2 x 11" white paper with 1 1/4" margins all around. References should be listed separately at the end of text, numbered in order of citation. Put reference numbers in the text in brackets at the end of the sentence before the period.

**Manuscript
editor:**

Gene Regenstreif, Managing Editor

Hospital and Health Services Administration, Health Administration Press, 1021 E. Huron

Ann Arbor, MI 48104-9990, U. S. A.

Publisher: Same as above

Human Systems Management

Primary readership: Academicians, businessmen

Review process: 3 external blind reviewers

Invited articles: 1-20%

Percentage of articles on accounting topics: 10

Approximate percentage of accounting-related articles devoted to:

Financial Accounting:		Managerial:	
Computers/Systems:	50	Tax:	
Auditing:		Education:	
Professional:	30	Other:	20

Approximate percentage of accounting-related articles characterized as primarily:

Empirical:	10	Experimental:	20
Analytical:	50	Descriptive:	10
Other:	10		

Language(s) in which articles are published: English

Accepts manuscripts in English for translation: N/A

Approximate acceptance rate: 60%

Review period: 1 month **Lead time to publication after acceptance:** 8 months

Circulation: Not specified **Frequency of publication:** Quarterly

Sponsoring organization:

Submission information:

Manuscript length: 20 printed pages

Number of copies: 3 **Submission fee:** None

Style: No footnotes should be included. Drawings for figures or diagrams will be included in the issue exactly as drawn by the author (except for the reduction in size). References should be listed alphabetically, with the authors' first name initials first, then complete spelling of the last name, i.e., J. W. Brown. In the text, references should be indicated by arabic numerals enclosed in square brackets.

Manuscript editor:

Manfred Kochen

Human Systems Management, MHRI, The University of Michigan

Ann Arbor, MI 48109, U. S. A.

Publisher: Elsevier Science Publishers B.V.

Box 211

1000 AE Amsterdam, Netherlands

In Business

Primary readership: Businessmen

Review process: Editorial only

Invited articles: 61-80%

**Percentage of articles
on accounting topics:** 10

Approximate percentage of accounting-related articles devoted to: Not specified

Financial Accounting: **Managerial:**
Computers/Systems: **Tax:**
Auditing: **Education:**
Professional:

Approximate percentage of accounting-related articles characterized as primarily: Not specified

Empirical: **Experimental:**
Analytical: **Descriptive:**

**Language(s) in which
articles are published:** English

Accepts manuscripts in English for translation: N/A

Approximate acceptance rate: 20%

Review period: Not specified **Lead time to publication after acceptance:** 4 months

Circulation: Not specified **Frequency of publication:** Bi-monthly

Sponsoring organization: None

Submission information:
Manuscript length: 1,000-1,500 words
Number of copies: 2 **Submission fee:** Not specified
Style: Not specified

**Manuscript
editor:** Nora Goldstein
In Business, P.O. Box 323
Emmaus, PA 18049, U. S. A.

Publisher: J. G. Press, Inc.
Box 351
Emmaus, PA 18049, U. S. A.

Income Tax Digest and Accountants Review

Primary readership: Accounting (or tax) practitioners, businessmen

Review process: Editorial only

Invited articles: N/A

**Percentage of articles
on accounting topics:**   100

Approximate percentage of accounting-related articles devoted to:

Financial Accounting:	**Managerial:**	
Computers/Systems:	**Tax:**	90
Auditing:	**Education:**	
Professional:	Other:	10

Approximate percentage of accounting-related articles characterized as primarily:

Empirical:	**Experimental:**
Analytical:	**Descriptive:**
Practice: 100	

**Language(s) in which
articles are published:**   English

Accepts manuscripts in English for translation: N/A

Approximate acceptance rate: Not specified

Review period: 1 month   **Lead time to publication after acceptance:** 2 months

Circulation: 1,000   **Frequency of publication:**   Monthly

Sponsoring organization: Fiscal Press LTD

> ### Submission information:

Manuscript length: 1,000-4,000 words
Number of copies: 1   **Submission fee:** None
Style: Not specified

**Manuscript
editor:**   Desmond Airey
Income Tax Digest and Accountants Review, Richmond House, 1 Richmond St.
Herne Bay, Kent CT6 5 LU, England

Publisher: Fiscal Press Ltd.
Fiscal House, 36 Lattimore Rd.
St. Albans, Herts. AL1 3XW, England

Indian Journal of Accounting

Primary readership: Academicians, practitioners

Review process: External reviewers (authors known)

Invited articles: Not specified

**Percentage of articles
on accounting topics:**   80

Approximate percentage of accounting-related articles devoted to:

Financial Accounting:	20	**Managerial:**	50
Computers/Systems:		**Tax:**	5
Auditing:		**Education:**	10
Professional:	10	**Other:**	5

Approximate percentage of accounting-related articles characterized as primarily:

Empirical:	5	**Experimental:**	
Analytical:	40	**Descriptive:**	40
Other:	15		

**Language(s) in which
articles are published:**   English

Accepts manuscripts in English for translation: N/A

Approximate acceptance rate: 75%

Review period: 1-2 months   **Lead time to publication after acceptance:** 3-6 months

Circulation: 1,000   **Frequency of publication:** Bi-annually

Sponsoring organization: Indian Accounting Association

Submission information:

Manuscript length: 15-20 typed double-spaced pages
Number of copies: 2   **Submission fee:** None
Style: Not specified

**Manuscript
editor:**   Dr. B. Banerjee, Professor of Commerce
Indian Journal of Accounting, Calcutta University
Calcutta 700073 India.

Publisher: Same as above

Indian Management

Primary readership: Academicians, accounting (or tax) practitioners, businessmen, managers all over India

Review process: 20 external reviewers (authors known)

Invited articles: 1-20%

**Percentage of articles
on accounting topics:**   20

Approximate percentage of accounting-related articles devoted to:

Financial Accounting:	5	**Managerial:**	
Computers/Systems:	10	**Tax:**	50
Auditing:	5	**Education:**	30
Professional:			

Approximate percentage of accounting-related articles characterized as primarily: Not specified

Empirical: **Experimental:**

Analytical: **Descriptive:**

Not specified.

**Language(s) in which
articles are published:**   English only

Accepts manuscripts in English for translation: N/A

Approximate acceptance rate: Depends on the inflow of articles.

Review period: 8 weeks   **Lead time to publication after acceptance:** 8 weeks

Circulation: 10,000   **Frequency of publication:**   Monthly

Sponsoring organization: All Indian Management Association

Submission information:

Manuscript length: 2,000-3,000 words

Number of copies: 2   **Submission fee:** None

Style: Easy and lucid language, original ideas, illustrated if possible.

**Manuscript
editor:**   Dr. Utpal K. Bannerjee (Editor in Chief) of Lalita Ramanathan
    All Indian Management Association, "Management House," 14, Institutional Area, Lodi Road
    New Delhi-3, India

Publisher: Y Ramaswamy
    Same as above

Industrial Accountant

Primary readership: Academicians, accounting (or tax) practitioners, members

Review process: Not specified

Invited articles: Not specified

**Percentage of articles
on accounting topics:**

Approximate percentage of accounting-related articles devoted to: Not specified

Financial Accounting:	**Managerial:**
Computers/Systems:	**Tax:**
Auditing:	**Education:**
Professional:	

Approximate percentage of accounting-related articles characterized as primarily: Not specified

Empirical:	**Experimental:**
Analytical:	**Descriptive:**

**Language(s) in which
articles are published:**   English

Accepts manuscripts in English for translation: N/A

Approximate acceptance rate: Not specified

Review period: 3 months   **Lead time to publication after acceptance:** 3-6 months

Circulation: 5,000   **Frequency of publication:**   Quarterly

Sponsoring organization: Institute of Cost and Management Accountants of Pakistan

Submission information:

Manuscript length: 5,000-10,000 words

Number of copies: 2   **Submission fee:** None

Style: Available upon request.

**Manuscript
editor:**   Asrar Jamil

Institute of Cost and Management Accountants of Pakistan, Box 7284, Soldier Bazar
Karachi 3, Pakistan

Publisher: Same as above

Industrial Management

Primary readership: Businessmen, academicians, computer specialists, all management interests

Review process: Editorial only, others if topic warrants

Invited articles: 1-20%

**Percentage of articles
on accounting topics:** 25

Approximate percentage of accounting-related articles devoted to:

Financial Accounting:		**Managerial:**	70
Computers/Systems:	30	**Tax:**	
Auditing:		**Education:**	
Professional:			

Approximate percentage of accounting-related articles characterized as primarily:

Empirical:	33	**Experimental:**	
Analytical:	33	**Descriptive:**	34

**Language(s) in which
articles are published:** English

Accepts manuscripts in English for translation: N/A

Approximate acceptance rate: 30%

Review period: 3-4 weeks   **Lead time to publication after acceptance:** 1-5 months

Circulation: 4,200   **Frequency of publication:** 6 times per year

Sponsoring organization: Institute of Industrial Engineers

Submission information:

Manuscript length: 6-30 typed double-spaced pages
Number of copies: 3   **Submission fee:** none
Style: Avoid jargon and wordiness

**Manuscript
editor:** Chuck Lopez, Managing Editor
Industrial Management, 25 Technology Park/Atlanta
Norcross, GA 30092, U. S. A.

Publisher: Same as above

Information & Management

Primary readership: Academicians, computer specialists

Review process: Not specified

Invited articles: 1-20%

**Percentage of articles
on accounting topics:**
Approximate percentage of accounting-related articles devoted to: Not specified

Financial Accounting:	**Managerial:**
Computers/Systems:	**Tax:**
Auditing:	**Education:**
Professional:	

Approximate percentage of accounting-related articles characterized as primarily: Not specified

Empirical:	**Experimental:**
Analytical:	**Descriptive:**

**Language(s) in which
articles are published:**   English

Accepts manuscripts in English for translation: N/A

Approximate acceptance rate: 50%

Review period: 3 months   **Lead time to publication after acceptance:** 9 months

Circulation: Not specified   **Frequency of publication:**   10 times per year

Sponsoring organization: IFIP

Submission information:

Manuscript length: No limit

Number of copies: 5   **Submission fee:** None

Style: Each diagram, figure, or illustration should be on a separate sheet and numbered consecutively and must be referenced at least once. References indicated by arabic numerals enclosed in square brackets. References listed alphabetically and numbered consecutively. Initials should precede the family name. Avoid footnotes if possible.

**Manuscript
editor:**   E. H. Sibley

George Mason University, Department of Computer and Information Science, 6600 University Drive

Fairfax, VA 22030, U. S. A.

Publisher: Elsevier Science Publishers B. V.

Box 211

1000 AE Amsterdam, Netherlands

126

Institute of Chartered Accountants of Sri Lanka

Primary readership: Not specified

Review process: Not specified

Invited articles: Not specified

Percentage of articles on accounting topics:
Approximate percentage of accounting-related articles devoted to: Not specified

Financial Accounting: | Managerial:
Computers/Systems: | Tax:
Auditing: | Education:
Professional:

Approximate percentage of accounting-related articles characterized as primarily: Not specified

Empirical: | Experimental:
Analytical: | Descriptive:

Language(s) in which articles are published: Sinhalese, Tamil, English

Accepts manuscripts in English for translation: Yes

Approximate acceptance rate: Not specified

Review period: Not specified **Lead time to publication after acceptance:** Not specified

Circulation: 1,000 **Frequency of publication:** Not specified

Sponsoring organization: Not specified

Submission information:
Manuscript length: Not specified
Number of copies: Not specified **Submission fee:** Not specified
Style: Not specified

Manuscript editor:
Editorial Board, Institute of Chartered Accountants of Sri Lanka
30A Longden Place
Colombo 7. Sri Lanka

Publisher: Same as above

Internal Auditing

Primary readership: Internal auditors

Review process: Editorial only

Invited articles: Not specified

**Percentage of articles
on accounting topics:**   100

Approximate percentage of accounting-related articles devoted to:

Financial Accounting:	**Managerial:**
Computers/Systems:	**Tax:**
Auditing: 100	**Education:**
Professional:	

Approximate percentage of accounting-related articles characterized as primarily:

Empirical:	**Experimental:**
Analytical:	**Descriptive:**
Practice-related articles: 100	

**Language(s) in which
articles are published:**   English

Accepts manuscripts in English for translation: N/A

Approximate acceptance rate: Not specified

Review period: 1 month   **Lead time to publication after acceptance:** 3 months

Circulation: 5,139   **Frequency of publication:**   Quarterly

Sponsoring organization:

Submission information:

Manuscript length: 3,200- 4,800 words

Number of copies: **Submission fee:** None

Style: Authors' guide available upon request.

**Manuscript
editor:**   Professor Michael Barrett, C.B.A.

Internal Auditing, (M/C 006) University of Illinois at Chicago, P.O. Box 4348
Chicago, IL 60680, U. S. A.

Publisher: Same as above

Internal Auditor, The

Primary readership: Academicians, businessmen, internal auditors, EDP auditors

Review process: 3 external blind reviewers

Invited articles: 1-20%

Percentage of articles on accounting topics:

Approximate percentage of accounting-related articles devoted to:

Financial Accounting:		**Managerial:**	
Computers/Systems:	40	**Tax:**	
Auditing:	40	**Education:**	10
Professional:	10		

Approximate percentage of accounting-related articles characterized as primarily:

Empirical:		**Experimental:**	10
Analytical:		**Descriptive:**	
Practitioner:	90		

Language(s) in which articles are published: English

Accepts manuscripts in English for translation: N/A

Approximate acceptance rate: 40%

Review period: 2 months   **Lead time to publication after acceptance:** 6-12 months

Circulation: 30,000   **Frequency of publication:** Bi-monthly

Sponsoring organization: Institute of Internal Auditing

Submission information:

Manuscript length: 18-25 typed (including exhibits) on 8 1/2 x 11" paper

Number of copies: Original and 3   **Submission fee:** None

Style: Manuscripts should be typed double-spaced, with margins no less than 1 1/4" wide. Letter-quality computer printouts are acceptable. Exhibits should be concise, separated from the text. The staff will prepare them for publications' specifications. Keep footnotes to a minimum. Include the footnote number in the text and group all footnotes at the end of the manuscript.

Manuscript editor:

Ceel Pasternak, Editor

Internal Auditor, 249 Maitland Avenue, P.O. Box 1119

Altamonte Springs, FL 32715-1119, U. S. A.

Publisher: Same as above

International Journal of Acct. Education and Research, The

Primary readership: Academicians, acccounting (or tax) practitioners

Review process: Not specified

Invited articles: Not specified

**Percentage of articles
on accounting topics:**   100

Approximate percentage of accounting-related articles devoted to:

Financial Accounting:	**Managerial:**	
Computers/Systems:	**Tax:**	
Auditing:	**Education:**	100
Professional:		

Approximate percentage of accounting-related articles characterized as primarily: Not specified

Empirical:	**Experimental:**
Analytical:	**Descriptive:**

**Language(s) in which
articles are published:**   English

Accepts manuscripts in English for translation: N?A

Approximate acceptance rate: 20-30%

Review period: 6 months   **Lead time to publication after acceptance:** 6 months

Circulation: 1,200   **Frequency of publication:**   Semiannually

Sponsoring organization: University of Illinois, Center for International Education and Research in Accounting

Submission information:

Manuscript length: 3,000 - 5,000 words

Number of copies: 2   **Submission fee:** Not specified

Style: Available upon request.

**Manuscript
editor:**   Manuscript Editor, Center for International Education and Research in Accounting
University of Illinois, 320 Commerce Bldg. (West), Box 109, 1206 S. Sixth St.
Champaign, IL 61820-6271, U. S. A.

Publisher: Same as above

International Journal of Government Auditing

Primary readership: Government auditors

Review process: Not specified

Invited articles: Not specified

**Percentage of articles
on accounting topics:**
Approximate percentage of accounting-related articles devoted to:

Financial Accounting:		**Managerial:**
Computers/Systems:		**Tax:**
Auditing:	100	**Education:**
Professional:		

Approximate percentage of accounting-related articles characterized as primarily: Not specified

Empirical:	**Experimental:**
Analytical:	**Descriptive:**

**Language(s) in which
articles are published:**   English, French, Spanish, German, Arabic

Accepts manuscripts in English for translation: N/A

Approximate acceptance rate: 60%

Review period: 2 months   **Lead time to publication after acceptance:** 3 months

Circulation: 8,000   **Frequency of publication:**   Quarterly

Sponsoring organization: Internal Organization of Supreme Audit Institutions

Submission information:
Manuscript length: 15 manuscript pages
Number of copies: Not specified   **Submission fee:** None
Style: Available upon request.

**Manuscript
editor:**   Elaine L. Orr

   U. S. General Accounting Office, Room 7131, 441 G. Street, N. W.
   Washington, DC 20548

Publisher: Not indicated

International Journal, The

Primary readership: Accounting (or tax) practitioners, lawyers, tax planners

Review process: Not specified

Invited articles: Not specified

**Percentage of articles
on accounting topics:**

Approximate percentage of accounting-related articles devoted to: Not specified

Financial Accounting:	**Managerial:**
Computers/Systems:	**Tax:**
Auditing:	**Education:**
Professional:	

Approximate percentage of accounting-related articles characterized as primarily: Not specified

Empirical:	**Experimental:**
Analytical:	**Descriptive:**

**Language(s) in which
articles are published:**   English

Accepts manuscripts in English for translation: N/A

Approximate acceptance rate: 50%

Review period: 4 - 6 weeks   **Lead time to publication after acceptance:** 1 month

Circulation: 2,000   **Frequency of publication:**   Monthly

Sponsoring organization: None

Submission information:

Manuscript length: 15 - 20 pages
Number of copies: Not specified   **Submission fee:**   None
Style: Available upon request.

**Manuscript
editor:**   Javed Khokhar, Esq.

     The International Journal, Tax Management, Inc., 1231 25th St., N. W., Suite 401
     Washington, DC 20037, U. S. A.

Publisher: Same as above

International Tax Journal

Primary readership: Accounting (or tax) practitioners, attorneys

Review process: Editorial only

Invited articles: 21-40%

**Percentage of articles
on accounting topics:**   10

Approximate percentage of accounting-related articles devoted to:

Financial Accounting:	**Managerial:**
Computers/Systems:	**Tax:** 100
Auditing:	**Education:**
Professional:	

Approximate percentage of accounting-related articles characterized as primarily: Not specified

Empirical:	**Experimental:**
Analytical:	**Descriptive:**

**Language(s) in which
articles are published:**   English

Accepts manuscripts in English for translation: N/A

Approximate acceptance rate: 60%

Review period: 2 months   **Lead time to publication after acceptance:** 2 months

Circulation: 2,000   **Frequency of publication:**   Quarterly

Sponsoring organization: Panel Publishers Inc.

Submission information:

Manuscript length: 10-40 pages

Number of copies: 2   **Submission fee:** None

Style: Manuscripts should be typed double-spaced with 1 inch margins on one side of the paper only, on 8 1/2 x 11" good-quality white bond. Type footnotes separately, double-spaced at the end of the text. Footnote and reference citations should generally follow the "Harvard Blue Book." Any artwork, e.g., charts or graphs, must be provided in camera-ready form. Contact the editor for more information concerning manuscript publication.

**Manuscript
editor:**   Richard Reichler

International Tax Journal, Panel Publishers Inc., 14 Plaza Rd.

Greenvale, NY 11548, U. S. A.

Publisher: Same as above

Interstate Tax Report

Primary readership: Accounting (or tax) practitioners

Review process: Not specified

Invited articles: Not specified

**Percentage of articles
on accounting topics:**

Approximate percentage of accounting-related articles devoted to:

Financial Accounting:		**Managerial:**	
Computers/Systems:		**Tax:**	100
Auditing:		**Education:**	
Professional:			

Approximate percentage of accounting-related articles characterized as primarily: Not specified

Empirical:	**Experimental:**
Analytical:	**Descriptive:**

**Language(s) in which
articles are published:**   English

Accepts manuscripts in English for translation:

Approximate acceptance rate: High for tax professionals, minimal for others.

Review period: 1 week   **Lead time to publication after acceptance:** 1 month

Circulation: 500   **Frequency of publication:**   Monthly

Sponsoring organization:

> ***Submission information:***

Manuscript length: 1,000 - 2,000 words

Number of copies: Not specified **Submission fee:** None

Style: All text in body of the article and all citations in footnotes. More information available upon request.

**Manuscript
editor:**   Robert Feinschreiber and Caryl Nackenson

Interstate Tax Report, Panel Publishers, Inc., 14 Plaza Rd.

Greenvale, NY 11548, U. S. A.

Publisher: Same as above

Issues in Accountability

Primary readership: Academicians, accounting (or tax) practitioners, businessmen, computer specialists

Review process: Editorial only, advisor as required.

Invited articles: 61-80%

**Percentage of articles
on accounting topics:**   85

Approximate percentage of accounting-related articles devoted to:

Financial Accounting:	55	**Managerial:**	16
Computers/Systems:	3	**Tax:**	
Auditing:	7	**Education:**	10
Professional:	8	Other:	1

Approximate percentage of accounting-related articles characterized as primarily:

Empirical:	20	**Experimental:**	20
Analytical:	40	**Descriptive:**	15
Other;	5		

**Language(s) in which
articles are published:**   English - after translated from foreign languages; articles reproduced in Japanese books.

Accepts manuscripts in English for translation: N/A

Approximate acceptance rate: 50%

Review period: 1 year   **Lead time to publication after acceptance:** 6 months

Circulation: About 450   **Frequency of publication:**   Intermittent

Sponsoring organization: None

Submission information:

Manuscript length: 20,000 words maximum

Number of copies: 1   **Submission fee:** None

Style: Preferred 2 sets camera-ready of Issue X, but new format for Issue XII were promised initially more frequently than has been possible. The Symposia concept has been retained, often with copyrights on relevant articles which have appeared elsewhere. The format changed from AL-2 col. to A5 with Issue XII.

**Manuscript
editor:**

D. A. R. Forrester

Issues in Accountability, 15 Spence Street

Glasgow G20 0AW, Scotland

Publisher: Same as above

Issues in Accounting Education

Primary readership: Academicians

Review process: 1 external blind reviewer

Invited articles: 0%

Percentage of articles on accounting topics: 100

Approximate percentage of accounting-related articles devoted to:

Financial Accounting:		Managerial:	
Computers/Systems:		Tax:	
Auditing:		Education:	100
Professional:			

Approximate percentage of accounting-related articles characterized as primarily:

Empirical:	25	Experimental:	25
Analytical:		Descriptive:	25
Pedagogical:	25		

Language(s) in which articles are published: English

Accepts manuscripts in English for translation: N/A

Approximate acceptance rate: 18%

Review period: 6 weeks   **Lead time to publication after acceptance:** 9 months

Circulation: 9,000   **Frequency of publication:** Semiannually

Sponsoring organization: American Accounting Association

Submission information:

Manuscript length:

Number of copies: 3   **Submission fee:** $25

Style: Follow the requirements in the Accounting Review.   Footnotes should be used for extensions whose inclusion in the body of the manuscript might disrupt continuity. Reference list must include only those works actually cited. Each table and figure should appear on a separate page and bear an arabic numeral and title. A helpful guide is the Elements of Style by William Strunk, Jr. and E. B. White.

Manuscript editor:

Robert W. Ingram

Issues in Accounting Education, P.O. Drawer AC, School of Accountancy, University of Alabama

Tuscaloosa, AL 35487, U. S. A.

Publisher: American Accounting Association

5717 Bessie Drive

Sarasota, FL 33583, U. S. A.

Journal fuer Betriebswirtschaft

Primary readership: Academicians, accounting (or tax) practitioners, businessmen, students

Review process: Editorial only

Invited articles: 21-40%

**Percentage of articles
on accounting topics:**   25

Approximate percentage of accounting-related articles devoted to:

Financial Accounting:	5	**Managerial:**	25
Computers/Systems:	10	**Tax:**	45
Auditing:	5	**Education:**	5
Professional:	5		

Approximate percentage of accounting-related articles characterized as primarily:

Empirical:	10	**Experimental:**	5
Analytical:	75	**Descriptive:**	10

**Language(s) in which
articles are published:**   German

Accepts manuscripts in English for translation: No

Approximate acceptance rate: Not specified

Review period: Not specified   **Lead time to publication after acceptance:**   Not specified

Circulation: 1,000   **Frequency of publication:**   Five times per year

Sponsoring organization: None

Submission information:

Manuscript length: 15 pages maximum
Number of copies: 2   **Submission fee:**   None
Style: Scientific construction desired.

**Manuscript
editor:**   Prof. Dr. Heinrich Stremitzer
       Wirtschaftsuniversitaet
       Wien, Austria

Publisher: Industrieverlag Peter Linde Gmb. H.
       Dominikanerbastei 10
       A 1010 Wien, Austria

Journal of Accountancy

Primary readership: Academicians, accounting (or tax) practitioners, CPAs

Review process: 3 external reviewers (authors known)

Invited articles: 21-40%

**Percentage of articles
on accounting topics:**   100

Approximate percentage of accounting-related articles devoted to:

Financial Accounting:	**Managerial:**
Computers/Systems:	**Tax:**
Auditing:	**Education:**
Professional:	Practical articles : 100

Approximate percentage of accounting-related articles characterized as primarily: Not specified

Empirical:	**Experimental:**
Analytical:	**Descriptive:**

**Language(s) in which
articles are published:**   English

Accepts manuscripts in English for translation: N/A

Approximate acceptance rate: 7%

Review period: 3 months maximum   **Lead time to publication after acceptance:** 2 months

Circulation: 286,109   **Frequency of publication:**   Monthly

Sponsoring organization: American Institute of CPAs

Submission information:

Manuscript length: 10-12 double-spaced pages, about 2,000-3,500 words

Number of copies: 5   **Submission fee:** None

Style: Manuscripts should be typed double-spaced on one side of the paper. Extensive documentation, footnotes, and bibliographies should be avoided. When feasible, authority for statements made should be included in the text. Contact the editor for more information concerning manuscript publication.

Manuscript editor: Diane Phillips, Assistant Manuscript Editor
Journal of Accountancy, AICPA, 1211 Avenue of the Americas
New York, NY 10036-8775, U. S. A.

Publisher: Same as above

Journal of Accounting and Economics

Primary readership: Academicians

Review process: 1 or 2 external blind reviewers

Invited articles: 1-20%

**Percentage of articles
on accounting topics:**   90

Approximate percentage of accounting-related articles devoted to:

Financial Accounting:	80	**Managerial:**	9
Computers/Systems:		**Tax:**	4
Auditing:	7	**Education:**	
Professional:			

Approximate percentage of accounting-related articles characterized as primarily:

Empirical:	80	**Experimental:**	
Analytical:	20	**Descriptive:**	

**Language(s) in which
articles are published:**   English

Accepts manuscripts in English for translation: N/A

Approximate acceptance rate: 8%

Review period: 4-5 weeks   **Lead time to publication after acceptance:** 4 months

Circulation: 1,000   **Frequency of publication:**   3 times per year

Sponsoring organization: None

Submission information:

Manuscript length: 20 pages, but it varies with topic

Number of copies: 3   **Submission fee:** $100 for subscribers, $130 for non-subscribers

Style: All pages should be numbered consecutively. References, tables, and legends for figures should be typed on separate pages. The legends and titles on tables must be sufficiently descriptive such that they are understandable without reference to the text. Footnotes should be kept to a minimum and be numbered consecutively throughout the text with superscript arabic numerals. See publication for more information.

Manuscript editor: Professor Ross L. Watts

William E. Simon Graduate School of Business Administration, University of Rochester

Rochester, NY 14627, U. S. A.

Publisher: Elsevier Science Publishers B.V.

Box 211

1000 AE Amsterdam, Netherlands

Journal of Accounting and EDP

Primary readership: Accounting (or tax) practitioners,computer specialists, auditors

Review process: 1 external reviewer (authors known)

Invited articles: 61-80%

**Percentage of articles
on accounting topics:** 10

Approximate percentage of accounting-related articles devoted to:

Financial Accounting:		**Managerial:**	
Computers/Systems:	90	**Tax:**	
Auditing:		**Education:**	
Professional:		**Other:**	10

Approximate percentage of accounting-related articles characterized as primarily: Not specified

Empirical:	**Experimental:**
Analytical:	**Descriptive:**

**Language(s) in which
articles are published:** English

Accepts manuscripts in English for translation: N/A

Approximate acceptance rate: 60%

Review period: 1 month   **Lead time to publication after acceptance:** 6 months

Circulation: 5,000   **Frequency of publication:** Quarterly

Sponsoring organization: None

Submission information:

Manuscript length: 15-20 pages

Number of copies: 2   **Submission fee:** None

Style: Articles should be typed double-spaced on 8 1/2 x 11" paper. All manuscripts are edited to conform to style. Contact the editor for more information concerning article publication.

**Manuscript
editor:** W. Ken Harmon

Journal of Accounting and EDP, School of Accountancy
University of Missouri, Columbia, MO 65211, U. S. A.

Publisher: Kim Horan Kelly

Journal of Accounting and EDP, Auerbach Publishers Inc. , One Penn Plaza
New York, NY   10119, U. S. A.

Journal of Accounting and Public Policy

Primary readership: Academicans

Review process: 2 external blind reviewers

Invited articles:

**Percentage of articles
on accounting topics:**   100

Approximate percentage of accounting-related articles devoted to: Not specified

Financial Accounting: **Managerial:**

Computers/Systems: **Tax:**

Auditing: **Education:**

Professional:

Approximate percentage of accounting-related articles characterized as primarily: Not specified

Empirical: **Experimental:**

Analytical: **Descriptive:**

**Language(s) in which
articles are published:**   English

Accepts manuscripts in English for translation: N/A

Approximate acceptance rate: Not specified

Review period: 6-10 weeks   **Lead time to publication after acceptance:** 1-3 months

Circulation: Not specified   **Frequency of publication:**   Quarterly

Sponsoring organization:

   Submission information:
Manuscript length: No limit
Number of copies: 3   **Submission fee:** None
Style: See journal or contact the editor for information concerning manuscript publication.

**Manuscript
editor:**   Professor Lawrence Gordon and Professor Stephen E. Loeb
   Journal of Accounting and Public Policy, College of Business and Management, University of Maryland
   College Park, MD 20742, U. S. A.

Publisher: Elsevier Science Publishing Co., Inc. (New York)
   52 Vanderbilt Ave.
   New York, NY 10017, U. S. A.

Journal of Accounting Education

Primary readership: Academicians

Review process: 2 external blind reviewers

Invited articles: 1-20%

**Percentage of articles
on accounting topics:** 100

Approximate percentage of accounting-related articles devoted to:

Financial Accounting:	**Managerial:**	
Computers/Systems:	**Tax:**	
Auditing:	**Education:**	100
Professional:		

Approximate percentage of accounting-related articles characterized as primarily: Not specified

Empirical: **Experimental:**
Analytical: **Descriptive:**

**Language(s) in which
articles are published:** English

Accepts manuscripts in English for translation: N/A

Approximate acceptance rate: 14%

Review period: 90 days   **Lead time to publication after acceptance:** 3-6 months

Circulation: 1,500   **Frequency of publication:** Semiannually

Sponsoring organization: James Madison University

Submission information:

Manuscript length: No limit

Number of copies: 4   **Submission fee:** $20 for non-subscribers, free to subscribers

Style: Indented quotations and footnotes should be single-spaced. References should be in square brackets in the body of the manuscript and should contain the author's name, year of publication of the literature cited, and page numbers, if appropriate. Reference list should be at the end of the manuscript and should be in alphabetical order by the last name of the first author. Footnotes should be used for extensions of the text.

**Manuscript
editor:** Kent St. Piene

Journal of Accounting Education, School of Accounting, James Madison University

Harrisonburg, VA 22107, U. S. A.

Publisher: Same as above

Journal of Accounting Literature

Primary readership: Academicians

Review process: External blind reviewers or 1 or 2 external reviewers

Invited articles: 0%

**Percentage of articles
on accounting topics:**   100

Approximate percentage of accounting-related articles devoted to: Not specified

Financial Accounting: **Managerial:**

Computers/Systems: **Tax:**

Auditing: **Education:**

Professional:

Approximate percentage of accounting-related articles characterized as primarily: Not specified

Empirical: **Experimental:**

Analytical: **Descriptive:**

**Language(s) in which
articles are published:**   English

Accepts manuscripts in English for translation: N/A

Approximate acceptance rate: 25%

Review period: 2 months   **Lead time to publication after acceptance:** 6-8 months

Circulation: 800   **Frequency of publication:**   Annually

Sponsoring organization: None

Submission information:

Manuscript length: Not to exceed 40 pages

Number of copies: 3   **Submission fee:** $25

Style: Same as The Accounting Review

**Manuscript
editor:**   A. Rashad Abdel Khalik

Journal of Accounting Literature, Fisher School of Accountancy, University of Florida

Gainesville, FL 32611, U. S. A.

Publisher: Society of Accounting Research Digest

Same as above

Journal of Accounting Research

Primary readership: Academicians, accounting (or tax) practitioners

Review process: 1 or 2 external reviewers (authors known)

Invited articles: Not specified

**Percentage of articles
on accounting topics:**   100

Approximate percentage of accounting-related articles devoted to: Not specified

Financial Accounting:	**Managerial:**
Computers/Systems:	**Tax:**
Auditing:	**Education:**
Professional:	

Approximate percentage of accounting-related articles characterized as primarily: Not specified

Empirical:	**Experimental:**
Analytical:	**Descriptive:**

**Language(s) in which
articles are published:**   English

Accepts manuscripts in English for translation: N/A

Approximate acceptance rate: Varies

Review period: Varies   **Lead time to publication after acceptance:** Varies

Circulation: 3,000   **Frequency of publication:**   3 times per year

Sponsoring organization: Institute of Professional Accounting

Submission information:

Manuscript length: Flexible

Number of copies: 2   **Submission fee:** $ 35

Style: Leave 1 1/2 inch margins all around. Footnotes are to be typed double-spaced and placed together at the end of the manuscript. References are to be typed double-spaced and placed at the end of the manuscript alphabetically and include only those cited in the text. Tables and figures should be typed on a separate sheet of paper. See publication for more information.

Manuscript editor: Prof. Katherine Schipper

Journal of Accounting Research, Graduate School of Business, University of Chicago, 1101 E. 58th St. Chicago, IL 60637, U. S. A.

Publisher: Same as above

Journal of Accounting, Auditing and Finance

Primary readership: Academicians, accounting (or tax) practitioners, bankers, lawyers, students

Review process: External blind reviewers

Invited articles: Not specified

**Percentage of articles
on accounting topics:**
Approximate percentage of accounting-related articles devoted to: Not specified

Financial Accounting:	**Managerial:**
Computers/Systems:	**Tax:**
Auditing:	**Education:**
Professional:	

Approximate percentage of accounting-related articles characterized as primarily: Not specified

Empirical:	**Experimental:**
Analytical:	**Descriptive:**

**Language(s) in which
articles are published:** English

Accepts manuscripts in English for translation: N/A

Approximate acceptance rate: 20%

Review period: 2-3 months **Lead time to publication after acceptance:** 4 months

Circulation: 2,500 **Frequency of publication:** Quarterly

Sponsoring organization: New York University

Submission information:

Manuscript length: 3,000 - 5,000 words

Number of copies: 3 **Submission fee:** None

Style: Footnotes at the end of the manuscript and numbered consecutively. Submit mathematical appendix where necessary.

**Manuscript
editor:** Hector Anton

The Vincent C. Ross Institute of Accounting Research, NYU, 300 Tish Hall, Washington Square
New York, NY 10003, U. S. A.

Publisher: Warren, Gorham & Lamont, Inc.
210 South St.
Boston, MA 02111, U. S. A.

Journal of Bank Research

Primary readership: Academicians, bank officers

Review process: Not specified

Invited articles: Not specified

**Percentage of articles
on accounting topics:**
Approximate percentage of accounting-related articles devoted to: Not specified

Financial Accounting:	**Managerial:**
Computers/Systems:	**Tax:**
Auditing:	**Education:**
Professional:	

Approximate percentage of accounting-related articles characterized as primarily: Not specified

Empirical:	**Experimental:**
Analytical:	**Descriptive:**

**Language(s) in which
articles are published:**   English

Accepts manuscripts in English for translation: N/A

Approximate acceptance rate: 15%

Review period: 2 months   **Lead time to publication after acceptance:** 3 - 6 months

Circulation: 2,500   **Frequency of publication:**   Quarterly

Sponsoring organization: Bank Administration Institute

Submission information:
Manuscript length: Not specified
Number of copies: 2   **Submission fee:** None
Style: Available upon request.

**Manuscript
editor:**   R. Gerald Fox
Journal of Bank Research, 60 E. Gould Center
Rolling Meadows, IL 60008, U. S. A.

Publisher: Same as above

Journal of Business

Primary readership: Academicians

Review process: 1-2 external reviewers (authors known)

Invited articles: 0%

**Percentage of articles
on accounting topics:**   5

Approximate percentage of accounting-related articles devoted to: Not specified

Financial Accounting:	**Managerial:**
Computers/Systems:	**Tax:**
Auditing:	**Education:**
Professional:	

Approximate percentage of accounting-related articles characterized as primarily:

Empirical:	80	**Experimental:**	
Analytical:	20	**Descriptive:**	

**Language(s) in which
articles are published:**   English

Accepts manuscripts in English for translation: N/A

Approximate acceptance rate: 20%

Review period: 2 months   **Lead time to publication after acceptance:** 6 months

Circulation: 5,000   **Frequency of publication:**   Quarterly

Sponsoring organization: University of Chicago

Submission information:

Manuscript length:

Number of copies: 3, 1 orignal   **Submission fee:** Not specified

Style: Right and left margins of at least 1 1/2". References should follow text, in alphabetical order by author's last name. Footnotes (typed paragraph style) should be placed together on typed sheets following the references. They should be numbered in order and correspond with the numbers in the text. Footnotes are not necessary if only used to refer to a work cited.

**Manuscript
editor:**   Albert Madansky

The Journal of Business, Graduate School of Business, University of Chicago, 1101 E. 58th St.

Chicago, IL 60637, U. S. A.

Publisher: The University of Chicago Press, Journals Division

P.O. Box 37005

Chicago, IL 60637, U. S. A.

Journal of Business Administration

Primary readership: Academicians, accounting (or tax) practitioners, businessmen, computer specialists

Review process: 10 external reviewers (authors known)

Invited articles: 21–40%

Percentage of articles on accounting topics: 10

Approximate percentage of accounting-related articles devoted to:

Financial Accounting:	35	**Managerial:**	40
Computers/Systems:	5	**Tax:**	5
Auditing:	5	**Education:**	
Professional:		Other:	10

Approximate percentage of accounting-related articles characterized as primarily:

Empirical:	40	**Experimental:**	
Analytical:	30	**Descriptive:**	25
Other:	5		

Language(s) in which articles are published: English, Bengali

Accepts manuscripts in English for translation: N/A

Approximate acceptance rate: 50%

Review period: 6 months   **Lead time to publication after acceptance:** 3 months

Circulation: 500   **Frequency of publication:**   Quarterly

Sponsoring organization: Institute of Business Administration, University of Dhaka, Bangladesh

Submission information:

Manuscript length: 25-30 double-spaced typed pages

Number of copies: 2   **Submission fee:** $10

Style: Not specified

Manuscript editor: Dr. Anwar Hossain, Director Programme, Research and Publication
Journal of Business Administration, Room No. 114, Institute of Business Administration, University of Dhaka
Dhaka-2, Bangladesh

Publisher: Same as above

Journal of Business and Economic Perspectives

Primary readership: Academicians

Review process: 3 external blind reviewers

Invited articles: 0%

**Percentage of articles
on accounting topics:**   25

Approximate percentage of accounting-related articles devoted to:

Financial Accounting:	10	**Managerial:**	30
Computers/Systems:	5	**Tax:**	20
Auditing:	5	**Education:**	10
Professional:	20		

Approximate percentage of accounting-related articles characterized as primarily:

Empirical:	50	**Experimental:**	20
Analytical:		**Descriptive:**	30

**Language(s) in which
articles are published:**   English

Accepts manuscripts in English for translation: N/A

Approximate acceptance rate: 20%

Review period: 3 months   **Lead time to publication after acceptance:** 6 months

Circulation: 2,000   **Frequency of publication:**   Semiannually

Sponsoring organization: University of Tennessee

Submission information:

Manuscript length: 10 typed double-spaced pages or fewer

Number of copies: 3   **Submission fee:** $5

Style: Same as the Journal of Economic Literature

**Manuscript
editor:**   Saul Z. Barr

    JBEP, School of Business, University of Tennessee

    Martin, TN 38238, U. S. A.

Publisher: Same as above

Journal of Business Finance and Accounting

Primary readership: Academicians, accounting practitioners, controllers, financial analysts

Review process: 2 or more external reviewers

Invited articles: Not specified

**Percentage of articles
on accounting topics:**   50

Approximate percentage of accounting-related articles devoted to: Not specified

Financial Accounting: **Managerial:**

Computers/Systems: **Tax:**

Auditing: **Education:**

Professional:

Approximate percentage of accounting-related articles characterized as primarily: Not specified

Empirical: **Experimental:**

Analytical: **Descriptive:**

**Language(s) in which
articles are published:**   English

Accepts manuscripts in English for translation: N/A

Approximate acceptance rate: 30%

Review period: 5 months   **Lead time to publication after acceptance:** 6-9 months

Circulation: 1,500   **Frequency of publication:**   Quarterly

Sponsoring organization: University of Warwick

Submission information:

Manuscript length: 4-8,000 words

Number of copies: 3   **Submission fee:** $30 ($15 for subscribers)

Style: Available upon request.

**Manuscript
editor:**   Professor R. J. Briston

Centre for Research in Industry and Business Administration

University of Warwick, Coventry. CV 4 7AL, England

Publisher: Basil Blackwell Ltd.

108 Cowley Rd.

Oxford OX4 1JF, England

Journal of Business Forecasting

Primary readership: Accounting (or tax) practitioners, businessmen

Review process: 2 external blind reviewers

Invited articles: 0%

Percentage of articles on accounting topics: 20

Approximate percentage of accounting-related articles devoted to:

Financial Accounting:	60	**Managerial:**	40
Computers/Systems:		**Tax:**	
Auditing:		**Education:**	
Professional:			

Approximate percentage of accounting-related articles characterized as primarily:

Empirical:	30	**Experimental:**	
Analytical:	30	**Descriptive:**	40

Language(s) in which articles are published: English

Accepts manuscripts in English for translation: N/A

Approximate acceptance rate: 50%

Review period: 3 months   **Lead time to publication after acceptance:** 3 months

Circulation: 3,500   **Frequency of publication:** Quarterly

Sponsoring organization: None

Submission information:

Manuscript length: 10-15 pages (double-spaced)

Number of copies: 3   **Submission fee:** None

Style: Contact the editor for a copy of the editorial policy statement before preparing an article for submission.

Manuscript editor:
Chaman L. Jain
Journal of Business Forecasting, St. John's University
Jamaica, NY 11439, U. S. A.

Publisher: Graceway Publishing Company, Inc.
P.O. Box 159, Station C
Flushing, NY 11367, U. S. A.

Journal of Business Research

Primary readership: Academicians

Review process: 2 external blind reviewers

Invited articles: 0%

Percentage of articles on accounting topics: 5

Approximate percentage of accounting-related articles devoted to:

Financial Accounting:	90	**Managerial:**	
Computers/Systems:		**Tax:**	
Auditing:		**Education:**	
Professional:		**Other:**	10

Approximate percentage of accounting-related articles characterized as primarily:

Empirical:	90	**Experimental:**	
Analytical:		**Descriptive:**	
Other:	10		

Language(s) in which articles are published: English

Accepts manuscripts in English for translation:

Approximate acceptance rate: 20%

Review period: 12 weeks   **Lead time to publication after acceptance:** 6 months

Circulation: 1,000   **Frequency of publication:** 6 times per year

Sponsoring organization: None

Submission information:

Manuscript length: 10-20 pages

Number of copies: 4   **Submission fee:** None

Style: Footnotes, tables, and references should be typed on separate pages. References to the literature are indicated in the text by full size numbers in brackets. Footnotes to the text are indicated by superior numbers, and will be set at the bottom of the journal page on which they are cited. Figures should be professionally done originals or glossies of originals. See recent publications for more information.

Manuscript editor:

Arch G. Woodside

Journal of Business Research, Freeman School of Business, Tulane University

New Orleans, LA 70118, U. S. A.

Publisher: Elsevier Science Publishing Co., Inc.

52 Vanderbilt Avenue

New York, NY 10017, U. S. A.

Journal of Business Strategy

Primary readership: Businessmen

Review process: Editorial only

Invited articles: 41-60%

**Percentage of articles
on accounting topics:**   7

Approximate percentage of accounting-related articles devoted to: Not specified

Financial Accounting: **Managerial:**

Computers/Systems: **Tax:**

Auditing: **Education:**

Professional:

Approximate percentage of accounting-related articles characterized as primarily: Not specified

Empirical: **Experimental:**

Analytical: **Descriptive:**

**Language(s) in which
articles are published:**   English

Accepts manuscripts in English for translation: N/A

Approximate acceptance rate: 20%

Review period: 1 month   **Lead time to publication after acceptance:** 6 months

Circulation: Not specified   **Frequency of publication:**   Quarterly

Sponsoring organization:

>   *Submission information:*

Manuscript length: 10 pages typed double-spaced

Number of copies: 2   **Submission fee:** None

Style: Contact editor for more information regarding manuscript publication.

**Manuscript
editor:**   Nancy Pratt

Journal of Business Strategy, Warren, Gorham & Lamont, Inc., One Penn Plaza
New York, NY 10119, U. S. A.

Publisher: Warren, Gorham & Lamont, Inc.
210 South St.
Boston, MA 02111, U. S. A.

Journal of Buyouts and Acquisitions, The

Primary readership: Not specified

Review process: Not specified

Invited articles: Not specified

**Percentage of articles
on accounting topics:**
Approximate percentage of accounting-related articles devoted to: Not specified

Financial Accounting: **Managerial:**
Computers/Systems: **Tax:**
Auditing: **Education:**
Professional:

Approximate percentage of accounting-related articles characterized as primarily: Not specified

Empirical: **Experimental:**
Analytical: **Descriptive:**

**Language(s) in which
articles are published:**   English

Accepts manuscripts in English for translation: N/A

Approximate acceptance rate: Not specified

Review period: Not specified   **Lead time to publication after acceptance:** Not specified

Circulation: Not specified   **Frequency of publication:**   Not specified

Sponsoring organization: None

Submission information:
Manuscript length: 1,500 to 3,500 words
Number of copies: Not specified   **Submission fee:** Not specified
Style: Not specified

**Manuscript
editor:**   Frederick J. Oshay
Buyouts Publications, Inc., 7124 Convoy Court
San Diego, CA   92111, U. S. A.

Publisher: Same as above

Journal of Commercial Bank Lending, The

Primary readership: Loan and credit officers

Review process: 1 external blind reviewers

Invited articles: 21-40%

**Percentage of articles
on accounting topics:**   10

Approximate percentage of accounting-related articles devoted to:

Financial Accounting:	100	**Managerial:**	
Computers/Systems:		**Tax:**	
Auditing:		**Education:**	
Professional:			

Approximate percentage of accounting-related articles characterized as primarily: Not specified

Empirical:	**Experimental:**
Analytical:	**Descriptive:**

**Language(s) in which
articles are published:**   English

Accepts manuscripts in English for translation: N/A

Approximate acceptance rate: 50%

Review period: 6 weeks   **Lead time to publication after acceptance:** 2 months

Circulation: 26,000   **Frequency of publication:**   Monthly

Sponsoring organization: Robert Morris Associates

Submission information:

Manuscript length: 15-25 double-spaced pages
Number of copies: 2   **Submission fee:** None
Style: For guidelines for publication, write to RMA .

**Manuscript
editor:**   Charlotte Weisman, Editor
The Journal of Commercial Bank Lending, RMA National , 1616 Philadelphia National Bank Blvd.
Philadelphia, PA 19107, U. S. A.

Publisher: Same as above

Journal of Corporate Taxation, The

Primary readership: Academicians, accounting (or tax) practitioners, lawyers

Review process: Not specified

Invited articles: Not specified

**Percentage of articles
on accounting topics:**

Approximate percentage of accounting-related articles devoted to:

Financial Accounting:		**Managerial:**	
Computers/Systems:		**Tax:**	100
Auditing:		**Education:**	
Professional:			

Approximate percentage of accounting-related articles characterized as primarily: Not specified

Empirical:	**Experimental:**
Analytical:	**Descriptive:**

**Language(s) in which
articles are published:**   English

Accepts manuscripts in English for translation:

Approximate acceptance rate: 40%

Review period: 1 month   **Lead time to publication after acceptance:** 3 - 6 months

Circulation: 5,000   **Frequency of publication:**   Quarterly

Sponsoring organization: None

Submission information:

Manuscript length: 5,000 - 10,000 words

Number of copies: Not specified   **Submission fee:**   None

Style: Footnotes separate from manuscript. More requirements available upon request.

**Manuscript
editor:**   Gersham Goldstein
The Journal of Corporate Taxation, 210 South St.
Boston, MA   02111, U. S. A.

Publisher: Warren, Gorham & Lamont, Inc.
Same as above

Journal of Cost Analysis

Primary readership: Academicians, accounting (or tax) practitioners, businessmen, computer specialists

Review process: Blind reviewers

Invited articles: 1-20%

**Percentage of articles
on accounting topics:**   50

Approximate percentage of accounting-related articles devoted to:

Financial Accounting:		**Managerial:**	90
Computers/Systems:	10	**Tax:**	
Auditing:		**Education:**	
Professional:			

Approximate percentage of accounting-related articles characterized as primarily:

Empirical:	50	**Experimental:**	
Analytical:	50	**Descriptive:**	

**Language(s) in which
articles are published:**   English

Accepts manuscripts in English for translation: N/A

Approximate acceptance rate: 20%

Review period: 3 to 6 months   **Lead time to publication after acceptance:** 1 year

Circulation: 2,500   **Frequency of publication:**   Annually

Sponsoring organization: Institute of Cost Analysis

Submission information:

Manuscript length: 20 pages
Number of copies: 5   **Submission fee:** None
Style: Not specified

**Manuscript
editor:**   Mr. Dallas Blevins
Station 6542, University of Montevallo
Montevallo, AL   35115-6542, U. S. A.

Publisher: Institute of Cost Analysis
7111 Marlan Dr.
Alexandria, VA   22307, U. S. A.

Journal of Cost Management for the Manufacturing Industry

Primary readership: Accounting (or tax) practitioners, businessmen

Review process: 3 external reviewers (authors known)

Invited articles: 81-99%

**Percentage of articles
on accounting topics:**   10

Approximate percentage of accounting-related articles devoted to:

Financial Accounting:	**Managerial:**	100
Computers/Systems:	**Tax:**	
Auditing:	**Education:**	
Professional:		

Approximate percentage of accounting-related articles characterized as primarily: Not specified

Empirical:	**Experimental:**
Analytical:	**Descriptive:**

**Language(s) in which
articles are published:**   English

Accepts manuscripts in English for translation: N/A

Approximate acceptance rate: 75%

Review period: 1 month   **Lead time to publication after acceptance:** 6 months

Circulation: N/A   **Frequency of publication:**   Quarterly

Sponsoring organization: CAM-I

Submission information:
Manuscript length: 15-20 pages, double-spaced
Number of copies: 2   **Submission fee:** None
Style: Will be edited to conform to style.

**Manuscript
editor:**   Kim Horan Kelly
Warren, Gorham & Lamont, Inc., One Penn Plaza
New York, NY 10119, U. S. A.

Publisher: Warren, Gorham & Lamont, Inc.
210 South St.
Boston, MA 02111, U. S. A.

Journal of Economics and Business

Primary readership: Academicians, research specialists

Review process: 3 external blind reviewers

Invited articles: 0%

**Percentage of articles
on accounting topics:**   10

Approximate percentage of accounting-related articles devoted to:

Financial Accounting:	75	**Managerial:**	25
Computers/Systems:		**Tax:**	
Auditing:		**Education:**	
Professional:			

Approximate percentage of accounting-related articles characterized as primarily:

Empirical:	100	**Experimental:**	
Analytical:		**Descriptive:**	

**Language(s) in which
articles are published:**   English

Accepts manuscripts in English for translation: N/A

Approximate acceptance rate: Varies by year

Review period: 8 weeks   **Lead time to publication after acceptance:** Up to 1 year

Circulation: 900 paid   **Frequency of publication:** Quarterly

Sponsoring organization: None

Submission information:

Manuscript length: None

Number of copies: Original and 3 **Submission fee:** $15

Style: See journal or contact the editor for information concerning manuscript publication.

**Manuscript
editor:** R. H. Deans

    Temple University, School of Business and Management, Speakman Hall, Rm. 201
    Philadelphia, PA 19122, U. S. A.

Publisher: Elsevier Science Publishing Co., Inc.
    52 Vanderbilt Ave.
    New York, NY 10017, U. S. A.

Journal of Education for Business

Primary readership: Academicians, businessmen

Review process: 2 external reviewers (authors known)

Invited articles: 1-20%

Percentage of articles on accounting topics: 25

Approximate percentage of accounting-related articles devoted to: Not specified

Financial Accounting: **Managerial:**

Computers/Systems: **Tax:**

Auditing: **Education:**

Professional:

Approximate percentage of accounting-related articles characterized as primarily: Not specified

Empirical: **Experimental:**

Analytical: **Descriptive:**

Language(s) in which articles are published: English

Accepts manuscripts in English for translation: N/A

Approximate acceptance rate: 30%

Review period: 6 weeks   **Lead time to publication after acceptance:** 3-6 months

Circulation: 5,000   **Frequency of publication:** Monthly - October through May

Sponsoring organization: None

Submission information:

Manuscript length: Not to exceed 2,500 words

Number of copies: 2   **Submission fee:** None

Style: Chicago Manual of Style

Manuscript editor: Gail Lowery

Journal of Education for Business, HELDREF Publications, 4000 Albemarle St., N.W. Washington, DC 20016, U. S. A.

Publisher: Same as above

Journal of Financial and Quantitative Analysis

Primary readership: Academicians, management scientists, students

Review process: Not specified

Invited articles: Not specified

Percentage of articles on accounting topics:

Approximate percentage of accounting-related articles devoted to: Not specified

Financial Accounting:	Managerial:
Computers/Systems:	Tax:
Auditing:	Education:
Professional:	

Approximate percentage of accounting-related articles characterized as primarily: Not specified

Empirical:	Experimental:
Analytical:	Descriptive:

Language(s) in which articles are published: English

Accepts manuscripts in English for translation: N/A

Approximate acceptance rate: Not specified

Review period: 3 to 6 months   **Lead time to publication after acceptance:** 1 year

Circulation: 2,400   **Frequency of publication:** 4 times per year

Sponsoring organization: University of Washington

Submission information:

Manuscript length: 10 - 20 pages

Number of copies: Not specified   **Submission fee:** $45 for non-subscribers; $30 for subscribers

Style: Available upon request.

Manuscript editor: Alfred N. Page

University of Washington, Graduate School of Business Administration, DJ-10, Mackenzie Hall, Seattle, WA 98195, U. S. A.

Publisher: Same as above

Journal of Financial Economics

Primary readership: Academicians, businessmen

Review process: Blind reviewers

Invited articles: 5%

**Percentage of articles
on accounting topics:**
Approximate percentage of accounting-related articles devoted to: Not specified

Financial Accounting: **Managerial:**
Computers/Systems: **Tax:**
Auditing: **Education:**
Professional:

Approximate percentage of accounting-related articles characterized as primarily: Not specified

Empirical: **Experimental:**
Analytical: **Descriptive:**

**Language(s) in which
articles are published:**   English

Accepts manuscripts in English for translation: N/A

Approximate acceptance rate: 15%

Review period: 6 weeks   **Lead time to publication after acceptance:** 2 - 4 months

Circulation: 1,700   **Frequency of publication:**   Quarterly

Sponsoring organization: University of Rochester

   Submission information:
Manuscript length: 1 - 50 pages
Number of copies: 3   **Submission fee:** $120 for subscribers; $150 for non-subscribers
Style: Available upon request.

**Manuscript
editor:**   Clifford W. Smith, Jr.
          Graduate School of Management, University of Rochester
          Rochester, NY 14627

Publisher: Same as above

Journal of Financial Software and Hardware, The

Primary readership: Businessmen, financial professionals

Review process: Not specified

Invited articles: Not specified

**Percentage of articles
on accounting topics:**
Approximate percentage of accounting-related articles devoted to:

Financial Accounting:		**Managerial:**	
Computers/Systems:	100	**Tax:**	
Auditing:		**Education:**	
Professional:			

Approximate percentage of accounting-related articles characterized as primarily: Not specified

Empirical:	**Experimental:**
Analytical:	**Descriptive:**

**Language(s) in which
articles are published:**   English

Accepts manuscripts in English for translation: N/A

Approximate acceptance rate: Not specified

Review period: 2 months   **Lead time to publication after acceptance:** 1 month

Circulation: 100,000   **Frequency of publication:**   Bi-monthly

Sponsoring organization:

 Submission information:
Manuscript length: 1,500 words
Number of copies: Not specified   **Submission fee:** None
Style: Available upon request.

**Manuscript
editor:**   Caroline Carr
Microthought Publication, 2811 Wilshire Blvd., Suite 640
Santa Monica, CA 90272

Publisher: Same as above

Journal of Futures Markets

Primary readership: Academicians, businessmen, brokers, students

Review process: Not specified

Invited articles: Not specified

**Percentage of articles
on accounting topics:**
Approximate percentage of accounting-related articles devoted to: Not specified

Financial Accounting:	**Managerial:**
Computers/Systems:	**Tax:**
Auditing:	**Education:**
Professional:	

Approximate percentage of accounting-related articles characterized as primarily: Not specified

Empirical:	**Experimental:**
Analytical:	**Descriptive:**

**Language(s) in which
articles are published:**   English

Accepts manuscripts in English for translation: N/A

Approximate acceptance rate: Not specified

Review period: Not specified   **Lead time to publication after acceptance:** 4-6 months

Circulation: Not specified   **Frequency of publication:**   Semiannually

Sponsoring organization: Columbia University

Submission information:

Manuscript length: 10-25 pages, double spaced on 8 1/2 by 11" paper

Number of copies: 3   **Submission fee:** None

Style: All figures must be cited in text and assigned arabic numerals and be submitted in camera-ready form after acceptance. Literature citations in the text should indicate the author and the year of publication. All literature citations should appear alphabetically under the heading "Bibliography" at the end of the text. Expository footnotes to the text are allowed, cited in text with a superscript arabic numerals .

**Manuscript
editor:**

Mark J. Powers, Editor

Journal of Futures Markets, 57 Glenmore Drive

Chatham, NJ 07928, U. S. A.

Publisher: John Wiley & Sons, Inc.

605 Third Ave.

New York, NY 10016, U. S. A.

Journal of Health Care Management

Primary readership: Health care personnel

Review process: Not specified

Invited articles: Not specified

**Percentage of articles
on accounting topics:**
Approximate percentage of accounting-related articles devoted to: Not specified

Financial Accounting: **Managerial:**
Computers/Systems: **Tax:**
Auditing: **Education:**
Professional:

Approximate percentage of accounting-related articles characterized as primarily: Not specified

Empirical: **Experimental:**
Analytical: **Descriptive:**

**Language(s) in which
articles are published:**   English

Accepts manuscripts in English for translation: N/A

Approximate acceptance rate: Not specified

Review period: Not specified   **Lead time to publication after acceptance:** Not specified

Circulation: Not specified   **Frequency of publication:**   Monthly

Sponsoring organization: The International Management Centre from Buckingham

Submission information:
Manuscript length: Not specified
Number of copies: Not specified   **Submission fee:**   None
Style: Not specified

**Manuscript
editor:**   Robin Gourlay
The International Management Centre from Buckingham, Castle Street, Buckingham
Buckinghamshire MK18 1BS, England

Publisher: Same as above

Journal of Information Systems

Primary readership: Academicians, accounting practitioners

Review process: 2 or more blind reviews

Invited articles: Not specified

**Percentage of articles
on accounting topics:**   100

Approximate percentage of accounting-related articles devoted to:

Financial Accounting:		**Managerial:**	
Computers/Systems:	100	**Tax:**	
Auditing:		**Education:**	
Professional:			

Approximate percentage of accounting-related articles characterized as primarily: Not specified

Empirical:	**Experimental:**
Analytical:	**Descriptive:**

**Language(s) in which
articles are published:**   English

Accepts manuscripts in English for translation: N/A

Approximate acceptance rate: 25%

Review period: 6-8 weeks   **Lead time to publication after acceptance:** 5-6 months

Circulation: 900-1,000   **Frequency of publication:** Semiannually

Sponsoring organization: IS/MAS Section of the American Accounting Association

Submission information:

Manuscript length: No limit

Number of copies: 4   **Submission fee:** $10

Style: Follow requirements published in The Accounting Review. All manuscripts should be typed on one side of 8 1/2 x 11" paper and double-spaced, except for indented quotations, footnotes, and references. Footnotes should be used for extensions whose inclusion in the body of the manuscript might disrupt continuity. Footnotes should be numbered consecutively. Reference list must include only those works actually cited.

**Manuscript
editor:**

Joseph W. Wilkinson

Journal of Information Systems, School of Accountancy, Arizona State University

Tempe, AZ 85287, U. S. A.

Publisher: American Accounting Association

5717 Bessie Drive

Sarasota, FL 33583, U. S. A.

Journal of International Business Studies

Primary readership: Academicians

Review process: 3 external blind reviewers

Invited articles: 0%

**Percentage of articles
on accounting topics:**   10

Approximate percentage of accounting-related articles devoted to:

Financial Accounting:	30	**Managerial:**	30
Computers/Systems:		**Tax:**	20
Auditing:	10	**Education:**	5
Professional:	5		

Approximate percentage of accounting-related articles characterized as primarily: Not specified

Empirical:	60	**Experimental:**	
Analytical:	30	**Descriptive:**	10

**Language(s) in which
articles are published:**   English

Accepts manuscripts in English for translation: N/A

Approximate acceptance rate: 10%

Review period: 2 months   **Lead time to publication after acceptance:** 8 months

Circulation: 2,800   **Frequency of publication:**   3 times per year

Sponsoring organization: University of South Carolina College of Business, and Academy of International Business (AIB)

Submission information:

Manuscript length: 30 pages (including figures, tables, etc.)

Number of copies: 4   **Submission fee:** $20 for AIB members; $30 for non-members

Style: Endnotes should be placed at the end of the manuscript and should precede the references; they should never be used in citing references. An alphabetical list of references should follow the endnotes at the end of the manuscript. Tables should be on separate sheets of paper and follow the references. Figures should be on separate sheets of paper and follow tables at the end of the manuscripts .

**Manuscript
editor:**   David A. Ricks, Editor in Chief

Journal of International Business Studies, University of South Carolina, College of Business

Columbia, SC 29208, U. S. A.

Publisher: Same as above

Journal of Management Studies

Primary readership: Academicians

Review process: 3 external blind reviewers

Invited articles: 0%, except for 1 guest-edited issue per annum = 6 papers

**Percentage of articles
on accounting topics:**   10

Approximate percentage of accounting-related articles devoted to: Not specified

Financial Accounting:	**Managerial:**
Computers/Systems:	**Tax:**
Auditing:	**Education:**
Professional:	

Approximate percentage of accounting-related articles characterized as primarily: Not specified

Empirical:	30	**Experimental:**	30
Analytical:	20	**Descriptive:**	10
Other:	10		

**Language(s) in which
articles are published:**   English

Accepts manuscripts in English for translation: N/A

Approximate acceptance rate: 30%

Review period: 2 months   **Lead time to publication after acceptance:** 1 year

Circulation: 1,500   **Frequency of publication:** 6 times per year

Sponsoring organization: Society for the Advancement of Management Education

Submission information:

Manuscript length: 5,000-7,000 words

Number of copies: 3   **Submission fee:** None

Style: Copies should be typed double-spaced with generous margins. Footnotes should be placed at the immediate end of the paper. References to books and articles headed "References" should be placed in alphabetical order at the end of the paper, following the footnotes. See publication for more information.

**Manuscript
editor:**

Professor A. G. Lockett

Journal of Management Studies, Manchester Business School, Booth St. West

Manchester MIS 6PB, England

Publisher: Basil Blackwell Publisher Ltd.

108 Cowley Road

Oxford OX4 1JF, England

Journal of Organizational Behavior Management

Primary readership: Academicians

Review process: 3 external reviewers, blind reviewers

Invited articles: 21-40%

**Percentage of articles
on accounting topics:**   0.1

Approximate percentage of accounting-related articles devoted to:

Financial Accounting:		**Managerial:**	
Computers/Systems:		**Tax:**	
Auditing:		**Education:**	
Professional:		Behavioral :	100

Approximate percentage of accounting-related articles characterized as primarily:

Empirical:		**Experimental:**	100
Analytical:		**Descriptive:**	

**Language(s) in which
articles are published:**   English

Accepts manuscripts in English for translation: N/A

Approximate acceptance rate: 20-30%

Review period: 6-8 weeks   **Lead time to publication after acceptance:** 6-7 months

Circulation: 450   **Frequency of publication:**   Semiannually

Sponsoring organization: None

Submission information:

Manuscript length: 15-20 pages
Number of copies: 4   **Submission fee:** None
Style: APA Style

**Manuscript
editor:**   Dr. Thomas C, Mawhinney
College of Business and Administration, University of Detroit
4001 West McNichols, Detroit MI 48221-9987, U. S. A.

Publisher: Same as above

Journal of Pension Planning and Compliance

Primary readership: Accounting (or tax) practitioners, attorneys

Review process: Editorial only

Invited articles: 41-60%

**Percentage of articles
on accounting topics:**   10

Approximate percentage of accounting-related articles devoted to:

Financial Accounting:	**Managerial:**	
Computers/Systems:	**Tax:**	50
Auditing:	**Education:**	
Professional:	**Other:**	50

Approximate percentage of accounting-related articles characterized as primarily: Not specified

Empirical:	**Experimental:**
Analytical:	**Descriptive:**

**Language(s) in which
articles are published:**   English

Accepts manuscripts in English for translation: N/A

Approximate acceptance rate: 75%

Review period: 2 months   **Lead time to publication after acceptance:** 2 months

Circulation: 2,000   **Frequency of publication:**   Quarterly

Sponsoring organization: Panel Publishers, Inc.

Submission information:

Manuscript length: 10-40 pages

Number of copies: 2   **Submission fee:** None

Style: Manuscripts should be typed on one side of the paper on 8 1/2 x 11" good-quality white bond. Use 1" margins and double spacing. Type footnotes separately, double-spaced, at the end of the main manuscript. Footnote and reference citations should generally follow the "Harvard Blue Book." Any artwork must be provided in camera-ready form.

Manuscript editor:

Scott P. Spector, Esq.

Journal of Pension Planning and Compliance, Panel Publishers, Inc., 14 Plaza Rd.

Greenvale, NY 11548, U. S. A.

Publisher: Same as above

Journal of Petroleum Accounting

Primary readership: Academicians, accounting (or tax) practitioners, oil and gas industry personnel

Review process: 1 external blind reviewer

Invited articles: 21-40%

**Percentage of articles
on accounting topics:**   85

Approximate percentage of accounting-related articles devoted to:

Financial Accounting:		**Managerial:**	
Computers/Systems:		**Tax:**	20
Auditing:		**Education:**	
Professional:		Oil and gas:	80

Approximate percentage of accounting-related articles characterized as primarily:

Empirical:	15	**Experimental:**	
Analytical:	50	**Descriptive:**	
Interpretation:	35		

**Language(s) in which
articles are published:**   English

Accepts manuscripts in English for translation: N/A

Approximate acceptance rate: 25-40%, depending on nature of article

Review period: 3 weeks to 3 months   **Lead time to publication after acceptance:** 3-6 months

Circulation: 1,000   **Frequency of publication:** 3 times per year

Sponsoring organization: Institute of Petroleum Accounting

Submission information:

Manuscript length: 1,000-10,000 words
Number of copies: 2   **Submission fee:** None
Style: Not specified

**Manuscript
editor:**   Edward B. Deakin
Journal of Petroleum Accounting, P.O. Box 13677, N. T. Station
Denton, TX 76205-3677, U. S. A.

Publisher: Professional Development Institute
P.O. Box 13288, North Texas State University
Denton, TX 76203-3288, U. S. A.

Journal of Property Management

Primary readership: Academicians, businessmen, real estate managers

Review process: 3 external blind reviewers

Invited articles: 41-60%

Percentage of articles on accounting topics: 10

Approximate percentage of accounting-related articles devoted to:

Financial Accounting:	10	**Managerial:**	20
Computers/Systems:	30	**Tax:**	40
Auditing:		**Education:**	
Professional:			

Approximate percentage of accounting-related articles characterized as primarily:

Empirical:		**Experimental:**	
Analytical:	5	**Descriptive:**	95

Language(s) in which articles are published: English

Accepts manuscripts in English for translation: N/A

Approximate acceptance rate: 67%

Review period: 6-8 weeks   **Lead time to publication after acceptance:** 2-4 months

Circulation: Not specified   **Frequency of publication:**   Bi-monthly

Sponsoring organization: Institute of Real Estate Management

Submission information:

Manuscript length: 1,500-3,500 words

Number of copies: 2   **Submission fee:** None

Style: Chicago Manual of Style

Manuscript editor: Mariwyn Evans
Journal of Property Management, 430 N. Michigan Ave.
Chicago, IL 60611, U. S. A.

Publisher: National Association of Realtors
Same as above

Journal of Real Estate Taxation, The

Primary readership: Academicians, accounting (or tax) practitioners, lawyers

Review process: Not specified

Invited articles: Not specified

**Percentage of articles
on accounting topics:**
Approximate percentage of accounting-related articles devoted to:

Financial Accounting:	**Managerial:**	
Computers/Systems:	**Tax:**	100
Auditing:	**Education:**	
Professional:		

Approximate percentage of accounting-related articles characterized as primarily: Not specified

Empirical:	**Experimental:**
Analytical:	**Descriptive:**

**Language(s) in which
articles are published:**   English

Accepts manuscripts in English for translation: N/A

Approximate acceptance rate: 50%

Review period: 1 month   **Lead time to publication after acceptance:** 3 - 6 months

Circulation: 9,000   **Frequency of publication:**   Quarterly

Sponsoring organization: None

Submission information:

Manuscript length: 5,000 to 10,000 words
Number of copies: Not specified   **Submission fee:**   None
Style: Available upon request.

**Manuscript
editor:**   Jill Koenigsberg, Accounting Editor
Warren, Gorham & Lamont, Inc., One Penn Plaza, 40th Floor
New York, NY 10119, U. S. A.

Publisher: Warren, Gorham & Lamont, Inc.
210 South St.
Boston, MA 02111, U. S. A.

Journal of Small Business Management

Primary readership: Academicians, businessmen

Review process: Not specified

Invited articles: Not specified

**Percentage of articles
on accounting topics:**
Approximate percentage of accounting-related articles devoted to: Not specified

Financial Accounting: **Managerial:**
Computers/Systems: **Tax:**
Auditing: **Education:**
Professional:

Approximate percentage of accounting-related articles characterized as primarily: Not specified

Empirical: **Experimental:**
Analytical: **Descriptive:**

**Language(s) in which
articles are published:**   English

Accepts manuscripts in English for translation: N/A

Approximate acceptance rate: 25%

Review period: 2 - 3 months   **Lead time to publication after acceptance:** 3 months

Circulation: 3,000   **Frequency of publication:**   Quarterly

Sponsoring organization: None

Submission information:
Manuscript length: 2,000 words
Number of copies: Not specified **Submission fee:** None
Style: Not specified

**Manuscript
editor:**   The Editor
Bureau of Business Research, West Virginia University, P.O. Box 6025
Morgantown, WV 26506-6025, U. S. A.

Publisher: Same as above

Journal of State Taxation

Primary readership: Accounting (or tax) practitioners

Review process: Editorial only

Invited articles: 21-40%

**Percentage of articles
on accounting topics:**   10

Approximate percentage of accounting-related articles devoted to:

Financial Accounting:	**Managerial:**
Computers/Systems:	**Tax:** 100
Auditing:	**Education:**
Professional:	

Approximate percentage of accounting-related articles characterized as primarily: Not specified

Empirical:	**Experimental:**
Analytical:	**Descriptive:**

**Language(s) in which
articles are published:**   English

Accepts manuscripts in English for translation: N/A

Approximate acceptance rate: 75%

Review period: 2 months   **Lead time to publication after acceptance:** 2 months

Circulation: 2,000   **Frequency of publication:**   Quarterly

Sponsoring organization: None

Submission information:

Manuscript length: 10-40 pages

Number of copies: 2   **Submission fee:** None

Style: Footnotes--whether legal citations or other references--type them separately, double-spaced, at the end of the manuscript. Footnote and reference citations should generally follow The Chicago Manual of Style; regulations and case citations should follow the "Harvard Blue Book." Any artwork should be provided in camera-ready form. Contact the editor for more information concerning manuscript publication.

**Manuscript
editor:**   James T. Collins, Editor

Journal of State Taxation, Panel Publishers, Inc., 14 Plaza Rd.

Greenvale, NY 11548, U. S. A.

Publisher: Same as above

Journal of Systems Management

Primary readership: Businessmen

Review process: 20 external reviewers (authors known)

Invited articles: 1-20%

**Percentage of articles
on accounting topics:**   25

Approximate percentage of accounting-related articles devoted to:

Financial Accounting:		**Managerial:**	
Computers/Systems:	100	**Tax:**	
Auditing:		**Education:**	
Professional:			

Approximate percentage of accounting-related articles characterized as primarily:

Empirical:		**Experimental:**	
Analytical:		**Descriptive:**	100

**Language(s) in which
articles are published:**   English

Accepts manuscripts in English for translation: N/A

Approximate acceptance rate: 33%

Review period: 4 weeks   **Lead time to publication after acceptance:** 3 months

Circulation: 13,000   **Frequency of publication:**   Monthly

Sponsoring organization: None

Submission information:

Manuscript length: 8 pages

Number of copies: 3 and original   **Submission fee:** None

Style: All figures, charts, diagrams, and tables should be referred to as "Figures" and numbered consecutively as they appear in the text. Their position in the article should be noted. Figures should be submitted on separate sheets of paper and should be numbered consecutively. Footnotes should be numbered consecutively and should be on a separate sheet of paper double-spaced at the end of the article.

**Manuscript
editor:**

A. James Andrews, Director of Publications

Journal of Systems Management, 24587 Bagley Rd.

Cleveland, OH 44138, U. S. A.

Publisher: Same as above

Journal of Taxation

Primary readership: Accounting (or tax) practitioners, lawyers

Review process: Not specified

Invited articles: Not specified

**Percentage of articles
on accounting topics:**   100

Approximate percentage of accounting-related articles devoted to:

Financial Accounting:	**Managerial:**	
Computers/Systems:	**Tax:**	100
Auditing:	**Education:**	
Professional:		

Approximate percentage of accounting-related articles characterized as primarily: Not specified

Empirical:	**Experimental:**
Analytical:	**Descriptive:**

**Language(s) in which
articles are published:**   English

Accepts manuscripts in English for translation: N/A

Approximate acceptance rate: 30%

Review period: 1 month   **Lead time to publication after acceptance:** 1 - 2 months

Circulation: 29,000   **Frequency of publication:**   Monthly

Sponsoring organization: None

Submission information:

Manuscript length: 3,000 - 6,000 words

Number of copies: 2   **Submission fee:** None

Style: Not specified

**Manuscript
editor:**   Ronald M. Klinger
Journal of Taxation, 1633 Broadway
New York, NY 10019, U. S. A.

Publisher: Warren, Gorham & Lamont, Inc.
210 South St.
Boston, MA 02111, U. S. A.

Journal of the American Society of CLU & ChFC

Primary readership: Academicians, accounting (or tax) practitioners, businessmen ,insurance businessmen, estate planners, financial planners

Review process: 8 external reviewers (authors known)

Invited articles: 21-40%

Percentage of articles on accounting topics: 30

Approximate percentage of accounting-related articles devoted to:

Financial Accounting:	5	**Managerial:**	
Computers/Systems:	5	**Tax:**	80
Auditing:		**Education:**	5
Professional:	5		

Approximate percentage of accounting-related articles characterized as primarily:

Empirical:	40	**Experimental:**	5
Analytical:	40	**Descriptive:**	15

Language(s) in which articles are published: English

Accepts manuscripts in English for translation: N/A

Approximate acceptance rate: 95%

Review period: 8 weeks   **Lead time to publication after acceptance:** 3-6 months

Circulation: 74,800   **Frequency of publication:** Bi-monthly

Sponsoring organization: American Society of CLU & ChFC

Submission information:

Manuscript length: 10-35 pages (double spaced)

Number of copies: 3   **Submission fee:** None

Style: All manuscripts should be typed double-spaced on one side of 8 1/2 by 11" paper. Footnotes should be used to provide simplified explanations or to provide references to cite bibliographical materials. Footnotes should be numbered consecutively.

Manuscript editor:
Kenneth Black, Jr., Editor

Journal of the American Society of CLU & ChFC, Georgia State University, Box 705, University Plaza Atlanta, GA 30303, U. S. A.

Publisher: American Society of CLU & ChFC
270 Bryn Mawr Avenue
Bryn Mawr, PA 19010-2195, U. S. A.

Journal of the American Taxation Association, The

Primary readership: Academicians, accounting (or tax) practitioners

Review process: 2-3 external blind reviewers

Invited articles: 0%

**Percentage of articles
on accounting topics:** 100

Approximate percentage of accounting-related articles devoted to:

Financial Accounting:	**Managerial:**
Computers/Systems:	**Tax:** 100
Auditing:	**Education:**
Professional:	

Approximate percentage of accounting-related articles characterized as primarily:

Empirical:	40	**Experimental:**	
Analytical:	30	**Descriptive:**	30

**Language(s) in which
articles are published:** English

Accepts manuscripts in English for translation: N/A

Approximate acceptance rate: 15%

Review period: 6-10 weeks **Lead time to publication after acceptance:** Varies, 1-8 months but should drop to 1-4 months in 1988

Circulation: 1,500 **Frequency of publication:** Semiannually, will be quarterly in 1988

Sponsoring organization: American Taxation Association

Submission information:

Manuscript length: 30-40 pages, including all tables, references, etc.

Number of copies: 3 **Submission fee:** None

Style: Contact the editor or see recent issue of the Journal.

**Manuscript
editor:** Silvia Madeo

School of Business Administration, University of Missouri - St. Louis

St. Louis, MO 63121-4499, U. S. A.

Publisher: Same as above

Journal of the Institute of Certified Financial Planners

Primary readership:	Academicians, accounting (or tax) practitioners, businessmen, financial planning practitioners
Review process:	11 external blind reviewers, 12 external reviewers (authors known)
Invited articles:	Varies

**Percentage of articles
on accounting topics:** 5

Approximate percentage of accounting-related articles devoted to:

Financial Accounting:	20	**Managerial:**	
Computers/Systems:		**Tax:**	80
Auditing:		**Education:**	
Professional:			

Approximate percentage of accounting-related articles characterized as primarily:

Empirical:		**Experimental:**	
Analytical:		**Descriptive:**	100

**Language(s) in which
articles are published:** English

Accepts manuscripts in English for translation: N/A

Approximate acceptance rate: 50%

Review period: 4-6 weeks   **Lead time to publication after acceptance:** Varies

Circulation: 9,000   **Frequency of publication:** Quarterly; and some special issues (i.e. Tax Reform of 1986)

Sponsoring organization: Institute of Certified Fianancial Planners

Submission Information:

Manuscript length: Not to exceed 30 typewritten pages

Number of copies: 3   **Submission fee:** None

Style: Manuscripts should be typed on one side of white paper (8 1/2 x 11"), double-spaced, and numbered consecutively. References should refer only to material cited within the text. List references in numerical order as they appear within the text, and place them on separate pages following the article. Tables should be placed on separate pages at the end of the manuscript and indicate their placement within the text.

Manuscript editor:

Bruce W. Most

ICFP, Two Denver Highlands, 10065 E. Harvard Ave., Suite 320

Denver, CO 80231-5942, U. S. A.

Publisher: Same as above

Knjigovoda

Primary readership: Not specified

Review process: Not specified

Invited articles: Not specified

**Percentage of articles
on accounting topics:**
Approximate percentage of accounting-related articles devoted to: Not specified

Financial Accounting:	**Managerial:**
Computers/Systems:	**Tax:**
Auditing:	**Education:**
Professional:	

Approximate percentage of accounting-related articles characterized as primarily: Not specified

Empirical:	**Experimental:**
Analytical:	**Descriptive:**

**Language(s) in which
articles are published:**   Serbo-Croatian

Accepts manuscripts in English for translation: Not specified

Approximate acceptance rate: Not specified

Review period: Not specified   **Lead time to publication after acceptance:** Not specified

Circulation: Not specified   **Frequency of publication:**   Not specified

Sponsoring organization: Not specified

     Submission information:

Manuscript length: Not specified

Number of copies: Not specified   **Submission fee:**   Not specified

Style: Not specified

**Manuscript
editor:**   Maria Ivkov
     Udruzenje Knijigovoda Hrvatske, 8. Maja 1945, 42
     Zagreb, Yugoslavia

Publisher: Same as above

Knjigovodstvo

Primary readership: Not specified

Review process: Not specified

Invited articles: Not specified

Percentage of articles on accounting topics:

Approximate percentage of accounting-related articles devoted to: Not specified

Financial Accounting:	**Managerial:**
Computers/Systems:	**Tax:**
Auditing:	**Education:**
Professional:	

Approximate percentage of accounting-related articles characterized as primarily: Not specified

Empirical:	**Experimental:**
Analytical:	**Descriptive:**

Language(s) in which articles are published: Serbo-Croatian (Cyrillic alphabet)

Accepts manuscripts in English for translation: Not specified

Approximate acceptance rate: Not specified

Review period: Not specified   **Lead time to publication after acceptance:** Not specified

Circulation: Not specified   **Frequency of publication:** Not specified

Sponsoring organization: Not specified

Submission information:

Manuscript length: Not specified

Number of copies: Not specified   **Submission fee:** Not specified

Style: Not specified

Manuscript editor:
Sergije Djurovc
Udruzenje Knjigovoda Srbije, Njegoseva 19, Box 403
Belgrade, Yugoslavia

Publisher: Same as above

Kostenrechnungspraxis

Primary readership:	Academicians, accounting (or tax) practitioners, businessmen
Review process:	Editorial only
Invited articles:	21-40%

**Percentage of articles
on accounting topics:** 90

Approximate percentage of accounting-related articles devoted to:

Financial Accounting:	10	**Managerial:**	50
Computers/Systems:	20	**Tax:**	
Auditing:		**Education:**	
Professional:	20		

Approximate percentage of accounting-related articles characterized as primarily:

Empirical:	10	**Experimental:**	
Analytical:	30	**Descriptive:**	60

**Language(s) in which
articles are published:** German, English (on rare occasions)

Accepts manuscripts in English for translation: Not specified

Approximate acceptance rate: 80%

Review period: 4 months   **Lead time to publication after acceptance:** 4 months

Circulation: 8,000   **Frequency of publication:** Bi-monthly

Sponsoring organization: None

Submission information:

Manuscript length: 5 pages
Number of copies: 2   **Submission fee:** None
Style: Not specified

**Manuscript
editor:** Professors Dr. Wolfgang Mannel and Dr. Wolfgang Becker
P.O. Box 3931
8500 Nuernberg, West Germany

Publisher: Gabler Verlag
Postfach 1546
62 Wiesbaden, West Germany

Kreditpraxis

Primary readership: Academicians, businessmen, bankers, financial managers

Review process: Editorial only

Invited articles: 81-99%

**Percentage of articles
on accounting topics:**   5

Approximate percentage of accounting-related articles devoted to: Not specified

Financial Accounting: **Managerial:**

Computers/Systems: **Tax:**

Auditing: **Education:**

Professional:

Approximate percentage of accounting-related articles characterized as primarily: Not specified

Empirical: **Experimental:**

Analytical: **Descriptive:**

**Language(s) in which
articles are published:**   German

Accepts manuscripts in English for translation: No

Approximate acceptance rate: 80%

Review period: 3 weeks   **Lead time to publication after acceptance:** 1-3 months

Circulation: 72,000   **Frequency of publication:**   6 issues per year

Sponsoring organization: None

Submission information:

Manuscript length: 10-15 pages

Number of copies: 1   **Submission fee:** None

Style: Not specified

**Manuscript
editor:**   Wolfgang Raab

Kreditpraxis, Gabler Verlag, Postfach 1546

6200 Wiesbaden, West Germany

Publisher: Same as above

Law Office Economics and Management

Primary readership: Lawyers, legal administrators

Review process: Editorial only

Invited articles: 21-40%

Percentage of articles on accounting topics: 40

Approximate percentage of accounting-related articles devoted to:

Financial Accounting:	10	Managerial:	20
Computers/Systems:	60	Tax:	5
Auditing:		Education:	
Professional:		Other:	5

Approximate percentage of accounting-related articles characterized as primarily: Not specified

Empirical: Experimental:

Analytical: Descriptive:

Language(s) in which articles are published: English

Accepts manuscripts in English for translation: N/A

Approximate acceptance rate: Not specified

Review period: 1 week   **Lead time to publication after acceptance:** 4 months

Circulation: 1,800   **Frequency of publication:**   Quarterly

Sponsoring organization: None

Submission information:

Manuscript length: 5-25 manuscript pages, double-spaced

Number of copies: 1   **Submission fee:** None

Style: Manuscripts should be typed double-spaced.

Manuscript editor: Paul S. Hoffman
Law Office Economics & Management, P.O. Box 40
Croton-on-Hudson, NY 10520, U. S. A.

Publisher: Same as above

Logistics and Transportation Review

Primary readership: Academicians, businessmen, government officials

Review process: 2-3 external blind reviewers

Invited articles: 1-20%

**Percentage of articles
on accounting topics:**   5

Approximate percentage of accounting-related articles devoted to: Not specified

Financial Accounting: **Managerial:**

Computers/Systems: **Tax:**

Auditing: **Education:**

Professional:

Approximate percentage of accounting-related articles characterized as primarily: Not specified

Empirical: **Experimental:**

Analytical: **Descriptive:**

**Language(s) in which
articles are published:**   English

Accepts manuscripts in English for translation: N/A

Approximate acceptance rate: 50%

Review period: 4 months   **Lead time to publication after acceptance:** 3-4 months

Circulation: 1,000   **Frequency of publication:**   Quarterly

Sponsoring organization: None

Submission information:

Manuscript length: Flexible, 6-50 pages

Number of copies: 3   **Submission fee:** None

Style: Any standard style accepted for initial review.

**Manuscript
editor:**

Professor W. G. Waters II, Editor

Logistics and Transportation Review, Faculty of Commerce, University of British Columbia
Vancouver V6T 1W5, Canada

Publisher: Same as above

Magazine of Bank Administration, The

Primary readership: Bank officers

Review process: Not specified

Invited articles: Not specified

**Percentage of articles
on accounting topics:**
Approximate percentage of accounting-related articles devoted to: Not specified

Financial Accounting:	**Managerial:**
Computers/Systems:	**Tax:**
Auditing:	**Education:**
Professional:	

Approximate percentage of accounting-related articles characterized as primarily: Not specified

Empirical:	**Experimental:**
Analytical:	**Descriptive:**

**Language(s) in which
articles are published:**   English

Accepts manuscripts in English for translation: N/A

Approximate acceptance rate: Not specified

Review period: 1 month   **Lead time to publication after acceptance:** 3 - 6 months

Circulation: 42,000   **Frequency of publication:**   Monthly

Sponsoring organization: Bank Administration Institute

Submission information:
Manuscript length: 2,000 words
Number of copies: Original   **Submission fee:** None
Style: Available upon request.

**Manuscript
editor:**   R. Gerald Fox
     The Magazine of Bank Administration, 60 E. Gould Center
     Rolling Meadows, IL 60008, U. S. A.

Publisher: Same as above

Malaysian Management Review

Primary readership: Managers, students of management and business studies

Review process: Editorial only

Invited articles: 21-40%

**Percentage of articles
on accounting topics:**   10

Approximate percentage of accounting-related articles devoted to:

Financial Accounting:	20	**Managerial:**	20
Computers/Systems:	10	**Tax:**	10
Auditing:	10	**Education:**	10
Professional:	10	**Other:**	10

Approximate percentage of accounting-related articles characterized as primarily:

Empirical:	20	**Experimental:**	10
Analytical:	10	**Descriptive:**	40
Other:	20		

**Language(s) in which
articles are published:**   English

Accepts manuscripts in English for translation:

Approximate acceptance rate: 50%

Review period: 2 months   **Lead time to publication after acceptance:** 1 month

Circulation: 3,500   **Frequency of publication:**   3 issues per year

Sponsoring organization: Malaysian Institute of Management

     Submission information:

Manuscript length: 6,000 words

Number of copies: 2   **Submission fee:** None

Style: Empirical, preferably related to the local management culture.

**Manuscript
editor:**

    Dr. Tarcisius Chin

    Malaysian Institute of Management, 227 Jalan Ampang

    50450 Kuala Lumpur, Malaysia

Publisher: Same as above

Management (Ireland)

Primary readership: Businessmen

Review process: Editorial only

Invited articles: 61-80%

Percentage of articles on accounting topics: 10

Approximate percentage of accounting-related articles devoted to:

Financial Accounting:	20	**Managerial:**	40
Computers/Systems:	40	**Tax:**	
Auditing:		**Education:**	
Professional:			

Approximate percentage of accounting-related articles characterized as primarily:

Empirical:		**Experimental:**	
Analytical:	25	**Descriptive:**	75

Language(s) in which articles are published: English

Accepts manuscripts in English for translation: N/A

Approximate acceptance rate: 75%

Review period: 1 month   **Lead time to publication after acceptance:** 3 months

Circulation: 8,000   **Frequency of publication:** Monthly

Sponsoring organization: Irish Management Institute

Submission information:

Manuscript length: 1,500 words

Number of copies: 1   **Submission fee:** None

Style: Not specified

Manuscript editor: Frank Corr
Management, Irish Management Institute, Sandyford Road.
Dublin 16, Ireland

Publisher: Lemma Publications Ltd.
22 Brookfield Ave.
Blackrock, Dublin, Ireland

Management Accountant

Primary readership: Accountants in industry, public accountants, academicians and students

Review process: External reviewers

Invited articles: Not specified

**Percentage of articles
on accounting topics:**   100

Approximate percentage of accounting-related articles devoted to: Not specified

Financial Accounting: **Managerial:**
Computers/Systems: **Tax:**
Auditing: **Education:**
Professional:

Approximate percentage of accounting-related articles characterized as primarily: Not specified

Empirical: **Experimental:**
Analytical: **Descriptive:**

**Language(s) in which
articles are published:**   English

Accepts manuscripts in English for translation: N/A

Approximate acceptance rate: Not specified

Review period: Not specified   **Lead time to publication after acceptance:** Not specified

Circulation: 29,000   **Frequency of publication:**   Monthly

Sponsoring organization: The Institute of Cost and Works Accountants of India

Submission information:
Manuscript length: Not specified
Number of copies: Not specified **Submission fee:** None
Style: Not specified

**Manuscript
editor:**   Dr. A. N. Dutta
The Institute of Cost and Works Accountants of India
12 Sudder Street, Calcutta 700016, India

Publisher: Same as above

Management Accounting (England)

Primary readership: Academicians, accounting (or tax) practitioners, businessmen, student accountants

Review process: Editorial only

Invited articles: 21-40%

Percentage of articles on accounting topics: 70

Approximate percentage of accounting-related articles devoted to:

Financial Accounting:	10	Managerial:	60
Computers/Systems:	10	Tax:	5
Auditing:		Education:	5
Professional:	10		

Approximate percentage of accounting-related articles characterized as primarily:

Empirical:	5	Experimental:	
Analytical:	5	Descriptive:	90

Language(s) in which articles are published: English

Accepts manuscripts in English for translation: N/A

Approximate acceptance rate: 40%

Review period: 6 weeks   **Lead time to publication after acceptance:** 2 months

Circulation: 65,000   **Frequency of publication:** Monthly

Sponsoring organization: Chartered Institute of Management Accountants

Submission information:

Manuscript length: 2,000-3,000 words

Number of copies: 2   **Submission fee:** None

Style: Not specified

Manuscript editor:
J. B. Hillary
Management Accounting, CIMA, 63 Portland Place
London W1N 4AB, England

Publisher: Same as above

Management Accounting (US)

Primary readership: Academicians, accounting (or tax) practitioners, businessmen

Review process: Editorial, 3 external blind reviewers (on request by academics only)

Invited articles: 0%

**Percentage of articles
on accounting topics:**   95

Approximate percentage of accounting-related articles devoted to:

Financial Accounting:	40	**Managerial:**	20
Computers/Systems:	10	**Tax:**	5
Auditing:	5	**Education:**	5
Professional:	15		

Approximate percentage of accounting-related articles characterized as primarily: Not specified

Empirical: **Experimental:**

Analytical: **Descriptive:**

**Language(s) in which
articles are published:**   English

Accepts manuscripts in English for translation: N/A

Approximate acceptance rate: 9%

Review period: 4-6 weeks   **Lead time to publication after acceptance:** 3-6 months

Circulation: 95,000   **Frequency of publication:**   Monthly

Sponsoring organization: National Association of Accountants

> **Submission information:**

Manuscript length: Maximum 8-10 pages, typed double-spaced
Number of copies: 3   **Submission fee:** None
Style: See recent issue of magazine.

**Manuscript
editor:**   Ms. Susan Jayson
Management Accounting, NAA, 10 Paragon Dr.
Montvale, NJ 07645-1760, U. S. A.

Publisher: Same as above

Management Science

Primary readership: Academicians, businessmen, management scientists

Review process: Not specified

Invited articles: Not specified

**Percentage of articles
on accounting topics:**
Approximate percentage of accounting-related articles devoted to: Not specified

Financial Accounting:	**Managerial:**
Computers/Systems:	**Tax:**
Auditing:	**Education:**
Professional:	

Approximate percentage of accounting-related articles characterized as primarily: Not specified

Empirical:	**Experimental:**
Analytical:	**Descriptive:**

**Language(s) in which
articles are published:**   English

Accepts manuscripts in English for translation: N/A

Approximate acceptance rate: 25%

Review period: 6 months   **Lead time to publication after acceptance:** 6 months

Circulation: 12,000   **Frequency of publication:**   Monthly

Sponsoring organization: The Institute of Management Sciences

Submission information:

Manuscript length: 10,000 words

Number of copies: 4   **Submission fee:** None

Style: Professionally drawn artwork should be included. Other requirements available upon request.

**Manuscript
editor:**   Donald Morrison
Management Science, 290 Westminster Street
Providence, RI 02903, U. S. A.

Publisher: Same as above

Management World

Primary readership: Academicians, businessmen

Review process: Editorial only

Invited articles: 1-20%

**Percentage of articles
on accounting topics:**   5

Approximate percentage of accounting-related articles devoted to:

Financial Accounting:		**Managerial:**	100
Computers/Systems:		**Tax:**	
Auditing:		**Education:**	
Professional:			

Approximate percentage of accounting-related articles characterized as primarily:

Empirical:		**Experimental:**	
Analytical:		**Descriptive:**	100

**Language(s) in which
articles are published:**   English

Accepts manuscripts in English for translation: N/A

Approximate acceptance rate: 50%

Review period: 3-4 weeks   **Lead time to publication after acceptance:** 6-8 months

Circulation: 13,000   **Frequency of publication:**   8 times per year

Sponsoring organization: Administrative Management Society

Submission information:

Manuscript length: 4-6 pages

Number of copies: 1   **Submission fee:** None

Style: Casual, easy-to-read style, no footnotes.

**Manuscript
editor:**   Michael Cregar
Management World, AMS, 2360 Maryland Rd.
Willow Grove, PA   19090, U. S. A.

Publisher: Same as above

Managerial and Decision Economics

Primary readership: Academicians, managers

Review process: Blind reviewers

Invited articles: Not specified

**Percentage of articles
on accounting topics:**
Approximate percentage of accounting-related articles devoted to: Not specified

Financial Accounting: **Managerial:**
Computers/Systems: **Tax:**
Auditing: **Education:**
Professional:

Approximate percentage of accounting-related articles characterized as primarily: Not specified

Empirical: **Experimental:**
Analytical: **Descriptive:**

**Language(s) in which
articles are published:**   English

Accepts manuscripts in English for translation: N/A

Approximate acceptance rate: Not specified

Review period: 6 weeks   **Lead time to publication after acceptance:** Fast

Circulation: Not specified   **Frequency of publication:**   Quarterly

Sponsoring organization: Business Economics Research Group, University of the Witwatersrand, Johannesburg, South Africa

        Submission information:

Manuscript length: Not specified

Number of copies: Four   **Submission fee:** None

Style: Citation in text by names of authors, followed by year of publication in parenthesis. Alphabetical list of references.

**Manuscript
editor:**
    For North America: Mark Hirschey

    Graduate School of Business Adminstration, University of Colorado at Denver

    1475 Lawrence Street, Denver, CO 80202, U. S. A.

Publisher: Not specified

Managerial Finance

Primary readership: Academicians, accounting (or tax) practitioners, businessmen

Review process: Editorial only

Invited articles: 41-60%

**Percentage of articles
on accounting topics:**   20

Approximate percentage of accounting-related articles devoted to:

Financial Accounting:	50	**Managerial:**	10
Computers/Systems:		**Tax:**	10
Auditing:	10	**Education:**	10
Professional:	10		

Approximate percentage of accounting-related articles characterized as primarily:

Empirical:	25	**Experimental:**	25
Analytical:	25	**Descriptive:**	25

**Language(s) in which
articles are published:**   English

Accepts manuscripts in English for translation: N/A

Approximate acceptance rate: 25%

Review period: 1 month   **Lead time to publication after acceptance:** 1 year

Circulation: 300   **Frequency of publication:**   Quarterly

Sponsoring organization: None

Submission information:
Manuscript length: 10,000 words
Number of copies: 2   **Submission fee:** None
Style: Sample copy available to authors.

**Manuscript
editor:**   Dr. R. Dobbins
Managerial Finance, Croft House Farm, Kildwick Grange, KILDWICK
Nr. Keighley, North Yorkshire BD20 9AD, England

Publisher: MCB University Press Ltd.
62 Toller Lane
Bradford BD8 9BY, England

Managing

Primary readership: Academicians, businessmen

Review process: Not specified

Invited articles: Not specified

Percentage of articles on accounting topics:
Approximate percentage of accounting-related articles devoted to: Not specified

Financial Accounting: **Managerial:**
Computers/Systems: **Tax:**
Auditing: **Education:**
Professional:

Approximate percentage of accounting-related articles characterized as primarily: Not specified

Empirical: **Experimental:**
Analytical: **Descriptive:**

Language(s) in which articles are published: English

Accepts manuscripts in English for translation: N/A

Approximate acceptance rate: Not specified

Review period: 90 days   **Lead time to publication after acceptance:** Up to 1 year

Circulation: 5,000   **Frequency of publication:**   Semiannually

Sponsoring organization: University of Pittsburgh

Submission information:
Manuscript length: 2,000 - 3,500 words
Number of copies: Not specified   **Submission fee:**   None
Style: Available upon request.

Manuscript editor: Karin Burgio Hoy
Graduate School of Business, University of Pittsburgh, 325 Mervis Hall
Pittsburgh, PA 15260, U. S. A.

Publisher: Same as above

Massachusetts CPA Review

Primary readership: Academicians, accounting (or tax) practitioners, businessmen

Review process: External blind reviewers

Invited articles: Not specified

**Percentage of articles
on accounting topics:** 100

Approximate percentage of accounting-related articles devoted to: Each issue is devoted to a particular area.

Financial Accounting: **Managerial:**

Computers/Systems: **Tax:**

Auditing: **Education:**

Professional:

Approximate percentage of accounting-related articles characterized as primarily: Not specified

Empirical: **Experimental:**

Analytical: **Descriptive:**

**Language(s) in which
articles are published:** English

Accepts manuscripts in English for translation: N/A

Approximate acceptance rate: Not specified

Review period: 6 weeks   **Lead time to publication after acceptance:** 6 weeks

Circulation: 7,000+   **Frequency of publication:** Quarterly

Sponsoring organization: Massachusetts Society of CPAs

Submission information:

Manuscript length: 1,500 words

Number of copies: 2   **Submission fee:** None

Style: Contact MSCPAs for information regarding manuscript publication.

**Manuscript
editor:**
Michael J. Klein
Massachusetts CPA Review, Massachusetts Society of CPAs, 3 Center Plaza
Boston, MA 02108, U. S. A.

Publisher: Same as above

Mergers & Acquisitions

Primary readership: Businessmen

Review process: Not specified

Invited articles: Not specified

**Percentage of articles
on accounting topics:**
Approximate percentage of accounting-related articles devoted to: Not specified

Financial Accounting:	**Managerial:**
Computers/Systems:	**Tax:**
Auditing:	**Education:**
Professional:	

Approximate percentage of accounting-related articles characterized as primarily: Not specified

Empirical:	**Experimental:**
Analytical:	**Descriptive:**

**Language(s) in which
articles are published:**   English

Accepts manuscripts in English for translation: N/A

Approximate acceptance rate: 70%

Review period: 4 weeks   **Lead time to publication after acceptance:** 2 weeks

Circulation: 5,500   **Frequency of publication:**   Bi-monthly

Sponsoring organization: None

     Submission information:

Manuscript length: 3,300 words maximum

Number of copies: 2   **Submission fee:** None

Style: Not specified

**Manuscript
editor:**   Martin Sikara

     M. L. R. Enterprises, Inc., 229 S. 18th St.

     Philadelphia, PA 19103, U. S. A.

Publisher: Same as above

MIS Quarterly

Primary readership: Academicians,computer specialists

Review process: 5 external blind reviewers plus 1 associate editor

Invited articles: 1-20%

Percentage of articles on accounting topics:

Approximate percentage of accounting-related articles devoted to:

Financial Accounting:		**Managerial:**	
Computers/Systems:	100	**Tax:**	
Auditing:		**Education:**	
Professional:			

Approximate percentage of accounting-related articles characterized as primarily: Not specified

Empirical:	**Experimental:**
Analytical:	**Descriptive:**

Language(s) in which articles are published: English

Accepts manuscripts in English for translation: N/A

Approximate acceptance rate: 15%

Review period: 3-4 months   **Lead time to publication after acceptance:** 6 months

Circulation: 3,600   **Frequency of publication:**   Quarterly

Sponsoring organization:

Submission information:

Manuscript length: 30-40 typed double-spaced papers

Number of copies: 8   **Submission fee:** None

Style: All manuscripts should be typed and double-spaced on one side of 8 1/2 x 11" paper. Citations should follow UPI or AP stylebook for bibliographies and references. See September 1986 issue for more information.

Manuscript editor:

F. Warren McFarlan, Senior Editor

MIS Quarterly,Harvard Business School, Soldiers Field

Boston, MA   02163, U. S. A.

Publisher: MIS Quarterly

MIS Research Center, School of Management, 271 19th Avenue S., University of Minnesota

Minneapolis, MN   55455, U. S. A.

Mississippi CPA Newsletter

Primary readership: Academicians, accounting (or tax) practitioners, computer specialists

Review process: Not specified

Invited articles: 21-40%

**Percentage of articles
on accounting topics:**   90

Approximate percentage of accounting-related articles devoted to: Not specified

Financial Accounting:	**Managerial:**
Computers/Systems:	**Tax:**
Auditing:	**Education:**
Professional:	

Approximate percentage of accounting-related articles characterized as primarily: Not specified

Empirical:	**Experimental:**
Analytical:	**Descriptive:**

**Language(s) in which
articles are published:**   English

Accepts manuscripts in English for translation: N/A

Approximate acceptance rate: 50%

Review period: 30-45 days   **Lead time to publication after acceptance:** Not specified

Circulation: 2,000   **Frequency of publication:**   Monthly

Sponsoring organization: Mississippi Society of CPAs

Submission information:

Manuscript length: 2 typed pages, double-spaced
Number of copies: 2   **Submission fee:** None
Style: Not specified

**Manuscript
editor:**   Robert L. Nickey

    Mississippi CPA Newsletter, Mississippi Society of CPAs, P.O. Box 16630
    Jackson, MS 39236, U. S. A.

Publisher: Same as above

Montana Business Quarterly

Primary readership: Businessmen

Review process: 2 external reviewers (authors known)

Invited articles: 61-80%

**Percentage of articles
on accounting topics:**   5

Approximate percentage of accounting-related articles devoted to:

Financial Accounting:	**Managerial:**
Computers/Systems: 50	**Tax:** 50
Auditing:	**Education:**
Professional:	

Approximate percentage of accounting-related articles characterized as primarily:

Empirical:	**Experimental:**
Analytical:	**Descriptive:** 100

**Language(s) in which
articles are published:**   English

Accepts manuscripts in English for translation: N/A

Approximate acceptance rate: 5% , for unsolicited articles

Review period: 1 month   **Lead time to publication after acceptance:** 2 months

Circulation: 1,500   **Frequency of publication:**   Quarterly

Sponsoring organization: Bureau of Business and Economic Research, University of Montana

Submission information:

Manuscript length: 12 pages, double-spaced

Number of copies: 2   **Submission fee:** None

Style: Chicago Manual of Style

**Manuscript
editor:**   Mary L. Lenihan

Montana Business Quarterly, Bureau of Business and Economic Research, University of Montana
Missoula, MT 59812, U. S. A.

Publisher: Same as above

Montana CPA

Primary readership: Accounting (or tax) practitioners

Review process: Editorial only

Invited articles: 61-80%

**Percentage of articles
on accounting topics:**   90

Approximate percentage of accounting-related articles devoted to:

Financial Accounting:	20	**Managerial:**	10
Computers/Systems:		**Tax:**	20
Auditing:	20	**Education:**	10
Professional:	10	Continuing professional education:	10

Approximate percentage of accounting-related articles characterized as primarily:

Empirical:		**Experimental:**	
Analytical:	50	**Descriptive:**	50

**Language(s) in which
articles are published:**   English

Accepts manuscripts in English for translation: N/A

Approximate acceptance rate: N/A

Review period: N/A   **Lead time to publication after acceptance:** N/A

Circulation: 1,101   **Frequency of publication:**   Bi-monthly

Sponsoring organization: Montana Society of CPAs

Submission information:

Manuscript length: No limit

Number of copies: 1   **Submission fee:** None

Style: Not specified

**Manuscript
editor:**   Jane Campbell, Executive Director
Montana CPA, Montana Society of CPAs, P.O. Box 138
Helena, MT 59624, U. S. A.

Publisher: Same as above

Motor Freight Controller Magazine

Primary readership: Accounting (or tax) practitioners, businessmen

Review process: Editorial only

Invited articles: 81-99%

Percentage of articles on accounting topics: 85

Approximate percentage of accounting-related articles devoted to:

Financial Accounting:	80	Managerial:	2
Computers/Systems:	10	Tax:	3
Auditing:	5	Education:	
Professional:			

Approximate percentage of accounting-related articles characterized as primarily: Looking for "how-to" articles

Empirical:		Experimental:	
Analytical:	5	Descriptive:	95

Language(s) in which articles are published: English

Accepts manuscripts in English for translation: N/A

Approximate acceptance rate: 75%

Review period: 2-3 weeks   **Lead time to publication after acceptance:** 1-2 months

Circulation: 1,300   **Frequency of publication:** Monthly

Sponsoring organization: National Accounting & Finance Council of the American Trucking Association

Submission information:

Manuscript length: 3-6 typed double-spaced pages

Number of copies: 2   **Submission fee:** None

Style: Not specified

Manuscript editor: Carla R. Bitterman

Motor Freight Controller, American Trucking Association, 2200 Mill Road
Alexandria, VA 22314, U. S. A.

Publisher: Same as above

Municipal Finance Journal

Primary readership: Accounting (or tax) practitioners, attorneys

Review process: Editorial only

Invited articles: 21-40%

**Percentage of articles
on accounting topics:**   10

Approximate percentage of accounting-related articles devoted to:

Financial Accounting:	**Managerial:**	
Computers/Systems:	**Tax:**	100
Auditing:	**Education:**	
Professional:		

Approximate percentage of accounting-related articles characterized as primarily: Not specified

Empirical:	**Experimental:**
Analytical:	**Descriptive:**

**Language(s) in which
articles are published:**   English

Accepts manuscripts in English for translation: N/A

Approximate acceptance rate: 70%

Review period: 2 months   **Lead time to publication after acceptance:** 2 months

Circulation: 1,500   **Frequency of publication:**   Quarterly

Sponsoring organization: None

Submission information:

Manuscript length: 10-40 pages

Number of copies: 2   **Submission fee:** Not specified

Style: Manuscripts should be typed double-spaced on one side of 8 1/2 by 11" good-quality bond paper with 1" margins all around. Type footnotes separately, double-spaced, at the end of the main manuscript. Footnote and reference citations should generally follow the "Harvard Blue Book." Any artwork, graphs, etc. must be provided in camera-ready form.

**Manuscript
editor:**   Edward D. Einowski, Esq.

Municipal Finance Journal, Panel Publishers Inc.,14 Plaza Rd.

Greenvale, NY 11548, U. S. A.

Publisher: Same as above

N.Y.U. Law Review

Primary readership: Academicians, lawyers, law students

Review process: Editorial only

Invited articles: 1-20%

**Percentage of articles
on accounting topics:**   2

Approximate percentage of accounting-related articles devoted to: Not specified

Financial Accounting: **Managerial:**

Computers/Systems: **Tax:**

Auditing: **Education:**

Professional:

Approximate percentage of accounting-related articles characterized as primarily: Not specified

Empirical: **Experimental:**

Analytical: **Descriptive:**

**Language(s) in which
articles are published:**   English

Accepts manuscripts in English for translation: N/A

Approximate acceptance rate: 25%

Review period: 1 week to 3
months   **Lead time to publication after acceptance:** 8 months to 1 1/2 years

Circulation: 3,100   **Frequency of publication:**   6 times per year

Sponsoring organization: N.Y.U. School of Law

   Submission information:

Manuscript length: No limit

Number of copies: 1   **Submission fee:** None

Style: All footnotes at the end; footnotes in "Harvard Blue Book" form.

**Manuscript
editor:**   Articles Editor
N.Y.U. Law Review, 110 West Third St.
New York, NY 10012, U. S. A.

Publisher: Same as above

National Public Accountant

Primary readership: Accounting (or tax) practitioners

Review process: 2 external blind reviewers

Invited articles: 1-20%

**Percentage of articles
on accounting topics:**   50

Approximate percentage of accounting-related articles devoted to:

Financial Accounting:	50	**Managerial:**	
Computers/Systems:	10	**Tax:**	30
Auditing:		**Education:**	
Professional:	10		

Approximate percentage of accounting-related articles characterized as primarily: Interested in practical articles only.

Empirical:	**Experimental:**
Analytical:	**Descriptive:**

**Language(s) in which
articles are published:**   English

Accepts manuscripts in English for translation: N/A

Approximate acceptance rate: 40%

Review period: 8-10 weeks   **Lead time to publication after acceptance:** 3 months

Circulation: 18,500   **Frequency of publication:**   Monthly

Sponsoring organization: National Society of Public Accountants

Submission information:

Manuscript length: No minimum or maximum length is required, average articles are 8-13 typed pages.

Number of copies: 3   **Submission fee:** None

Style: Manuscripts should be typed double-spaced, and may include tables, charts, graphs, illustrations, and pictures. Exceptionally long articles may run as a two-part story.

**Manuscript
editor:**   Susan Cappitelli

National Public Accountant, 1010 N. Fairfax St.

Alexandria, VA 22314, U. S. A.

Publisher: Same as above

National Tax Journal

Primary readership: Accounting (or tax) practitioners

Review process: Not specified

Invited articles: Not specified

**Percentage of articles
on accounting topics:**   100

Approximate percentage of accounting-related articles devoted to:

Financial Accounting:	**Managerial:**
Computers/Systems:	**Tax:** 100
Auditing:	**Education:**
Professional:	

Approximate percentage of accounting-related articles characterized as primarily: Not specified

Empirical:	**Experimental:**
Analytical:	**Descriptive:**

**Language(s) in which
articles are published:**   English

Accepts manuscripts in English for translation: N/A

Approximate acceptance rate: Less than 20%

Review period: 3 - 4 months   **Lead time to publication after acceptance:** 3 months

Circulation: 4,000   **Frequency of publication:**   Quarterly

Sponsoring organization: Massachusetts Institute of Technology

Submission information:

Manuscript length: Not specified

Number of copies: 3   **Submission fee:** None

Style: Available upon request.

**Manuscript
editor:**   Daniel M. Holland

Sloan School of Management, Massachusetts Institute of Technology, 50 Memorial Drive
Cambridge, MA 02139, U. S. A.

Publisher: National Tax Association - Tax Institute of America
21 E. State St.
Columbus, OH 43215, U. S. A.

Neue Juristische Wochenschrift

Primary readership: Academicians, accounting (tax) practitioners, businessmen

Review process: Editorial review only

Invited articles: 21-40%

**Percentage of articles
on accounting topics:**   15

Approximate percentage of accounting-related articles devoted to:

Financial Accounting:	**Managerial:**
Computers/Systems:	**Tax:** 100
Auditing:	**Education:**
Professional:	

Approximate percentage of accounting-related articles characterized as primarily: Not specified

Empirical:	**Experimental:**
Analytical:	**Descriptive:**

**Language(s) in which
articles are published:**   German

Accepts manuscripts in English for translation: No

Approximate acceptance rate: 30%

Review period: 4-5 months   **Lead time to publication after acceptance:** 3-4 months

Circulation: 55,000   **Frequency of publication:**   Weekly

Sponsoring organization: None

Submission information:

Manuscript length: 10-15 pages

Number of copies: 1   **Submission fee:** None

Style: None

**Manuscript
editor:**   Prof. Dr. Hermann Weber
Palmengartenstr. 14
6000 Frankfurt 1, West Germany

Publisher: Not specified

Nevada Review of Business and Economics

Primary readership: Academicians, businessmen

Review process: 2 (including editor) external reviewers (authors known)

Invited articles: 1-20%

Percentage of articles on accounting topics: 20

Approximate percentage of accounting-related articles devoted to:

Financial Accounting:		**Managerial:**	
Computers/Systems:	50	**Tax:**	50
Auditing:		**Education:**	
Professional:			

Approximate percentage of accounting-related articles characterized as primarily:

Empirical:	50	**Experimental:**	
Analytical:		**Descriptive:**	25
Other:	25		

Language(s) in which articles are published: English

Accepts manuscripts in English for translation: N/A

Approximate acceptance rate: 60%

Review period: 1-2 months   **Lead time to publication after acceptance:** 6 months

Circulation: 2,000   **Frequency of publication:**   Quarterly

Sponsoring organization: Bureau of Business and Economic Research, University of Nevada-Reno

Submission information:

Manuscript length: 15-30 pages

Number of copies: 2   **Submission fee:** None

Style: To be fulfilled only after acceptance of article.

Manuscript editor:

Thomas F. Cargill

Bureau of Business and Economic Research, University of Nevada

Reno, NV 89557-0016, U. S. A.

Publisher: Same as above

New Accountant

Primary readership: Accounting (or tax) practitioners, academicians, accounting seniors, graduates and faculty

Review process: Editorial only

Invited articles: 41-60%

**Percentage of articles
on accounting topics:** 90

Approximate percentage of accounting-related articles devoted to:

Financial Accounting:	1	**Managerial:**	1
Computers/Systems:	10	**Tax:**	2
Auditing:	2	**Education:**	2
Professional:	80	**Career planning:**	2

Approximate percentage of accounting-related articles characterized as primarily:

Empirical:	**Experimental:**	
Analytical:	**Descriptive:**	100

**Language(s) in which
articles are published:** English

Accepts manuscripts in English for translation: N/A

Approximate acceptance rate: 20%

Review period: 2-3 months   **Lead time to publication after acceptance:** No fixed time

Circulation: 55,000   **Frequency of publication:** 6 times per year (Sept., Oct., Nov., Jan., Feb., Mar.)

Sponsoring organization:

Submission information:

Manuscript length: 1,800-2,000 words

Number of copies: 2   **Submission fee:** None

Style: Conversational tone, no footnotes, no more than 2 charts, illustrations, or examples.

**Manuscript
editor:** Louise Dratler Haberman, Managing Editor
New Accountant, 33 Village Square
Glen Cove, NY 11542, U. S. A.

Publisher: Same as above

New Management

Primary readership:	Academicians, businessmen

Review process: Editorial only

Invited articles: 61-80%

**Percentage of articles
on accounting topics:**   3

Approximate percentage of accounting-related articles devoted to:

Financial Accounting:	**Managerial:**
Computers/Systems:	**Tax:**
Auditing:	**Education:**
Professional:	

Approximate percentage of accounting-related articles characterized as primarily: Not specified

Empirical:	**Experimental:**
Analytical:	**Descriptive:**

**Language(s) in which
articles are published:**   English

Accepts manuscripts in English for translation: N/A

Approximate acceptance rate: 25%

Review period: 6-9 months   **Lead time to publication after acceptance:** 3-6 months

Circulation: 5,000-6,000   **Frequency of publication:**   Quarterly

Sponsoring organization: University of Southern California

Submission information:

Manuscript length: 2,000 words or fewer
Number of copies: 2   **Submission fee:** None
Style: Not specified

**Manuscript
editor:**   Alice Short
    New Management, University of Southern California, University Park
    Los Angeles, CA 90064-1421, U. S. A.

Publisher: Wilson Learning Corporation
    6950 Washington Avenue South
    Eden Prairie, MN 55344, U. S. A.

NewsAccount

Primary readership: Academicians, accounting (or tax) practitioners

Review process: Not specified

Invited articles: Not specified

**Percentage of articles
on accounting topics:** 100

Approximate percentage of accounting-related articles devoted to: Not specified

Financial Accounting: **Managerial:**
Computers/Systems: **Tax:**
Auditing: **Education:**
Professional:

Approximate percentage of accounting-related articles characterized as primarily: Not specified

Empirical: **Experimental:**
Analytical: **Descriptive:**

**Language(s) in which
articles are published:** English

Accepts manuscripts in English for translation: N/A

Approximate acceptance rate: 50%

Review period: 8 weeks **Lead time to publication after acceptance:** 4 weeks

Circulation: 6,500 **Frequency of publication:** 1 issue every 6 weeks

Sponsoring organization: Colorado Society of CPAs

Submission information:
Manuscript length: 400 words maximum
Number of copies: 1 **Submission fee:** None
Style: Not specified

**Manuscript
editor:** Anne Marie Glennon
NewsAccount, Colorado SCPAS, 7720 E. Belleview Ave., # 46B
Englewood, CO 80111, U. S. A.

Publisher: Same as above

Newsledger

Primary readership: Members of the Society only

Review process: editorial,1 external blind reviewers

Invited articles: Not specified

**Percentage of articles
on accounting topics:**   95

Approximate percentage of accounting-related articles devoted to:

Financial Accounting:	10	**Managerial:**	10
Computers/Systems:	5	**Tax:**	20
Auditing:	5	**Education:**	10
Professional:	10	**Other:**	30

Approximate percentage of accounting-related articles characterized as primarily:

Empirical:		**Experimental:**	5
Analytical:	10	**Descriptive:**	80
Other:	5		

**Language(s) in which
articles are published:**   English

Accepts manuscripts in English for translation: N/A

Approximate acceptance rate: N/A

Review period: 1 month   **Lead time to publication after acceptance:** Not specified

Circulation: N/A   **Frequency of publication:**   Monthly

Sponsoring organization: Arizona Society of CPAs

Submission information:

Manuscript length: 10 pages or fewer, typed double-spaced
Number of copies: 2   **Submission fee:** None
Style: Simple and direct

**Manuscript
editor:**   Derrick Schnebett, ASCPA Communications Manager
Newsledger, P.O. Box 24049
Tempe, AZ 85282, U. S. A.

Publisher: Same as above

Newspaper Financial Executive Journal

Primary readership: Accounting (or tax) practitioners, businessmen

Review process: Editorial only

Invited articles: 1-20%

**Percentage of articles
on accounting topics:**   50

Approximate percentage of accounting-related articles devoted to:

Financial Accounting:	10	**Managerial:**	20
Computers/Systems:	20	**Tax:**	20
Auditing:	10	**Education:**	10
Professional:	10		

Approximate percentage of accounting-related articles characterized as primarily:

Empirical:		**Experimental:**	
Analytical:	30	**Descriptive:**	70

**Language(s) in which
articles are published:**   English

Accepts manuscripts in English for translation: N/A

Approximate acceptance rate: 25%

Review period: 1 month   **Lead time to publication after acceptance:** 40 days

Circulation: 12,000   **Frequency of publication:**   Monthly

Sponsoring organization: International Newpaper Financial Executives

Submission information:

Manuscript length: 2-5 typed double-spaced pages

Number of copies: 1   **Submission fee:** None

Style: Contact the editor for information concerning manuscript publication.

**Manuscript
editor:**   Daniel Dildine

Newspaper Financial Executive Journal, P.O. Box 17573, Dulles Airport
Washington, DC 20041 , U. S. A.

Publisher: International Newspaper Financial Executives
The Newspaper Center, 11600 Sunrise Valley Drive
Reston, VA

Nigerian Accountant, The

Primary readership: Academicians, accounting (or tax) practitioners, businessmen, computer specialists, students

Review process: Editorial only

Invited articles: 41-60%

Percentage of articles on accounting topics: 50

Approximate percentage of accounting-related articles devoted to: Not specified

Financial Accounting: **Managerial:**

Computers/Systems: **Tax:**

Auditing: **Education:**

Professional:

Approximate percentage of accounting-related articles characterized as primarily: Not specified

Empirical: **Experimental:**

Analytical: **Descriptive:**

Language(s) in which articles are published: English

Accepts manuscripts in English for translation: N/A

Approximate acceptance rate: 70 %

Review period: 1-6 months   **Lead time to publication after acceptance:** 3 months

Circulation: 15,000   **Frequency of publication:** Quarterly

Sponsoring organization: The Institute of Chartered Accountants of Nigeria

Submission information:

Manuscript length: maximum 12 typewritten double-spaced pages

Number of copies: 2   **Submission fee:** None

Style: Not specified

Manuscript editor:
Sola M. O. Olukota, Editor
The Nigerian Accountant, ICAN, P.O. Box 1580
Lagos, Nigeria

Publisher: Same as above

Northeast Journal of Business & Economics, The

Primary readership: Academicians

Review process: 2 external blind reviewers

Invited articles: 0%

**Percentage of articles
on accounting topics:**   10

Approximate percentage of accounting-related articles devoted to: Not specified

Financial Accounting: **Managerial:**

Computers/Systems: **Tax:**

Auditing: **Education:**

Professional:

Approximate percentage of accounting-related articles characterized as primarily: Not specified

Empirical: **Experimental:**

Analytical: **Descriptive:**

**Language(s) in which
articles are published:**   English

Accepts manuscripts in English for translation: N/A

Approximate acceptance rate: 30%

Review period: 2-3 months   **Lead time to publication after acceptance:** 2-3 months

Circulation: 2,000   **Frequency of publication:**   Semiannually

Sponsoring organization: College of Business Administration, University of Rhode Island, and the Northeast Business & Economics Association

Submission information:

Manuscript length: 10-20 pages, typed double-spaced

Number of copies: 4   **Submission fee:** None

Style: References should be listed alphabetically at the end of the manuscript and numbered sequentially throughout the text. Content footnotes should appear at the end of the paper before "References" under the heading "Footnotes" but they should be used at a minimum. All tables, graphs, etc. should be labeled "Exhibits" and numbered serially with respect to the first textual reference. See publication for more information.

Manuscript editor: Peter Koveos and Blair Lord

Research Center in Business and Economics, 210 Ballentine, University of Rhode Island

Kingston, RI 02881, U. S. A.

Publisher: Same as above

Nursing Homes and Senior Citizen Care

Primary readership: Nursing home administrators

Review process: 1 external reviewer (authors known)

Invited articles: 1-20%

Percentage of articles on accounting topics: 5

Approximate percentage of accounting-related articles devoted to:

Financial Accounting:	**Managerial:**	40
Computers/Systems:	**Tax:**	
Auditing:	**Education:**	
Professional: 60		

Approximate percentage of accounting-related articles characterized as primarily: Not specified

Empirical:	**Experimental:**
Analytical:	**Descriptive:**

Language(s) in which articles are published: English

Accepts manuscripts in English for translation: N/A

Approximate acceptance rate: 60%

Review period: 2 weeks   **Lead time to publication after acceptance:** Varies, depends on backlog of accepted material

Circulation: 4,000+   **Frequency of publication:** Bi-monthly

Sponsoring organization: None

Submission information:

Manuscript length: Not to exceed 3,000 words

Number of copies: 1   **Submission fee:** None, we pay for accepted manuscript

Style: Not specified

Manuscript editor:

William D. Magnes, Editor in Chief

Nursing Homes and Senior Citizen Care, Centaur & Company, 5 Willowbrook Court
Potomac, MD 20854, U. S. A.

Publisher: Same as above

Ohio CPA Journal, The

Primary readership: Academicians, accounting (or tax) practitioners, businessmen, computer specialists, members of OSCPA

Review process: 2 external blind reviewers

Invited articles: 1-20%

Percentage of articles on accounting topics: 100

Approximate percentage of accounting-related articles devoted to: Varies each issue

Financial Accounting:	**Managerial:**	
Computers/Systems:	**Tax:**	
Auditing:	**Education:**	
Professional:		

Approximate percentage of accounting-related articles characterized as primarily: Depends on articles submitted

Empirical:	**Experimental:**
Analytical:	**Descriptive:**

Language(s) in which articles are published: English

Accepts manuscripts in English for translation: N/A

Approximate acceptance rate: 20%

Review period: 2 months   **Lead time to publication after acceptance:** 1-3 months

Circulation: 13,000   **Frequency of publication:** Quarterly

Sponsoring organization: Ohio Society of CPAs

Submission information:

Manuscript length: 5-8 pages, double-spaced

Number of copies: 3   **Submission fee:** None

Style: Manuscripts should be typed double-spaced, on 8 1/2 x 11" paper. Reference footnotes should be numbered consecutively and grouped on a separate page. A bibliography or reference list should not be submitted. Each table and figure should appear on a separate page and should be titled and numbered consecutively using arabic numerals; each figure or table must be referred to in the text. Contact the editor for more information.

Manuscript editor:

Michael Pearson, CPA, Editor

The Ohio CPA Journal, P.O. Box 1810, Metro Place South

Dublin, OH   43017-7810, U. S. A.

Publisher: Same as above

Oil and Gas Tax Quarterly

Primary readership: Academicians, accounting (or tax) practitioners, businessmen, lawyers

Review process: Editorial, external blind reviewers

Invited articles: 1-20%

**Percentage of articles
on accounting topics:** 90

Approximate percentage of accounting-related articles devoted to:

Financial Accounting:	5	**Managerial:**	
Computers/Systems:		**Tax:**	80
Auditing:	5	**Education:**	
Professional:		**Other :**	10

Approximate percentage of accounting-related articles characterized as primarily:

Empirical:	10	**Experimental:**	10
Analytical:	15	**Descriptive:**	60
Other:	5		

**Language(s) in which
articles are published:** English

Accepts manuscripts in English for translation: N/A

Approximate acceptance rate: 35%

Review period: 2 months **Lead time to publication after acceptance:** 2-3 months

Circulation: 5,000 **Frequency of publication:** Quarterly

Sponsoring organization: Texas A & M University

Submission information:

Manuscript length: 14-17 typed double-spaced

Number of copies: 2 **Submission fee:** None

Style: Contact the editor for information concerning manuscript publication.

**Manuscript
editor:** D. Larry Crumbley

Oil and Gas Tax Quarterly, Dept. of Accounting, Texas A & M University
College Station, TX 77843, U. S. A.

Publisher: Matthew Bender & Co., Inc.
235 E. 45th St.
New York, NY 10017, U. S. A.

Oklahoma Business Bulletin

Primary readership:	Businessmen
Review process:	6 external blind reviewers
Invited articles:	41-60%

**Percentage of articles
on accounting topics:** 20

Approximate percentage of accounting-related articles devoted to:

Financial Accounting:	10	**Managerial:**	
Computers/Systems:	30	**Tax:**	20
Auditing:		**Education:**	25
Professional:		Impact of tax laws :	15

Approximate percentage of accounting-related articles characterized as primarily:

Empirical:	20	**Experimental:**	15
Analytical:	30	**Descriptive:**	35

**Language(s) in which
articles are published:** English

Accepts manuscripts in English for translation: N/A

Approximate acceptance rate: 70%

Review period: 2 weeks	**Lead time to publication after acceptance:** 3 months
Circulation: 3,120	**Frequency of publication:** Monthly

Sponsoring organization: University of Oklahoma

Submission information:

Manuscript length: 16 pages, typed double-spaced

Number of copies: 3   **Submission fee:** None

Style: Not specified

**Manuscript
editor:** Alice Watkins
Center for Economic and Business Research, 307 W. Brooks, Room 4
Norman, OK 73069, U. S. A.

Publisher: Same as above

Oklahoma Law Review

Primary readership: Attorneys, judges

Review process: Editorial only

Invited articles: 5%

**Percentage of articles
on accounting topics:**   10

Approximate percentage of accounting-related articles devoted to:

Financial Accounting:	**Managerial:**	
Computers/Systems:	**Tax:**	100
Auditing:	**Education:**	
Professional:		

Approximate percentage of accounting-related articles characterized as primarily:

Empirical:	**Experimental:**
Analytical: 100	**Descriptive:**

**Language(s) in which
articles are published:**   English

Accepts manuscripts in English for translation: N/A

Approximate acceptance rate: 15%

Review period: 1 week   **Lead time to publication after acceptance:** 4 months

Circulation: 1,250   **Frequency of publication:**   Quarterly

Sponsoring organization: Oklahoma College of Law

Submission information:

Manuscript length: No limit

Number of copies: 2   **Submission fee:** None

Style: Typed double-spaced, including footnotes. Footnotes should be included on a separate sheet of paper. Follow the "Harvard Blue Book" as a guide to the style requirements.

**Manuscript
editor:**   Greg Pilcher

Oklahoma Law Review, College of Law, University of Oklahoma, 300 Timberdell Rd.
Norman, OK 73019, U. S. A.

Publisher: Same as above

Outlook

Primary readership: Accounting (or tax) practitioners

Review process: Not specified

Invited articles: 100%

**Percentage of articles
on accounting topics:**   100

Approximate percentage of accounting-related articles devoted to: Not specified

Financial Accounting:	**Managerial:**
Computers/Systems:	**Tax:**
Auditing:	**Education:**
Professional:	

Approximate percentage of accounting-related articles characterized as primarily: Not specified

Empirical:	**Experimental:**
Analytical:	**Descriptive:**

**Language(s) in which
articles are published:**   English

Accepts manuscripts in English for translation: N/A

Approximate acceptance rate: 0%

Review period: Not specified   **Lead time to publication after acceptance:** Not specified

Circulation: 27,000   **Frequency of publication:**   Quarterly

Sponsoring organization: California Society of CPAs

Submission information:

Manuscript length: Not specified

Number of copies: Not specified   **Submission fee:** Not specfied

Style: Not specified

**Manuscript
editor:**   Linda Fresques
          Outlook, 1000 Welch Rd.
          Palo Alto, CA 94006, U. S. A.

Publisher: Same as above

Pacific Northwest Executive

Primary readership: Businessmen, business and government policy decision makers

Review process: Not specified

Invited articles: Not specified

**Percentage of articles
on accounting topics:**
Approximate percentage of accounting-related articles devoted to: Not specified

Financial Accounting:	**Managerial:**
Computers/Systems:	**Tax:**
Auditing:	**Education:**
Professional:	

Approximate percentage of accounting-related articles characterized as primarily: Not specified

Empirical:	**Experimental:**
Analytical:	**Descriptive:**

**Language(s) in which
articles are published:**   English

Accepts manuscripts in English for translation: N/A

Approximate acceptance rate: 30%

Review period: 1 month   **Lead time to publication after acceptance:** Up to one year

Circulation: 25,000   **Frequency of publication:**   Quarterly

Sponsoring organization: Seafirst Bank

Submission information:

Manuscript length: 2,000-5,000 words

Number of copies: 1   **Submission fee:** None

Style: In-depth, non-academic, not newspaper or popular magazine style. Articles should have relevance for the Pacific Northwest area. Articles must be typewritten double-spaced on one side of the paper, with at least 1" margins. Submission of floppy discs with ASCII or Microsoft Word files in PC- or MS-DOS format is encouraged. Graphics and tables should be provided, but do not have to be camera-ready.

**Manuscript
editor:**   Professor J. J. Sullivan

Pacific Northwest Executive, 336 Lewis Hall DJ-10, University of Washington

Seattle, WA 98195, U. S. A.

Publisher: Same as above

Password, The

Primary readership: Academicians, accounting (or tax) practitioners, businessmen, computer specialists, EDP audit professionals

Review process: Editorial only

Invited articles: Not specified

Percentage of articles on accounting topics: 25

Approximate percentage of accounting-related articles devoted to:

Financial Accounting:		**Managerial:**	
Computers/Systems:		**Tax:**	
Auditing:	80	**Education:**	10
Professional:	10		

Approximate percentage of accounting-related articles characterized as primarily:

Empirical:	25	**Experimental:**	25
Analytical:		**Descriptive:**	50

Language(s) in which articles are published: English

Accepts manuscripts in English for translation: N/A

Approximate acceptance rate: 100%

Review period: 1 month   **Lead time to publication after acceptance:** 1 month

Circulation: 1,100   **Frequency of publication:** Monthly

Sponsoring organization: EDP Auditors Association-Australia

Submission information:

Manuscript length: 500-1,000 words

Number of copies: 1   **Submission fee:** None

Style: Not specified

Manuscript editor:
Gary Benbow
The Password, P.O. Box 723F   GPO Melbourne
Victoria, 3000, Australia

Publisher: Same as above

Pennsylvania CPA Journal

Primary readership: Accounting (or tax) practitioners

Review process: Not specified

Invited articles: 0%

**Percentage of articles
on accounting topics:**   100

Approximate percentage of accounting-related articles devoted to:

Financial Accounting:	25	**Managerial:**	
Computers/Systems:		**Tax:**	25
Auditing:	25	**Education:**	
Professional:	25		

Approximate percentage of accounting-related articles characterized as primarily: Not specified

Empirical:	**Experimental:**
Analytical:	**Descriptive:**

**Language(s) in which
articles are published:**   English

Accepts manuscripts in English for translation: N/A

Approximate acceptance rate: Not specified

Review period: Not specified   **Lead time to publication after acceptance:** Not specified

Circulation: 17,000   **Frequency of publication:**   Quarterly

Sponsoring organization: Pennsylvania Institute of CPAs

Submission information:

Manuscript length: 1,500-2,000 words

Number of copies: 2   **Submission fee:** Not specified

Style: Contact the editor for information concerning manuscript publication.

**Manuscript
editor:**   Pat Walker
Pennsylvania CPA Journal, 1608 Walnut St., Third Floor
Philadelphia, PA   19103, U. S. A.

Publisher: Same as above

Pension World

Primary readership: Pension industry professionals

Review process: 1-3 external blind reviewers

Invited articles: Varies

**Percentage of articles
on accounting topics:**   10

Approximate percentage of accounting-related articles devoted to: Limited to pension-related topics

Financial Accounting: **Managerial:**

Computers/Systems: **Tax:**

Auditing: **Education:**

Professional:

Approximate percentage of accounting-related articles characterized as primarily:

Empirical: **Experimental:**

Analytical: **Descriptive:**   100

**Language(s) in which
articles are published:**   English

Accepts manuscripts in English for translation: N/A

Approximate acceptance rate: Varies

Review period: 6 weeks   **Lead time to publication after acceptance:** 6 weeks

Circulation: 28,000   **Frequency of publication:**   Monthly

Sponsoring organization:

Submission information:

Manuscript length: 2,000-2,500 words (8-12 pages, typed double-spaced)

Number of copies: 1   **Submission fee:** None

Style: Articles should be typed double-spaced. Paragraphs should be indented. Footnotes should be used sparingly, but when used should contain complete citations and should be listed at the end of the article. Contact the editor for more information concerning manuscript publication.

Manuscript editor: Kathleen Crighton, Associate Publisher/Editor

Pension World, 6255 Barfield Rd.

Atlanta, GA 30328, U. S. A.

Publisher: Communication Channels, Inc.

Same as above

Planning Review

Primary readership: Businessmen

Review process: 3 external blind reviewers

Invited articles: 61-80%

**Percentage of articles
on accounting topics:**   5

Approximate percentage of accounting-related articles devoted to: Not specified

Financial Accounting:	**Managerial:**
Computers/Systems:	**Tax:**
Auditing:	**Education:**
Professional:	

Approximate percentage of accounting-related articles characterized as primarily: Not specified

Empirical:	**Experimental:**
Analytical:	**Descriptive:**

**Language(s) in which
articles are published:**   English

Accepts manuscripts in English for translation: N/A

Approximate acceptance rate: 10%

Review period: 6 weeks   **Lead time to publication after acceptance:** 6 months

Circulation: 10,000   **Frequency of publication:**   Bi-monthly

Sponsoring organization: The Planning Forum

Submission information:

Manuscript length: 3,000 words or fewer

Number of copies: 4   **Submission fee:** None

Style: Manuscripts should be submitted typed double-spaced on 8 1/2 x 11" paper. References should be limited to those essential to the subject. Illustrative material (e.g., tables, charts, and figures) should be inserted within the text where applicable. Contact the editor for more information concerning manuscript publication.

Manuscript editor: Robert Randall
Planning Review, 320 Riverside Dr.
New York, NY 10025, U. S. A.

Publisher: The Planning Forum
5500 College Corner Pike, P.O. Box 70
Oxford, OH 45056, U. S. A.

Practical Lawyer, The

Primary readership: Lawyers

Review process: Not specified

Invited articles: Not specified

Percentage of articles on accounting topics:
Approximate percentage of accounting-related articles devoted to: Not specified

Financial Accounting: Managerial:
Computers/Systems: Tax:
Auditing: Education:
Professional:

Approximate percentage of accounting-related articles characterized as primarily: Not specified

Empirical: Experimental:
Analytical: Descriptive:

Language(s) in which articles are published: English

Accepts manuscripts in English for translation: N/A

Approximate acceptance rate: 50%

Review period: 6 weeks   **Lead time to publication after acceptance:** 3 months

Circulation: Not specified   **Frequency of publication:** 8 times per year

Sponsoring organization: American Law Institute - American Bar Association

Submission information:
Manuscript length: 15-30 double-spaced typed pages
Number of copies: 3   **Submission fee:** None
Style: Typed double-spaced

Manuscript editor:
Mark T. Carroll
The Practical Lawyer, ALI-ABA, 4025 Chestnut St.
Philadelphia, PA 19104, U. S. A.

Publisher: ALI-ABA
Same as above

Production and Inventory Management

Primary readership: Academicians, management consultants, APICS members

Review process: Not specified

Invited articles: Not specified

**Percentage of articles
on accounting topics:**

Approximate percentage of accounting-related articles devoted to: Not specified

Financial Accounting:	**Managerial:**
Computers/Systems:	**Tax:**
Auditing:	**Education:**
Professional:	

Approximate percentage of accounting-related articles characterized as primarily: Not specified

Empirical:	**Experimental:**
Analytical:	**Descriptive:**

**Language(s) in which
articles are published:**   English

Accepts manuscripts in English for translation: N/A

Approximate acceptance rate: 40%

Review period: 6 months   **Lead time to publication after acceptance:** 6 months

Circulation: 60,000   **Frequency of publication:** Quarterly

Sponsoring organization: American Production and Inventory Control Society

Submission information:

Manuscript length: 15 pages

Number of copies: Not specified   **Submission fee:** None

Style: Available upon request.

**Manuscript
editor:** Robert E. D. Woolsey

American Production & Inventory Management Control Society, Inc., 500 W. Annandale Rd.
Falls Church, VA 22046, U. S. A.

Publisher: Same as above

Psychometrika

Primary readership: Academicians, employees of agencies for psychological and educational testing

Review process: 3 external blind reviewers

Invited articles: 1-20%

Percentage of articles on accounting topics: 1

Approximate percentage of accounting-related articles devoted to:

Financial Accounting:	**Managerial:**	
Computers/Systems:	**Tax:**	
Auditing:	**Education:**	
Professional:	**Math.models:**	100

Approximate percentage of accounting-related articles characterized as primarily: Not specified

Empirical:	**Experimental:**
Analytical:	**Descriptive:**

Language(s) in which articles are published: English

Accepts manuscripts in English for translation: N/A

Approximate acceptance rate: 32%

Review period: 3-7 months   **Lead time to publication after acceptance:** 5 months

Circulation: 2,200   **Frequency of publication:** Quarterly

Sponsoring organization: Psychometric Society

Submission information:

Manuscript length: 5-30 typed double-spaced pages

Number of copies: 4   **Submission fee:** $30

Style: Manuscripts should be typed double-spaced throughout, including title page, abstract, key words, text, quotations, references, and footnotes. Also allow for wide margins. Follow the style recommended in the Publication Manual of the American Psychological Association. Contact the editor for more information concerning manuscript publication.

Manuscript editor:
Ivo W. Molenaar

Psychometrika, Vakgroen, Sem FSW, Oude Boceringestraat 23

9712 G C Groningen, Netherlands

Publisher: Same as above

Public Budgeting & Finance

Primary readership: Academicians, accounting (or tax) practitioners, government financial and budget practitioners

Review process: 2 external blind reviewers

Invited articles: 1-20%

Percentage of articles on accounting topics: 20

Approximate percentage of accounting-related articles devoted to:

Financial Accounting:	10	**Managerial:**	
Computers/Systems:		**Tax:**	20
Auditing:	70	**Education:**	
Professional:			

Approximate percentage of accounting-related articles characterized as primarily: Not specified

Empirical:	**Experimental:**
Analytical:	**Descriptive:**

Language(s) in which articles are published: English

Accepts manuscripts in English for translation: N/A

Approximate acceptance rate: 35%

Review period: 2 months **Lead time to publication after acceptance:** 3-6 months

Circulation: 4,500 **Frequency of publication:** Quarterly

Sponsoring organization: Public Financial Publications

Submission information:

Manuscript length: 25 pages or fewer, typed double-spaced

Number of copies: 3 **Submission fee:** None

Style: All material should be typed double-spaced with ample margins. Footnotes should be limited to essential entries and should be typed double-spaced on a separate page and placed following the last page of text. Authors should be guided by the Chicago Manual of Style for endnotes, abstract, etc.

Manuscript editor:

Professor Jesse Burkhead (1 copy)

Maxwell School, Syracuse University

Syracuse, NY 13244-1090, U. S. A.

Publisher: AND: Professor James Edwin Kee (2 copies)

Department of Public Administration, 302 Montoe Hall, George Washington University

Washington, DC 20052, U. S. A.

Quarterly Journal of Business and Economics

Primary readership: Academicians

Review process: Not specified

Invited articles: Not specified

**Percentage of articles
on accounting topics:**
Approximate percentage of accounting-related articles devoted to: Not specified

Financial Accounting:	**Managerial:**
Computers/Systems:	**Tax:**
Auditing:	**Education:**
Professional:	

Approximate percentage of accounting-related articles characterized as primarily: Not specified

Empirical:	**Experimental:**
Analytical:	**Descriptive:**

**Language(s) in which
articles are published:**   English

Accepts manuscripts in English for translation: N/A

Approximate acceptance rate: 25 to 30%

Review period: 3 - 6 months   **Lead time to publication after acceptance:** 6 - 9 months

Circulation: 1,000   **Frequency of publication:**   Quarterly

Sponsoring organization: University of Nebraska

Submission information:

Manuscript length: 4,000 - 8,000 words

Number of copies: 3   **Submission fee:** $20

Style: See journal.

**Manuscript
editor:**   George M. McCabe

University of Nebraska, College of Business Administration, #200

Lincoln, NB 68588, U. S. A.

Publisher: American Association for Budget and Program Analysis

Transaction Periodicals Consortium, Rutgers University

New Brunswick, NJ 08903, U. S. A.

Rachunkowosc

Primary readership: Not specified

Review process: Not specified

Invited articles: Not specified

**Percentage of articles
on accounting topics:**
Approximate percentage of accounting-related articles devoted to: Not specified

Financial Accounting:	**Managerial:**
Computers/Systems:	**Tax:**
Auditing:	**Education:**
Professional:	

Approximate percentage of accounting-related articles characterized as primarily: Not specified

Empirical:	**Experimental:**
Analytical:	**Descriptive:**

**Language(s) in which
articles are published:**   Polish

Accepts manuscripts in English for translation: Not specified

Approximate acceptance rate: Not specified

Review period: Not specified   **Lead time to publication after acceptance:** Not specified

Circulation: 41,000   **Frequency of publication:**   Not specified

Sponsoring organization: Not specified

Submission information:
Manuscript length: Not specified
Number of copies: Not specified   **Submission fee:** Not specified
Style: Not specified

**Manuscript
editor:**   The Editor
Panstwowe Wydawnictwo Ekonomiczne, Niecala 4a
Warsaw, Poland

Publisher: Ars Polona-Ruch
Krakowskic Przedmicsclez
Warsaw, Poland

Rand Journal of Economics, The

Primary readership: Academicians, businessmen, students

Review process: Not specified

Invited articles: Not specified

**Percentage of articles
on accounting topics:**
Approximate percentage of accounting-related articles devoted to: Not specified

Financial Accounting:	**Managerial:**
Computers/Systems:	**Tax:**
Auditing:	**Education:**
Professional:	

Approximate percentage of accounting-related articles characterized as primarily: Not specified

Empirical:	**Experimental:**
Analytical:	**Descriptive:**

**Language(s) in which
articles are published:**   English

Accepts manuscripts in English for translation: N/A

Approximate acceptance rate: 12%

Review period: 4 - 6 weeks   **Lead time to publication after acceptance:** 6 months

Circulation: 22,000   **Frequency of publication:**   Quarterly

Sponsoring organization: None

Submission information:

Manuscript length: 15 - 30 pages

Number of copies: 3   **Submission fee:** $30

Style: References, footnotes, figures, and tables on separate sheets. More information available upon request.

**Manuscript
editor:**   Dr. Stephen W. Salant
The Rand Journal of Economics, P.O. Box 2138
Santa Monica, CA 90406-2138, U. S. A.

Publisher: Rand Corporation
2100 M St., N. W.,
Washington, DC 20037, U. S. A.

Real Estate Accounting & Taxation

Primary readership: Real estate accountants, lawyers, developers, businessmen

Review process: Editorial only

Invited articles: Not specified

**Percentage of articles
on accounting topics:** 80

Approximate percentage of accounting-related articles devoted to: Not specified

Financial Accounting: **Managerial:**
Computers/Systems: **Tax:**
Auditing: **Education:**
Professional:

Approximate percentage of accounting-related articles characterized as primarily: Should be "how-to" articles

Empirical: **Experimental:**
Analytical: **Descriptive:**

**Language(s) in which
articles are published:** English

Accepts manuscripts in English for translation: N/A

Approximate acceptance rate: Varies

Review period: Varies   **Lead time to publication after acceptance:** 3 months

Circulation: 2,500   **Frequency of publication:** Quarterly

Sponsoring organization: None

Submission information:
Manuscript length: Varies
Number of copies: 2   **Submission fee:** None
Style: "How-to" articles, not theoretical.

**Manuscript
editor:** Jill Koenigsberg, Accounting Editor
Real Estate Accounting & Taxation, Warren, Gorham & Lamont, Inc., One Penn Plaza, 40th Floor
New York, NY 10119, U. S. A.

Publisher: Warren, Gorham & Lamont, Inc.
210 South St.
Boston, MA 02111, U. S. A.

Real Estate Business

Primary readership: Real estate sales associates, brokers

Review process: 3 external blind reviewers

Invited articles: 21-40%

**Percentage of articles
on accounting topics:**   5

Approximate percentage of accounting-related articles devoted to:

Financial Accounting:	1	**Managerial:**	3
Computers/Systems:	2	**Tax:**	
Auditing:		**Education:**	
Professional:	80	**Other :**	14

Approximate percentage of accounting-related articles characterized as primarily:

Empirical:	**Experimental:**	
Analytical:	**Descriptive:**	100

**Language(s) in which
articles are published:**   English

Accepts manuscripts in English for translation: N/A

Approximate acceptance rate: 70%

Review period: 6 weeks   **Lead time to publication after acceptance:** 3 months

Circulation: 20,000   **Frequency of publication:**   Quarterly

Sponsoring organization: Realtors National Marketing Institute

Submission information:

Manuscript length: 10-30 pages

Number of copies: 4   **Submission fee:** None

Style: All articles should be typed double-spaced on plain 8 1/2 by 11" paper. Footnotes (where needed) should be numbered along with all facts of publication or sources of quotations. Submit charts, graphs, and photographs whenever possible to emphasize and clarify points.

**Manuscript
editor:**   Colleen Redmond

Real Estate Business, 430 N. Michigan Ave. Suite 500

Chicago, IL 60611, U. S. A.

Publisher: Same as above

Research in Accounting Regulation

Primary readership: Academicians, accounting practitioners, regulators

Review process: 2 external blind reviewers

Invited articles: 1-20%

**Percentage of articles
on accounting topics:**   70

Approximate percentage of accounting-related articles devoted to:

Financial Accounting:	**Managerial:**	
Computers/Systems:	**Tax:**	
Auditing:	**Education:**	
Professional:	**Regulation:**	100

Approximate percentage of accounting-related articles characterized as primarily:

Empirical:	10	**Experimental:**	20
Analytical:	30	**Descriptive:**	30
Other:	10		

**Language(s) in which
articles are published:**   English

Accepts manuscripts in English for translation: N/A

Approximate acceptance rate: 50%

Review period: 2 months   **Lead time to publication after acceptance:** 8 months

Circulation: New in 1987   **Frequency of publication:**   Annually

Sponsoring organization:

Submission information:

Manuscript length: 25 pages, double-spaced
Number of copies: 3   **Submission fee:** None
Style: Style requirements should conform to the style used in The Accounting Review.

**Manuscript
editor:**   Gary John Previts

    Department of Accountancy, Weatherhead School of Management, Case Western Reserve University
    Cleveland, OH 44106, U. S. A.

Publisher: JAI Press

    P.O. Box 1678, 36 Sherwood Place
    Greenwich, CT 06836, U. S. A.

Research in Governmental and Nonprofit Accounting

Primary readership: Academicians

Review process: Editorial, 2-3 blind reviews

Invited articles: 21-40%

**Percentage of articles
on accounting topics:**   100

Approximate percentage of accounting-related articles devoted to:

Financial Accounting:	30	**Managerial:**	20
Computers/Systems:		**Tax:**	
Auditing:	20	**Education:**	
Professional:		**Other:**	30

Approximate percentage of accounting-related articles characterized as primarily:

Empirical:	60	**Experimental:**	
Analytical:	40	**Descriptive:**	

**Language(s) in which
articles are published:**   English

Accepts manuscripts in English for translation: N/A

Approximate acceptance rate: 25-30%

Review period: 4-6 weeks   **Lead time to publication after acceptance:** 10-15 months

Circulation: New journal   **Frequency of publication:**   Annually

Sponsoring organization: University of Illinois

Submission information:
Manuscript length: Not specified
Number of copies: 3   **Submission fee:** None
Style: Available upon request.

**Manuscript
editor:**   James L. Chan

Office for Governmental and Accounting Research in Education, University of Illinois,
Chicago, IL 60680-4348, U. S. A.

Publisher: JAI Press
P.O. Box 1678, 36 Sherwood Place
Greenwich, CT 06836, U. S. A.

Review of Business and Economic Research

Primary readership: Academicians

Review process: 2 external blind reviewers

Invited articles: 0%

Percentage of articles on accounting topics: 10

Approximate percentage of accounting-related articles devoted to: Not specified

Financial Accounting: **Managerial:**

Computers/Systems: **Tax:**

Auditing: **Education:**

Professional:

Approximate percentage of accounting-related articles characterized as primarily: Not specified

Empirical: **Experimental:**

Analytical: **Descriptive:**

Language(s) in which articles are published: English

Accepts manuscripts in English for translation: N/A

Approximate acceptance rate: 10%

Review period: 3-6 months   **Lead time to publication after acceptance:** 6 months to 1 year

Circulation: 1,000   **Frequency of publication:** Semiannually

Sponsoring organization: None

Submission information:

Manuscript length: Not exceeding 15 pages

Number of copies: 3   **Submission fee:** $10 (1 year subscription)

Style: Footnotes should be double-spaced and grouped at the end of the article. Tables and references should be typed in a form suitable for camera reproduction and should be single-spaced, with double-spaced between sections of tables and items in the list of references. Any standard, internally consistent style is acceptable.

Manuscript editor: J. P. Simpson

Division of Business and Economic Research, University of New Orleans

New Orleans, LA 70148, U. S. A.

Publisher: Same as above

Review of Taxation of Individuals, The

Primary readership: Accounting (or tax) practitioners,lawyers

Review process: Not specified

Invited articles: Not specified

**Percentage of articles
on accounting topics:**   100

Approximate percentage of accounting-related articles devoted to:

Financial Accounting:	**Managerial:**	
Computers/Systems:	**Tax:**	100
Auditing:	**Education:**	
Professional:		

Approximate percentage of accounting-related articles characterized as primarily: Not specified

Empirical:	**Experimental:**
Analytical:	**Descriptive:**

**Language(s) in which
articles are published:**   English

Accepts manuscripts in English for translation: N/A

Approximate acceptance rate: 50%

Review period: 1 month   **Lead time to publication after acceptance:** 3 - 6 months

Circulation: 3,000   **Frequency of publication:**   Quarterly

Sponsoring organization:

   Submission information:

Manuscript length: 5,000 to 10,000 words
Number of copies: Not specified **Submission fee:** None
Style: Footnotes separate from the manuscript; more information available upon request.

**Manuscript
editor:**   James. S. Halper
210 South St.
Boston, MA   02111, U. S. A.

Publisher: Warren, Gorham & Lamont, Inc.
Same as above

Revision og Regnskabsvesen

Primary readership: Academicians, accounting (or tax) practitioners, businessmen

Review process: Not specified

Invited articles: 41-60%

**Percentage of articles
on accounting topics:** 80

Approximate percentage of accounting-related articles devoted to:

Financial Accounting:	25	**Managerial:**	25
Computers/Systems:		**Tax:**	25
Auditing:	25	**Education:**	
Professional:			

Approximate percentage of accounting-related articles characterized as primarily:

Empirical:	25	**Experimental:**	25
Analytical:	25	**Descriptive:**	25

**Language(s) in which
articles are published:** Danish

Accepts manuscripts in English for translation: Yes

Approximate acceptance rate: 80%

Review period: Not specified   **Lead time to publication after acceptance:** 1 week

Circulation: 6,000   **Frequency of publication:** Monthly

Sponsoring organization: The Association of Chartered Accountants

Submission information:

Manuscript length:
Number of copies: 1   **Submission fee:** None, an honorarium is paid to author.
Style: Not specified

**Manuscript
editor:**
Viggo Gunni Pedersen
Revision og Regnskabvesen, Bredgade 32
1260 Kobenhaven K. Denmark

Publisher: Same as above

Revisjon og Regnskap

Primary readership: Academicians, accounting (or tax) practitioners, businessmen, computer specialists

Review process: Not specified

Invited articles: Not specified

**Percentage of articles
on accounting topics:**

Approximate percentage of accounting-related articles devoted to: Not specified

Financial Accounting:	**Managerial:**
Computers/Systems:	**Tax:**
Auditing:	**Education:**
Professional:	

Approximate percentage of accounting-related articles characterized as primarily: Not specified

Empirical:	**Experimental:**
Analytical:	**Descriptive:**

**Language(s) in which
articles are published:**   Norwegian

Accepts manuscripts in English for translation: Not specified

Approximate acceptance rate: Not specified

Review period: Not specified   **Lead time to publication after acceptance:** Not specified

Circulation: Not specified   **Frequency of publication:**   8 issues per year

Sponsoring organization: Norges Statsautoriserte Revisorers Forening

     Submission information:

Manuscript length: Not specified

Number of copies: Not specified   **Submission fee:** Not specified

Style: Not specified

**Manuscript
editor:**   Hans Cordt-Hansen

     Revisjon og Regnskap, Norges Statsautoriserte Revisorers Forening, Uranienborg Terrassee 9
     0351 Oslo 3, Norway

Publisher: Same as above

Revisorbladet

Primary readership: Not specified

Review process: Not specified

Invited articles: Not specified

**Percentage of articles
on accounting topics:**
Approximate percentage of accounting-related articles devoted to: Not specified

Financial Accounting:	**Managerial:**
Computers/Systems:	**Tax:**
Auditing:	**Education:**
Professional:	

Approximate percentage of accounting-related articles characterized as primarily: Not specified

Empirical:	**Experimental:**
Analytical:	**Descriptive:**

**Language(s) in which
articles are published:**   Danish

Accepts manuscripts in English for translation: Not specified

Approximate acceptance rate: Not specified

Review period: Not specified   **Lead time to publication after acceptance:** Not specified

Circulation: 4,000   **Frequency of publication:**   Not specified

Sponsoring organization: Not specified

Submission information:
Manuscript length: Not specified
Number of copies: Not specified **Submission fee:** Not specified
Style: Not specified

**Manuscript
editor:**   Henning Moelgaard
    Roerningen af Registrerede Revisorer, Flintholm Alle 57
    2000 Koebenhaun F, Denmark

Publisher: Same as above

Revue du Tresor, La

Primary readership: Practitioners

Review process: Editorial

Invited articles: 41-60%

**Percentage of articles
on accounting topics:**   50

Approximate percentage of accounting-related articles devoted to:

Financial Accounting: 100   **Managerial:**

Computers/Systems: **Tax:**

Auditing: **Education:**

Professional:

Approximate percentage of accounting-related articles characterized as primarily: Not specified

Empirical: **Experimental:**

Analytical: **Descriptive:**

**Language(s) in which
articles are published:**   French

Accepts manuscripts in English for translation: No

Approximate acceptance rate: Not specified

Review period: Not specified   **Lead time to publication after acceptance:** 3 months

Circulation: Not specified   **Frequency of publication:**   Monthly

Sponsoring organization: Not specified

   Submission information:

Manuscript length: 4 pages

Number of copies: 2   **Submission fee:** none

Style: Not specified

**Manuscript
editor:**   Sarl de Editors du Tresor

   LaRevue du Tresor, 26, rue de Lille

   75007 - Paris, France

Publisher: Same as above

Revue Francaise de Comptabilite

Primary readership: Not specified

Review process: Not specified

Invited articles: Not specified

**Percentage of articles
on accounting topics:**

Approximate percentage of accounting-related articles devoted to: Not specified

Financial Accounting:	**Managerial:**	
Computers/Systems:	**Tax:**	
Auditing:	**Education:**	
Professional:		

Approximate percentage of accounting-related articles characterized as primarily: Not specified

Empirical:	**Experimental:**
Analytical:	**Descriptive:**

**Language(s) in which
articles are published:** French (summaries in English)

Accepts manuscripts in English for translation: Not specified

Approximate acceptance rate: Not specified

Review period: Not specified   **Lead time to publication after acceptance:** Not specified

Circulation: 24,000   **Frequency of publication:** Not specified

Sponsoring organization: Ordre des Experts Comptables et des Comptables Agrees Conseil Superieur

Submission information:

Manuscript length: Not specified
Number of copies: Not specified   **Submission fee:** Not specified
Style: Not specified

**Manuscript
editor:** Philippe Dantou

Ordre des Experts Comptables et des Comptables Agrees Conseil Superieur, 109 bd. Malesherbes
75008 Paris, France

Publisher: Same as above

Roeh Hacheshbon

Primary readership: Not specified

Review process: Not specified

Invited articles: Not specified

**Percentage of articles
on accounting topics:**

Approximate percentage of accounting-related articles devoted to: Not specified

Financial Accounting:	**Managerial:**
Computers/Systems:	**Tax:**
Auditing:	**Education:**
Professional:	

Approximate percentage of accounting-related articles characterized as primarily: Not specified

Empirical:	**Experimental:**
Analytical:	**Descriptive:**

**Language(s) in which
articles are published:**   Hebrew

Accepts manuscripts in English for translation: Not specified

Approximate acceptance rate: Not specified

Review period: Not specified   **Lead time to publication after acceptance:** Not specified

Circulation: 2,700   **Frequency of publication:** Not specified

Sponsoring organization: Institute of Certified Public Accountants in Israel

      Submission information:

Manuscript length: Not specified

Number of copies: Not specified   **Submission fee:** Not specified

Style: Not specified

**Manuscript
editor:**   Isaac L. Halifi

    Institute of Certified Public Accountants in Israel, Box 29281, 1 Montefiore St.

    Tel Aviv, Israel

Publisher: Same as above

SAM Advanced Management Journal

Primary readership: Academicians, businessmen

Review process: 15 external blind reviewers

Invited articles: 1-20%

**Percentage of articles
on accounting topics:**   10

Approximate percentage of accounting-related articles devoted to: Not specified

Financial Accounting:	**Managerial:**
Computers/Systems:	**Tax:**
Auditing:	**Education:**
Professional:	

Approximate percentage of accounting-related articles characterized as primarily: Not specified

Empirical:	**Experimental:**
Analytical:	**Descriptive:**

**Language(s) in which
articles are published:**   English

Accepts manuscripts in English for translation: N/A

Approximate acceptance rate: 30%

Review period: Not specified   **Lead time to publication after acceptance:** 3 months

Circulation: 10,000   **Frequency of publication:**   Quarterly

Sponsoring organization: Society for Advancement of Management

Submission information:

Manuscript length: 10-15 pages

Number of copies: 1   **Submission fee:** None

Style: Articles should be typed double-spaced with 1" margins all around. Graphs and illustrations should be kept to a minimum and included only when deemed essential. Full references should be made when other studies are cited.

**Manuscript
editor:**   Dr. Moustafa H. Abdelsamad

SAM Advanced Management Journal, Virginia Commonwealth University, 1054 Floyd Ave.
Richmond, VA 23284, U. S. A.

Publisher: Society for Advancement of Management
2113 Victory Parkway
Cincinnati, OH 45206, U. S. A.

Schweizer Treuhaender, Der/ Expert-Comptable Suisse, L'

Primary readership: Academicians, accounting (or tax) practitioners, businessmen, computer specalists, auditors fiduciary consultants

Review process: Editorial only

Invited articles: 81-99%

Percentage of articles on accounting topics: 25

Approximate percentage of accounting-related articles devoted to: Distributed evenly

Financial Accounting: **Managerial:**

Computers/Systems: **Tax:**

Auditing: **Education:**

Professional:

Approximate percentage of accounting-related articles characterized as primarily: Distributed evenly

Empirical: **Experimental:**

Analytical: **Descriptive:**

Language(s) in which articles are published: German, French, English (on occasion)

Accepts manuscripts in English for translation: Subject to negotiation

Approximate acceptance rate: N/A

Review period: N/A **Lead time to publication after acceptance:** 2 to 4 months, subject to prior agreement

Circulation: 7,500 **Frequency of publication:** 11 issues per year

Sponsoring organization: Schweizer Treuhand und Revisionskammer

Submission information:

Manuscript length: 3 to 6 pages

Number of copies: 2 **Submission fee:** Subject to negotiation, usually none

Style: Manuscript should be typed and properly legible, with a lead of approximately 5 lines

Manuscript editor:
Dr. Margit Pfaffli-Huber
Am Limmatquai 120
8000 Zuerich, Switzerland

Publisher: Schweizer Treuhand und Revisionskammer
Same as above

Simulation and Games

Primary readership: Academicians

Review process: 2-3 external blind reviewers

Invited articles: 1-20%

**Percentage of articles
on accounting topics:** 5

Approximate percentage of accounting-related articles devoted to: Not specified

Financial Accounting:	**Managerial:**
Computers/Systems:	**Tax:**
Auditing:	**Education:**
Professional:	

Approximate percentage of accounting-related articles characterized as primarily: Not specified

Empirical:	**Experimental:**
Analytical:	**Descriptive:**

**Language(s) in which
articles are published:**   English

Accepts manuscripts in English for translation: N/A

Approximate acceptance rate: 25%

Review period: 3 months   **Lead time to publication after acceptance:** 6-9 months

Circulation: 3,000   **Frequency of publication:**   Quarterly

Sponsoring organization: ABSEL, NASAGA, and ISAGA

Submission information:

Manuscript length: 15-30 manuscript pages

Number of copies: 3   **Submission fee:** None

Style: Manuscripts should be typed double-spaced with footnotes, references, tables, charts, and as abstract of up to 100 words, on separate pages. Footnotes and bibliographic citations should follow the current journal style; a style sheet may be obtained from the Editor.

**Manuscript
editor:**   Dr. Cathy Greenblat
Simulation and Games, Sociology Dept., Rutgers University
New Brunswick, NJ 08903, U. S. A.

Publisher: Sage Publications, Inc.
2111 West Hillcrest Drive
Newbury Park, CA 91320, U. S. A.

Singapore Accountant

Primary readership: Academicians, accounting (or tax) practitioners, businessmen, computer specialists

Review process: Editorial only

Invited articles: 1-20%

**Percentage of articles
on accounting topics:**   90

Approximate percentage of accounting-related articles devoted to: Not specified

Financial Accounting:	**Managerial:**
Computers/Systems:	**Tax:**
Auditing:	**Education:**
Professional:	

Approximate percentage of accounting-related articles characterized as primarily: Not specified

Empirical:	**Experimental:**
Analytical:	**Descriptive:**

**Language(s) in which
articles are published:**   English

Accepts manuscripts in English for translation: N/A

Approximate acceptance rate: 50%

Review period: 2 months   **Lead time to publication after acceptance:** 3-6 months

Circulation: 10,000   **Frequency of publication:**   Monthly

Sponsoring organization: Singapore Society of Accountants

Submission information:

Manuscript length: Not specified

Number of copies: 2   **Submission fee:** None

Style: References (in alphabetical order) listed at end of paper and should include only those cited in paper; include abstract of not more than 100 words. Set within quotes all quotations of passages in their original wording, spelling, and punctuation where they are fewer than three lines. If extracts exceed three lines, the passage should be in a separate indented paragraph without quotation marks.

**Manuscript
editor:**   The Editorial Board

Singapore Accountant, Singapore Society of Accountants, 15 Beach Road #05-03, Beach Centre

Singapore 0718, Singapore

Publisher: Singapore Publishers Pte. Ltd.

25 First Lok Yang Rd., P.O. Box 261, Jurong Town

Singapore 1961, Singapore

Sloan Management Review

Primary readership: Academicians, businessmen

Review process: 2 external blind reviewers

Invited articles: 1-20%

**Percentage of articles
on accounting topics:** 1

Approximate percentage of accounting-related articles devoted to: Not specified

Financial Accounting:	**Managerial:**
Computers/Systems:	**Tax:**
Auditing:	**Education:**
Professional:	

Approximate percentage of accounting-related articles characterized as primarily: Not specified

Empirical:	**Experimental:**
Analytical:	**Descriptive:**

**Language(s) in which
articles are published:** English

Accepts manuscripts in English for translation: N/A

Approximate acceptance rate: 15%

Review period: 6-8 weeks   **Lead time to publication after acceptance:** 3 months

Circulation: 20,000   **Frequency of publication:** Quarterly

Sponsoring organization: Massachusetts Institute of Technology

Submission information:

Manuscript length: 15-25 typewritten pages, including references.

Number of copies: 3   **Submission fee:** None

Style: Manuscripts should be typed double-spaced. Figures and tables should be numbered and include English captions, one figure or table per sheet of paper. Footnotes, containing all bibliographic information, should be consecutively numbered and presented in a single list at the end of the paper. References should be prepared according to the Chicago Manual of Style format.

**Manuscript
editor:** Rosemary Brutico,Managing Editor

Alfred P. Sloan School of Management, Massachusetts Institute of Technology, 50 Memorial Dr.

Cambridge, MA 02139, U. S. A.

Publisher: Same as above

Social Accounting Monitor

Primary readership: Not specified

Review process: Not specified

Invited articles: Not specified

**Percentage of articles
on accounting topics:**
Approximate percentage of accounting-related articles devoted to: Not specified

Financial Accounting: **Managerial:**

Computers/Systems: **Tax:**

Auditing: **Education:**

Professional:

Approximate percentage of accounting-related articles characterized as primarily: Not specified

Empirical: **Experimental:**

Analytical: **Descriptive:**

**Language(s) in which
articles are published:**   Not specified

Accepts manuscripts in English for translation: Not specified

Approximate acceptance rate: Not specified

Review period: Not specified   **Lead time to publication after acceptance:** Not specified

Circulation: 600   **Frequency of publication:**   Not specified

Sponsoring organization: Not specified

Submission information:

Manuscript length: Not specified
Number of copies: Not specified   **Submission fee:**   Not specified
Style: Not specified

**Manuscript
editor:**   James Guthrie and M. R. Mathews
University of New South Wales, School of Accountancy
Kensington, N. S. W. 2033, Australia

Publisher: Same as above

South African Chartered Accountant

Primary readership: Not specified

Review process: Not specified

Invited articles: Not specified

Percentage of articles on accounting topics:
Approximate percentage of accounting-related articles devoted to: Not specified

Financial Accounting:	**Managerial:**
Computers/Systems:	**Tax:**
Auditing:	**Education:**
Professional:	

Approximate percentage of accounting-related articles characterized as primarily: Not specified

Empirical:	**Experimental:**
Analytical:	**Descriptive:**

Language(s) in which articles are published: Afrikaans , English

Accepts manuscripts in English for translation: Yes

Approximate acceptance rate: Not specified

Review period: Not specified **Lead time to publication after acceptance:** Not specified

Circulation: 15,500 **Frequency of publication:** Not specified

Sponsoring organization: South African Institute of Chartered Accountants

Submission information:
Manuscript length: Not specified
Number of copies: Not specified **Submission fee:** Not specified
Style: Not specified

Manuscript editor: Derrick Robson
South African Institute of Chartered Accountants, Box 964
Johannesburg 2000, South Africa

Publisher: Same as above

Southwest Journal of Business and Economics

Primary readership: Academicians, businessmen

Review process: 2 external blind reviewers

Invited articles: 1-20%

Percentage of articles on accounting topics: 10

Approximate percentage of accounting-related articles devoted to:

Financial Accounting:	33	**Managerial:**	33
Computers/Systems:		**Tax:**	34
Auditing:		**Education:**	
Professional:			

Approximate percentage of accounting-related articles characterized as primarily:

Empirical:	25	**Experimental:**	30
Analytical:	30	**Descriptive:**	15

Language(s) in which articles are published: English

Accepts manuscripts in English for translation: N/A

Approximate acceptance rate: 10%

Review period: 65 days   **Lead time to publication after acceptance:** 1 year

Circulation: 2,000   **Frequency of publication:** Quarterly

Sponsoring organization:

Submission information:

Manuscript length: 3,000-3,500 words

Number of copies: 3   **Submission fee:** None

Style: Copies should be typed double-spaced, 25 lines per page on standard size paper. An alphabetical (last name first) numbered list of references cited in the text should be included on a separate page at the end of the article. Tables, graphs, etc. should only be used if they contribute significantly to the article and increase its readability. See publication for more information.

Manuscript editor:

Glenn L. Palmore, Director

Bureau of Business & Economic Research, University of Texas at El Paso

El Paso, TX 79968-0541, U. S. A.

Publisher: Same as above

Sovremeno Pretprijatie

Primary readership: Not specified

Review process: Not specified

Invited articles: Not specified

**Percentage of articles
on accounting topics:**
Approximate percentage of accounting-related articles devoted to: Not specified

Financial Accounting:	**Managerial:**
Computers/Systems:	**Tax:**
Auditing:	**Education:**
Professional:	

Approximate percentage of accounting-related articles characterized as primarily: Not specified

Empirical:	**Experimental:**
Analytical:	**Descriptive:**

**Language(s) in which
articles are published:**   Macedonian (Cyrillic alphabet)

Accepts manuscripts in English for translation: Not specified

Approximate acceptance rate: Not specified

Review period: Not specified   **Lead time to publication after acceptance:** Not specified

Circulation: 1,000   **Frequency of publication:**   Not specified

Sponsoring organization: Not specified

Submission information:
Manuscript length: Not specified
Number of copies: Not specified   **Submission fee:** Not specified
Style: Not specified

**Manuscript
editor:**   Boris Stojmenov
Zdruzenie na Smetkovodsveno-Finansiskite Rabotnici na Makedonija, Box 267
Skopje, Yugoslavia

Publisher: Same as above

St. John's Law Review

Primary readership: Academicians, businessmen, legal practitioners

Review process: Editorial only

Invited articles: 21-40%

**Percentage of articles
on accounting topics:**
Approximate percentage of accounting-related articles devoted to: Varies

Financial Accounting: **Managerial:**

Computers/Systems: **Tax:**

Auditing: **Education:**

Professional:

Approximate percentage of accounting-related articles characterized as primarily: Not specified

Empirical: **Experimental:**

Analytical: **Descriptive:**

**Language(s) in which
articles are published:**   English

Accepts manuscripts in English for translation: N/A

Approximate acceptance rate: 5

Review period: 2-3 weeks   **Lead time to publication after acceptance:** 6 months

Circulation: Not specified   **Frequency of publication:**   Quarterly

Sponsoring organization: St. John's University

  Submission information:
Manuscript length: Varies
Number of copies: 1   **Submission fee:** None
Style: Not specified

**Manuscript
editor:**   Lawrence Pasini
St. John's Law Review, Fromkes Hall, Grand Central & Utopia Pkwys
Jamaica, NY 11439, U. S. A.

Publisher: Same as above

Szamvitel Es Ugyviteltechnika

Primary readership: Not specified

Review process: Not specified

Invited articles: Not specified

**Percentage of articles
on accounting topics:**
Approximate percentage of accounting-related articles devoted to: Not specified

Financial Accounting: **Managerial:**
Computers/Systems: **Tax:**
Auditing: **Education:**
Professional:

Approximate percentage of accounting-related articles characterized as primarily: Not specified

Empirical: **Experimental:**
Analytical: **Descriptive:**

**Language(s) in which
articles are published:**   Hungarian (summaries in English, French, German, and Russian)

Accepts manuscripts in English for translation: Not specified

Approximate acceptance rate: Not specified

Review period: Not specified   **Lead time to publication after acceptance:**   Not specified

Circulation: Not specified   **Frequency of publication:**   Not specified

Sponsoring organization: Not specified

   Submission information:
Manuscript length: Not specified
Number of copies: Not specified   **Submission fee:**   Not specified
Style: Not specified

**Manuscript
editor:**
      Dr. Rezso Scholtz
      Lapkiado Vallalat, Lenin korut 9-11
      1073 Budapest 7, Hungary

Publisher: Same as above

Tax Adviser, The

Primary readership: Accounting (or tax) practitioners

Review process: 1 external blind reviewer (per manuscript)

Invited articles: 1-20%

**Percentage of articles
on accounting topics:**   100

Approximate percentage of accounting-related articles devoted to:

Financial Accounting:	**Managerial:**
Computers/Systems:	**Tax:** 100
Auditing:	**Education:**
Professional:	

Approximate percentage of accounting-related articles characterized as primarily:

Empirical:	**Experimental:**
Analytical: 100	**Descriptive:**

**Language(s) in which
articles are published:**   English

Accepts manuscripts in English for translation: N/A

Approximate acceptance rate: 50%

Review period: 4 weeks   **Lead time to publication after acceptance:** 6-8 months

Circulation: 26,000   **Frequency of publication:**   Monthly

Sponsoring organization: AICPA

Submission information:

Manuscript length: Features: 15 page minimum plus footnotes; Tax Clinic: 5-6 pages, double-spaced

Number of copies: 2   **Submission fee:** None

Style: All articles should be typed on one side of 8 1/2 by 11" white paper, double-spaced, with a left-hand margin of 2 inches. Type all footnotes double-spaced and appropriately numbered on the last pages of the manuscript. Citations should be confined to footnotes. Contact the editor for more information concerning manuscript publication.

**Manuscript
editor:**   Debra Weingarten

The Tax Adviser, 1211 Ave. of the Americas

New York, NY 10036, U. S. A.

Publisher: Same as above

Tax Executive, The

Primary readership: Accounting (or tax) practitioners, lawyers

Review process: Not specified

Invited articles: Not specified

**Percentage of articles
on accounting topics:** 100

Approximate percentage of accounting-related articles devoted to:

Financial Accounting:	**Managerial:**	
Computers/Systems:	**Tax:**	100
Auditing:	**Education:**	
Professional:		

Approximate percentage of accounting-related articles characterized as primarily: Not specified

Empirical:	**Experimental:**
Analytical:	**Descriptive:**

**Language(s) in which
articles are published:** English

Accepts manuscripts in English for translation:

Approximate acceptance rate: 50%

Review period: 2 months   **Lead time to publication after acceptance:** 3 - 9 months

Circulation: 4,500   **Frequency of publication:** Quarterly

Sponsoring organization: None

Submission information:

Manuscript length: 3,000 - 10,000 words
Number of copies: Not specified **Submission fee:** None
Style: Not specified

**Manuscript
editor:** Timothy J. McCormally

Tax Executives Institute, 1300 N. 17th St., Suite 1300
Arlington, Va 22209, U. S. A.

Publisher: Same as above

Tax Law Review

Primary readership: Academicians, lawyers, accounting (or tax) practitioners

Review process: Not specified

Invited articles: Not specified

**Percentage of articles
on accounting topics:**   100

Approximate percentage of accounting-related articles devoted to:

Financial Accounting:	**Managerial:**
Computers/Systems:	**Tax:** 100
Auditing:	**Education:**
Professional:	

Approximate percentage of accounting-related articles characterized as primarily: Not specified

Empirical:	**Experimental:**
Analytical:	**Descriptive:**

**Language(s) in which
articles are published:**   English

Accepts manuscripts in English for translation: N/A

Approximate acceptance rate: Not specified

Review period: 1 to 2 months   **Lead time to publication after acceptance:** 3 - 6 months

Circulation: 5,000   **Frequency of publication:**   Quarterly

Sponsoring organization: None

Submission information:

Manuscript length: 10,000 - 20,000 words

Number of copies: Not specified   **Submission fee:** None

Style: Footnotes should be separate from the manuscript. More information available upon request.

**Manuscript
editor:**   John P. Steines
Tax Law Review, 210 South St.
Boston, MA 02111, U. S. A.

Publisher: Warren, Gorham & Lamont, Inc.
Same as above

Tax Lawyer, The

Primary readership: Accounting (or tax) practitioners, tax lawyers

Review process: Editorial only

Invited articles: 1-20%

**Percentage of articles
on accounting topics:**   50

Approximate percentage of accounting-related articles devoted to: Not specified

Financial Accounting:	**Managerial:**
Computers/Systems:	**Tax:**
Auditing:	**Education:**
Professional:	

Approximate percentage of accounting-related articles characterized as primarily: Not specified

Empirical:	**Experimental:**
Analytical:	**Descriptive:**

**Language(s) in which
articles are published:**   English

Accepts manuscripts in English for translation: N/A

Approximate acceptance rate: Not specified

Review period: 4 weeks   **Lead time to publication after acceptance:** 2-6 months

Circulation: 30,000   **Frequency of publication:**   Quarterly

Sponsoring organization: American Bar Association

Submission information:

Manuscript length: 50 manuscript pages

Number of copies: 1   **Submission fee:** None

Style: Not specified

**Manuscript
editor:**
George Howell III
The Tax Lawyer, Hunter & Williams, P.O. Box 1535
Richmond, VA 23212, U. S. A.

Publisher: American Bar Association - Taxation Section
1800 M St, N. W., 2nd Floor Lobby
Washington, DC 20036, U. S. A.

Tax Management International Journal

Primary readership: Not specified

Review process: Not specified

Invited articles: Not specified

**Percentage of articles
on accounting topics:**
Approximate percentage of accounting-related articles devoted to:

Financial Accounting:	**Managerial:**	
Computers/Systems:	**Tax:**	100
Auditing:	**Education:**	
Professional:		

Approximate percentage of accounting-related articles characterized as primarily: Not specified

Empirical:	**Experimental:**
Analytical:	**Descriptive:**

**Language(s) in which
articles are published:**   English

Accepts manuscripts in English for translation: N/A

Approximate acceptance rate: 85%

Review period: 1 month   **Lead time to publication after acceptance:** 6 weeks

Circulation: 5,000   **Frequency of publication:**   Monthly

Sponsoring organization: None

       Submission information:
Manuscript length: 12 pages
Number of copies: Not specified   **Submission fee:**   Not specified
Style: Available upon request.

**Manuscript
editor:**
    Managing Editor
    Tax Management, Inc., 1231 25th St. , N. W., Suite 401
    Washington, DC 20037

Publisher: Same as above

Taxation for Accountants

Primary readership: Accounting (or tax) practitioners

Review process: Not specified

Invited articles: Not specified

**Percentage of articles
on accounting topics:**   100

Approximate percentage of accounting-related articles devoted to:

Financial Accounting:	**Managerial:**	
Computers/Systems:	**Tax:**	100
Auditing:	**Education:**	
Professional:		

Approximate percentage of accounting-related articles characterized as primarily: Not specified

Empirical:	**Experimental:**
Analytical:	**Descriptive:**

**Language(s) in which
articles are published:**   English

Accepts manuscripts in English for translation: N/A

Approximate acceptance rate: 50%; 75% for invited articles

Review period: 1 month   **Lead time to publication after acceptance:** 2 months

Circulation: 18,500   **Frequency of publication:**   Monthly

Sponsoring organization:

Submission information:

Manuscript length: 3,500 words

Number of copies: **Submission fee:** None

Style: Available upon request.

**Manuscript
editor:**   Norman A. Kanter
    Taxation for Accountants, 1633 Broadway
    New York, NY 10019, U. S. A.

Publisher: Warren, Gorham & Lamont, Inc.
    210 South St.
    Boston, MA 02111, U. S. A.

Taxes - The Tax Magazine

Primary readership: Accounting (or tax) practitioners, lawyers

Review process: Not specified

Invited articles: Not specified

Percentage of articles on accounting topics:

Approximate percentage of accounting-related articles devoted to:

Financial Accounting:	**Managerial:**
Computers/Systems:	**Tax:** 100
Auditing:	**Education:**
Professional:	

Approximate percentage of accounting-related articles characterized as primarily: Not specified

Empirical:	**Experimental:**
Analytical:	**Descriptive:**

Language(s) in which articles are published: English

Accepts manuscripts in English for translation: N/A

Approximate acceptance rate: 33%

Review period: 2 weeks   **Lead time to publication after acceptance:** 1 - 3 months

Circulation: 12,500   **Frequency of publication:**   Monthly

Sponsoring organization: None

     Submission information:

Manuscript length: 2,500 - 10,000 words

Number of copies: 1   **Submission fee:** None

Style: Not specified

Manuscript editor:

Gene O. Sjostrand

Commerce Clearing House, Inc., 4025 West Peterson Ave.

Chicago, IL 60646, U. S. A.

Publisher: Same as above

Tennessee CPA

Primary readership: Academicians, accounting (or tax) practitioners

Review process: Editorial only

Invited articles: 1-20%

**Percentage of articles
on accounting topics:**   50

Approximate percentage of accounting-related articles devoted to:

Financial Accounting:	5	**Managerial:**	5
Computers/Systems:	5	**Tax:**	15
Auditing:	5	**Education:**	25
Professional:	5	**Other:**	35

Approximate percentage of accounting-related articles characterized as primarily:

Empirical:		**Experimental:**	10
Analytical:	10	**Descriptive:**	80

**Language(s) in which
articles are published:**   English

Accepts manuscripts in English for translation: N/A

Approximate acceptance rate: N/A

Review period: 3 days   **Lead time to publication after acceptance:** 21 days

Circulation: 4,300   **Frequency of publication:**   Monthly

Sponsoring organization: Tennessee Society of CPAs

Submission information:

Manuscript length: 1-2 pages typed manuscript

Number of copies: 1   **Submission fee:** None

Style: AP style preferred

**Manuscript
editor:**   Kirkland T. Byars

Tennessee CPA, 2000 Richard Jones Rd., Suite 105, P.O. Box 150549
Nashville, TN 37215, U. S. A.

Publisher: Same as above

Trusts and Estates

Primary readership: Accounting (or tax) practitioners, attorneys, bank trust officers

Review process: 2-4 external reviewers (authors known)

Invited articles: 61-80%

**Percentage of articles
on accounting topics:** 20

Approximate percentage of accounting-related articles devoted to: Not specified

Financial Accounting: **Managerial:**

Computers/Systems: **Tax:**

Auditing: **Education:**

Professional:

Approximate percentage of accounting-related articles characterized as primarily: Not specified

Empirical: **Experimental:**

Analytical: **Descriptive:**

**Language(s) in which
articles are published:** English

Accepts manuscripts in English for translation: N/A

Approximate acceptance rate: 25%

Review period: 8 weeks   **Lead time to publication after acceptance:** 8 weeks

Circulation: 12,000   **Frequency of publication:** Monthly

Sponsoring organization: None

Submission information:

Manuscript length: 8-35 pages, typed double-spaced

Number of copies: 4   **Submission fee:** None

Style: Articles are to be typed double-spaced on one side of the paper which is either 8 1/2 x 11" or 8 1/2 x 14 " in length. Citations may be included either in footnotes (appear at the end of the article) or in parentheses (must be within the text). If charts or tables accompany the article, they should be referred to as Chart I, Chart II, etc., and appear as a group at the end of the article.

**Manuscript
editor:** Michael S. Klim

Trusts and Estates, 6255 Barfield Rd.

Atlanta, GA 30328, U. S. A.

Publisher: Same as above

Valuation

Primary readership: Businessmen

Review process: 3-4 external reviewers (authors known)

Invited articles: 1-20%

**Percentage of articles
on accounting topics:**
Approximate percentage of accounting-related articles devoted to: Not specified

Financial Accounting: **Managerial:**

Computers/Systems: **Tax:**

Auditing: **Education:**

Professional:

Approximate percentage of accounting-related articles characterized as primarily: Not specified

Empirical: **Experimental:**

Analytical: **Descriptive:**

**Language(s) in which
articles are published:**   English

Accepts manuscripts in English for translation: N/A

Approximate acceptance rate: 50%

Review period: 3 months   **Lead time to publication after acceptance:** 3-6 months

Circulation: 6,000   **Frequency of publication:**   Semiannually

Sponsoring organization: American Society of Appraisers

Submission information:

Manuscript length: Minimum of 2,500 words

Number of copies: 4   **Submission fee:** None

Style: Articles should be typed double-spaced on 8 1/2 x11" paper. Illustrations, when used, should be black and white, with appropriate captions and references noted thereon.

**Manuscript
editor:**   Shirley A. Belz

Valuation, American Society of Appraisers, International Headquarters, P.O. Box 17265
Washington, DC   20041, U. S. A.

Publisher: Same as above

Vikalpa: The Journal for Decision Makers

Primary readership: Academicians, accounting (or tax) practitioners, businessmen, computer specialists, policy makers in government / non-government organizations

Review process: Editorial only, external reviewers (authors known)

Invited articles: 21-40%

Percentage of articles on accounting topics: 20

Approximate percentage of accounting-related articles devoted to:

Financial Accounting:	33	Managerial:	34
Computers/Systems:	33	Tax:	
Auditing:		Education:	
Professional:			

Approximate percentage of accounting-related articles characterized as primarily:

Empirical:	25	Experimental:	20
Analytical:	25	Descriptive:	30

Language(s) in which articles are published: English

Accepts manuscripts in English for translation: N/A

Approximate acceptance rate: 20%

Review period: 3 months   **Lead time to publication after acceptance:** Three months, at most

Circulation: 2,000   **Frequency of publication:** Quarterly

Sponsoring organization: Indian Institute of Management, Ahmedabad

Submission information:

Manuscript length: 6-30 pages

Number of copies: 3   **Submission fee:** None

Style: Useful to managers and non-technical but rigorous.

Manuscript editor: K. R. S. Murthy
Vikalpa, Indian Institute of Management
Ahmedabad 380015, India

Publisher: Same as above

Virginia Accountant Quarterly, The

Primary readership: Academicians, accounting (or tax) practitioners, computer specialists

Review process: 2 external blind reviewers, 2 external reviewers (co-editors make final decision)

Invited articles: 10%

**Percentage of articles
on accounting topics:**   80

Approximate percentage of accounting-related articles devoted to: Not specified

Financial Accounting: **Managerial:**

Computers/Systems: **Tax:**

Auditing: **Education:**

Professional:

Approximate percentage of accounting-related articles characterized as primarily:

Empirical: **Experimental:**

Analytical: **Descriptive:**   100

**Language(s) in which
articles are published:**   English

Accepts manuscripts in English for translation: N/A

Approximate acceptance rate: 35%

Review period: 6 weeks   **Lead time to publication after acceptance:** 4 weeks

Circulation: 4,500   **Frequency of publication:**   Quarterly

Sponsoring organization: Virginia Society of CPAs

Submission information:

Manuscript length: 3,000-4,000 words

Number of copies: 4   **Submission fee:** None

Style: Manuscripts should be typed on plain 8 1/2 x 11" paper, double-spaced, with 1" margins all around. All citations should be placed at the end of the article. Contact the editor for more information concerning manuscript publication.

**Manuscript
editor:**
Sara E. Mullen

The Virginia Accountant Quarterly, VSCPA, P.O. Box 31635

Richmond, VA 23294-1635, U. S. A.

Publisher: Virginia Society of CPAs

4309 Cox Road

Glen Allen, VA 23060, U. S. A.

Washington and Lee Law Review

Primary readership: Academicians, judges, attorneys, law libraries

Review process: Editorial only

Invited articles: 21-40%

**Percentage of articles
on accounting topics:** 20

Approximate percentage of accounting-related articles devoted to:

Financial Accounting:	**Managerial:**	
Computers/Systems:	**Tax:**	75
Auditing:	**Education:**	
Professional:	Legal aspects:	25

Approximate percentage of accounting-related articles characterized as primarily:

Empirical:	**Experimental:**	
Analytical:	100	**Descriptive:**	

**Language(s) in which
articles are published:** English

Accepts manuscripts in English for translation: N/A

Approximate acceptance rate: 10%

Review period: 2 weeks   **Lead time to publication after acceptance:** 2 months

Circulation: 1,400   **Frequency of publication:** Quarterly

Sponsoring organization: Washington and Lee School of Law

Submission information:

Manuscript length: 10-125 pages, typed double-spaced

Number of copies: 1   **Submission fee:** None

Style: Footnotes should conform to "A Uniform System of Citation."

**Manuscript
editor:** Tyler P. Brown, Editor in Chief

Washington and Lee Law Review, Lewis Hall, Washington and Lee University
Lexington, VA 24450, U. S. A.

Publisher: Same as above

West Virginia CPA, The

Primary readership: Accounting (or tax) practitioners, CPAs

Review process: Editorial only

Invited articles: 1-20%

**Percentage of articles
on accounting topics:**   10

Approximate percentage of accounting-related articles devoted to:

Financial Accounting:	**Managerial:**
Computers/Systems:	**Tax:**
Auditing:	**Education:**
Professional:	**Varies:** 100

Approximate percentage of accounting-related articles characterized as primarily:

Empirical:	**Experimental:**
Analytical:	**Descriptive:** 100

**Language(s) in which
articles are published:**   English

Accepts manuscripts in English for translation: N/A

Approximate acceptance rate: 90%

Review period: 2 months   **Lead time to publication after acceptance:** 1 month

Circulation: 3,500   **Frequency of publication:**   Quarterly

Sponsoring organization: West Virginia Society of CPAs

Submission information:
Manuscript length: 1,000 words
Number of copies: 2   **Submission fee:** None
Style: AP style

**Manuscript
editor:**   Mary R. Neale

The West Virginia CPA, West Virginia Society of CPAs, P.O. Box 1142
Charleston, WV 25324, U. S. A.

Publisher: Same as above

Wirtschaftspruefung, Die

Primary readership: Academicians, accounting (or tax) practitioners, businessmen

Review process: Editorial only

Invited articles: 1-20%

Percentage of articles on accounting topics: 90

Approximate percentage of accounting-related articles devoted to:

Financial Accounting:	50	Managerial:	
Computers/Systems:		Tax:	10
Auditing:	30	Education:	5
Professional:	5		

Approximate percentage of accounting-related articles characterized as primarily:

Empirical:	20	Experimental:	10
Analytical:	50	Descriptive:	20

Language(s) in which articles are published: German

Accepts manuscripts in English for translation: No

Approximate acceptance rate: 50%

Review period: 2 weeks   **Lead time to publication after acceptance:** 4 months

Circulation: 10,000   **Frequency of publication:** Bi-weekly

Sponsoring organization: German Institute of Chartered Accountants

Submission information:

Manuscript length: 15 - 30 pages (typed)

Number of copies: 1   **Submission fee:** None, author's honorarium

Style: None

Manuscript editor:
Dr. Hans Havermann
Am Bonneshof 5
D-4000 Duesseldorf 30, West Germany

Publisher: Institut der Wirtschaftspruefer
Same as above

Wirtschaftstreuhaender, Der

Primary readership: Not specified

Review process: Not specified

Invited articles: Not specified

**Percentage of articles
on accounting topics:**
Approximate percentage of accounting-related articles devoted to: Not specified

Financial Accounting:	**Managerial:**
Computers/Systems:	**Tax:**
Auditing:	**Education:**
Professional:	

Approximate percentage of accounting-related articles characterized as primarily: Not specified

Empirical:	**Experimental:**
Analytical:	**Descriptive:**

**Language(s) in which
articles are published:**   German

Accepts manuscripts in English for translation: Not specified

Approximate acceptance rate: Not specified

Review period: Not specified   **Lead time to publication after acceptance:** Not specified

Circulation: 4,100   **Frequency of publication:**   Not specified

Sponsoring organization: Not specified

Submission information:
Manuscript length: Not specified
Number of copies: Not specified   **Submission fee:** Not specified
Style: Not specified

**Manuscript
editor:**   Edeltrude Arthofer, Friedrich Rudy
Florianigasse 21
A-1080 Vienna, Austria

Publisher: Same as above

Wirtschaftswissenschaftliches Studium

Primary readership: Academicians, students

Review process: Editorial, external reviewers

Invited articles: 81-99%

**Percentage of articles
on accounting topics:**   20

Approximate percentage of accounting-related articles devoted to:

Financial Accounting:	10	Managerial:	30
Computers/Systems:	20	Tax:	20
Auditing:	10	Education:	10
Professional:			

Approximate percentage of accounting-related articles characterized as primarily:

Empirical:	20	Experimental:	
Analytical:	50	Descriptive:	30

**Language(s) in which
articles are published:**   German

Accepts manuscripts in English for translation: No

Approximate acceptance rate: 50%

Review period: 2 weeks   **Lead time to publication after acceptance:** 8 months

Circulation: 3,000   **Frequency of publication:**   Monthly

Sponsoring organization: None

Submission information:

Manuscript length: Up to 15 pages

Number of copies: 1   **Submission fee:** None

Style: Not specified

**Manuscript
editor:**   Professor Dr. Erwin Dichtl
Universitat Mannheim, Postfach 2428
6800 Mannheim 1, West Germany

Publisher: Verlage: C. H. Beck - Franz Vahlen
Wilhelm Str. 9
8 Muenchen 40, West Germany

Wisconsin CPA

Primary readership:　　WICPA members

Review process:　　Editorial only

Invited articles:　　Not specified

**Percentage of articles
on accounting topics:**　　15

Approximate percentage of accounting-related articles devoted to:　　Not specified

Financial Accounting:　　　　　　**Managerial:**

Computers/Systems:　　　　　　**Tax:**

Auditing:　　　　　　　　　　**Education:**

Professional:

Approximate percentage of accounting-related articles characterized as primarily: Not specified

Empirical:　　　　　　　　**Experimental:**

Analytical:　　　　　　　　**Descriptive:**

**Language(s) in which
articles are published:**　　English

Accepts manuscripts in English for translation:　　N/A

Approximate acceptance rate:　　Not specified

Review period:　Not specified　　**Lead time to publication after acceptance:**　Not specified

Circulation:　　Not specified　　**Frequency of publication:**　　Semiannually

Sponsoring organization:　　Wisconsin Institute of CPAs

Submission information:

Manuscript length:　　800 words

Number of copies:　　2　　　　**Submission fee:**　None

Style:　　Not specified

**Manuscript
editor:**　　Susan A. Murphy

　　　　　Wisconsin CPA, WICPA, 180 N. Executive Dr.

　　　　　Brookfield, WI　53005, U. S. A.

Publisher:　Same as above

Woman CPA, The

Primary readership: Academicians, accounting (or tax) practitioners, businessmen, computer specialists

Review process: 2 external blind reviewers

Invited articles: 1-20%

Percentage of articles on accounting topics: 70

Approximate percentage of accounting-related articles devoted to:

Financial Accounting:	25	Managerial:	10
Computers/Systems:	15	Tax:	15
Auditing:	15	Education:	10
Professional:	10		

Approximate percentage of accounting-related articles characterized as primarily:

Empirical:	20	Experimental:	10
Analytical:	30	Descriptive:	40

Language(s) in which articles are published: English

Accepts manuscripts in English for translation: N/A

Approximate acceptance rate: 20-25%

Review period: 7 weeks   **Lead time to publication after acceptance:** 3-18 months

Circulation: Not specified   **Frequency of publication:** Quarterly

Sponsoring organization: American Woman's Society of CPAs and the Amercian Society of Women Accountants

Submission information:

Manuscript length: 10-15 double-spaced, typewritten pages

Number of copies: 3   **Submission fee:** None

Style: Each table and figure should be on a separate page and bear an arabic numeral and a title. A reference should appear in the text for each table or figure. The work should be cited by the author's name and year of publication in the body of the text. Textual footnotes should be used for definitions and explanations whose inclusion in the body of the manuscript might disrupt continuity. A list of references should follow the text.

Manuscript editor: Dr. Roland L. Madison

The Woman CPA, 20700 Northpark Blvd., John Carroll University
Cleveland, OH 44118, U. S. A.

Publisher: The Woman CPA
3998 Ridgedale Drive
Cincinnati, OH 45247, U. S. A.

Women in Business

Primary readership: Association members

Review process: Editorial only

Invited articles: 1-20%

**Percentage of articles
on accounting topics:**   5

Approximate percentage of accounting-related articles devoted to:

Financial Accounting:	**Managerial:**
Computers/Systems:	**Tax:** 100
Auditing:	**Education:**
Professional:	

Approximate percentage of accounting-related articles characterized as primarily: Not specified

Empirical:	**Experimental:**
Analytical:	**Descriptive:**

**Language(s) in which
articles are published:**   English

Accepts manuscripts in English for translation: N/A

Approximate acceptance rate: 5%

Review period: 1 week   **Lead time to publication after acceptance:** 2-4 months

Circulation: 113,000   **Frequency of publication:** Bi-monthly

Sponsoring organization: American Business Women's Association

Submission information:

Manuscript length: 1,000 to 1,500 words

Number of copies: 1   **Submission fee:** None

Style: Not specified

**Manuscript
editor:**   Laura Lickert, Associate Editor
Women in Business, 9100 Ward Parkway, P.O. Box 8728
Kansas City, Missouri 64114-0728, U. S. A.

Publisher: Same as above

World Accounting Report

Primary readership: Accounting (or tax) practitioners, businessmen

Review process: Editorial only

Invited articles: 61-80%

**Percentage of articles
on accounting topics:**   100

Approximate percentage of accounting-related articles devoted to:

Financial Accounting:	30	**Managerial:**	10
Computers/Systems:	5	**Tax:**	10
Auditing:	10	**Education:**	5
Professional:	30		

Approximate percentage of accounting-related articles characterized as primarily:

Empirical:		**Experimental:**	
Analytical:		**Descriptive:**	100

**Language(s) in which
articles are published:**   English, French

Accepts manuscripts in English for translation: N/A

Approximate acceptance rate: Not specified

Review period: 1 day   **Lead time to publication after acceptance:** 3 weeks

Circulation: N/A   **Frequency of publication:**   Monthly

Sponsoring organization: None

Submission information:

Manuscript length: Not specified

Number of copies: 1   **Submission fee:** None

Style: Not specified

**Manuscript
editor:**   Leon Hopkins

World Accounting Report, Chapter Three Publications, Ltd., 8A Hythe St.
Dartford, Kent, DA1 1BY, England

Publisher: Same as above

Yale Law Journal

Primary readership: Academicians, lawyers

Review process: Editorial only

Invited articles: 1-20%

**Percentage of articles
on accounting topics:**

Approximate percentage of accounting-related articles devoted to: Accounting articles if they contain legal elements

Financial Accounting:	**Managerial:**
Computers/Systems:	**Tax:**
Auditing:	**Education:**
Professional:	

Approximate percentage of accounting-related articles characterized as primarily: Not specified

Empirical:	**Experimental:**
Analytical:	**Descriptive:**

**Language(s) in which
articles are published:**   English

Accepts manuscripts in English for translation: N/A

Approximate acceptance rate: 1%

Review period: 3-9 weeks   **Lead time to publication after acceptance:** 2-4 months

Circulation: 4,000   **Frequency of publication:**   8 times per year

Sponsoring organization:

Submission information:

Manuscript length: 40-60 journal pages

Number of copies: 1   **Submission fee:** None

Style: Consult the "Harvard Blue Book."

**Manuscript
editor:**   Articles Editor
Yale Law Journal, 401-A Yale Station
New Haven, CT 06520, U. S. A.

Publisher: Same as above

Zeitschrift fuer Interne Revision (ZIR)

Primary readership: Academicians, accounting (or tax) practitioners, internal and external auditors

Review process: Editorial only

Invited articles: 1-20%

**Percentage of articles
on accounting topics:**   50

Approximate percentage of accounting-related articles devoted to:

Financial Accounting:		**Managerial:**	
Computers/Systems:		**Tax:**	
Auditing:	95	**Education:**	5
Professional:			

Approximate percentage of accounting-related articles characterized as primarily:

Empirical:	30	**Experimental:**	
Analytical:		**Descriptive:**	70

**Language(s) in which
articles are published:**   German

Accepts manuscripts in English for translation: Yes

Approximate acceptance rate: 70%

Review period: 1 month   **Lead time to publication after acceptance:** 6 months

Circulation: 3,000   **Frequency of publication:**   Quarterly

Sponsoring organization: Deutsches Institut fuer Interne Revision

Submission information:

Manuscript length: No limit
Number of copies: 2   **Submission fee:** None
Style: None

**Manuscript
editor:**

Winfried Hohloch

c/o Deutsches Institut fuer Interne Revision e. V. (IIR), POB 101139
D-6000 Frankfurt 1, West Germany

Publisher: Same as above

II. JOURNALS LISTED BY COUNTRY

*Note: If the editorial address and the publisher's
address are in different countries, the editorial
address is the basis for listing in this section*

AUSTRALIA

Abacus
Accounting, Auditing and Accountability Journal
Accounting and Finance
Australian Accountant
Australian Journal of Management
Australian Tax Forum
Chartered Accountant in Australia, The
Password, The
Social Accounting Monitor

AUSTRIA

Journal fuer Betriebswirtschaft
Wirtschaftstreuhaender, Der

BANGLADESH

Cost and Management
Journal of Business Administration

CANADA

Bilans
Business Quarterly
CA Magazine
CGA Magazine
CMA – The Management Accounting Magazine
Contemporary Accounting Research
Logistics and Transportation Review

DENMARK

Revision og Regnskabsvasen
Revisorbladet

EGYPT

Accounting, Business and Insurance

FRANCE

Bulletin Comptable & Financier
Comptabilite Et Mecanographie
Economie Et Comptabilite
Revue du Tresor, La
Revue Francaise de Comptabilite

GREAT BRITAIN

Accountancy
Accountancy Age
Accountant (England)
Accountant's Magazine, The
Accounting and Business Research
Accounting Technician
Accounting, Organizations and Society
Administrative Accountant
Audit Report
British Accounting Review
British Tax Review
Certified Accountant
Executive Accountant
Financial Accountability & Management
Income Tax Digest and Accountants Review
Issues in Accountability
Journal of Business Finance and Accounting
Journal of Health Care Management
Journal of Management Studies
Management Accounting (England)
Managerial Finance
World Accounting Report

HONG KONG

Asian Finance
Hong Kong Manager, The

HUNGARY

Szamvitel Es Ugyviteltechnika

INDIA

Bombay Chartered Accountant Journal
Chartered Accountant, The
Cost and Management
Indian Journal of Accounting
Indian Management
Management Accountant
Vikalpa: The Journal for Decision Makers

INDONESIA

Akuntansi and Administrators

IRELAND

Accountancy Ireland
Management (Ireland)

ISRAEL

Roeh Hacheshbon

ITALY

Esso Italiana Informazioni Economiche

JAPAN

Annals of the School of Business Admin., Kobe University

MALAYSIA

Malaysian Management Review

MEXICO

Contaduria Administrcion

NETHERLANDS

Accountant (Netherlands)
European Taxation
Psychometrika

NEW ZEALAND

Accountants' Journal (New Zealand)

NIGERIA

Nigerian Accountant, The

NORWAY

Revisjon og Regnskap

PAKISTAN

Industrial Accountant

PHILIPPINES

Accountants' Journal (Philippines)

POLAND

Rachunkowosc

SINGAPORE

Asia Pacific Journal of Management
Singapore Accountant

SRI LANKA

Institute of Chartered Accountants of Sri Lanka

SOUTH AFRICA

South African Chartered Accountant

SWITZERLAND

Schweizer Treuhaender, Der / L'Expert-Comptable Suisse

UNITED STATES

Academic Computing
Accounting Educators' Journal
Accounting Historians Journal, The
Accounting Horizons
Accounting News
Accounting Review, The
Accounting, Organizations and Society

UNITED STATES (CONTINUED)

Advances in Accounting
Advances in Accounting Information Systems
Advances in International Accounting
Advances in Public Interest Accounting
AEDS Journal
Akron Business and Economic Review
American Business Law Journal
American Economist, The
American Journal of Small Business
API Account
Applied Business and Administration Quarterly
Arkansas Business and Economic Review
Armed Forces Comptroller
Attorney – CPA, The
Auditing: A Journal of Practice and Theory
Bankers Magazine
Behavioral Research in Accounting
Broadcast Financial Journal
Business
Business and Economic Review
Business and Professional Ethics Journal
Business and Society
Business Horizons
Business Insights
Buyouts and Acquisitions
California Management Review
Certificate
Columbia Journal of World Business
COM-AND, Computer Audit News & Developments
COM-SAC, Computer Security, Auditing & Controls
Commercial Investment Real Estate Journal
Compensation Planning Journal
Computers in Accounting
Connecticut CPA Quarterly, The
Controllers' Quarterly
Cooperative Accountant
Coordinator
Corporate Accounting
CPA Marketing Report

UNITED STATES (CONTINUED)

CPA Journal, The
CPA Personnel Report
Current Accounts
Data Management
Decision Sciences
Defense Management Journal
Detroit Business Review
Directors & Boards
Estate Planning
Estates
Examiner, The
Financial Analysts Journal
Financial Management
Financial Planning Today
Financial Review, The
Georgia Journal of Accounting
Government Accountants Journal, The
Government Finance Review
Governmental Finance
Harvard Business Review
Healthcare Financial Management
Hospital & Health Services Administration
Human Systems Management
In Business
Industrial Management
Information & Management
Internal Auditing
Internal Auditor, The
International Journal of Accounting Educ
    Research, The
International Journal of Government A
International Journal, The
International Tax Journal
Interstate Tax Report
Issues in Accounting Education
Journal of Accountancy
Journal of Accounting and Econ
Journal of Accounting and EDP
Journal of Accounting and Pu

UNITED STATES (CONTINUED)

Journal of Accounting Education
Journal of Accounting Literature
Journal of Accounting Research
Journal of Accounting, Auditing and Finance
Journal of Bank Research
Journal of Business and Economic Perspectives
Journal of Business
Journal of Business Forecasting
Journal of Business Research
Journal of Business Strategy
Journal of Buyouts and Acquisitions, The
Journal of Commercial Bank Lending, The
Journal of Corporate Taxation, The
Journal of Cost Analysis
Journal of Cost Management for the Manufacturing Industry
Journal of Economics and Business
Journal of Education for Business
Journal of Financial and Quantitative Analysis
Journal of Financial Economics
Journal of Financial Software and Hardware, The
Journal of Futures Markets
Journal of Information Systems
Journal of International Business Studies
Journal of Organizational Behavior Management
Journal of Pension Planning and Compliance
Journal of Petroleum Accounting
Journal of Property Management
Journal of Real Estate Taxation, The
Journal of Small Business Management
Journal of State Taxation
Journal of Systems Management
Journal of Taxation
Journal of the American Society of CLU & ChFC
Journal of the American Taxation Association, The
Journal of the Institute of Certified Financial Planners
Office Economics and Management
ne of Bank Administration, The

UNITED STATES (CONTINUED)

Management Accounting (US)
Management Science
Management World
Managerial and Decision Economics
Managerial Finance
Managing
Massachusetts CPA Review
Mergers & Acquisitions
MIS Quarterly
Mississippi CPA Newsletter
Montana Business Quarterly
Montana CPA
Motor Freight Controller Magazine
Municipal Finance Journal
N.Y.U. Law Review
National Public Accountant
National Tax Journal
Nevada Review of Business and Economics
New Accountant
New Management
NewsAccount
Newsledger
Newspaper Financial Executive Journal
Northeast Journal of Business & Economics, The
Nursing Homes and Senior Citizen Care
Ohio CPA Journal, The
Oil and Gas Tax Quarterly
Oklahoma Business Bulletin
Oklahoma Law Review
Outlook
Pacific Northwest Executive
Pennsylvania CPA Journal
Pension World
Planning Review
Practical Lawyer, The
Production and Inventory Management

UNITED STATES (CONTINUED)

Public Budgeting & Finance
Quarterly Journal of Business and Economics
Rand Journal of Economics, The
Real Estate Accounting & Taxation
Real Estate Business
Research in Accounting Regulation
Research in Governmental and Nonprofit Accounting
Review of Business and Economic Research
Review of Taxation of Individuals, The
SAM Advanced Management Journal
Simulation and Games
Sloan Management Review
Southwest Journal of Business and Economics
St. John's Law Review
Tax Adviser, The
Tax Executive, The
Tax Law Review
Tax Lawyer, The
Tax Management International Journal
Taxation for Accountants
Taxes - The Tax Magazine
Tennessee CPA
Trusts and Estates
Valuation
Virginia Accountant Quarterly, The
Washington and Lee Law Review
West Virginia CPA, The
Wisconsin CPA
Woman CPA, The
Women in Business
Yale Law Journal

USSR

Bookkeeping Science

WEST GERMANY

Betrieb, Der
Bilanz & Buchhaltung
Controller Magazin
Kostenrechnungspraxis
Kreditpraxis
Neue Juristische Wochenschrift
Wirtschaftsprufung, Die
Wirtschaftswissenschaftliches Studium
Zeitschrift fuer Interne Revision (ZIR)

YUGOSLAVIA

Knjigovoda
Knjigovodstvo
Sovremeno Pretprijatie

ABOUT THE AUTHORS

J. David Spiceland, Ph.D., CPA, is Center of Excellence Research Professor in the School of Accountancy at Memphis State University. Dr. Spiceland is the author of numerous accounting articles in academic and professional journals. He has also served as the editor of a professional journal.

Surendra P. Agrawal, Ph.D., CPA, CMA, is Professor of Accountancy at Memphis State University. Professor Agrawal has published numerous accounting articles in academic and professional journals.